France–Germany in the Twenty-First Century

France–Germany in the
Twenty-First Century

Edited by

Patrick McCarthy

palgrave

First published 2001 by
PALGRAVE™
175 Fifth Avenue, New York, N.Y.10010 and
Houndmills, Basingstoke, Hampshire RG21 6XS.
Companies and representatives throughout the world

PALGRAVE™ is the new global publishing imprint of St. Martin 's Press LLC Scholarly and Reference Division and Palgrave Publishers Ltd (formerly Macmillan Press Ltd).

ISBN 0–312–22814–7 hardback

Library of Congress Cataloging-in-Publication Data
France-Germany in the twenty-first century / edited by Patrick McCarthy.
    p. cm.
Includes bibliographical references and index.
    ISBN 0–312–22814–7
    1. France—Foreign relations—Germany. 2. Germany—Foreign relations—France. 3. Heads of state—France—Attitudes. 4. Heads of state—Germany—Attitudes. 5. World politics. I. Title: France-Germany in the twenty-first century. II. McCarthy, Patrick, 1941-
DC59.8.G3 F686   2001
327.44043—dc21

                                                                00–059143

A catalogue record for this book is available from the British Library.

Design by Letra Libre, Inc.

First edition: January 2001
10 9 8 7 6 5 4 3 2 1

Printed in the United States of America.

For Isak Jones
who arrived only a short time
before the euro but is much stronger;
and for
Jakob Jones
who arrived in the year 2000.

Contents

About the Contributors

DAVID CALLEO is Dean Acheson Professor of European Studies at the School of Advanced International Studies, the Johns Hopkins University.

ANJA DALGAARD-NIELSEN is pursuing her doctorate in European Studies at SAIS.

ULRIKE GUEROT teaches European Studies at SAIS.

ERIK JONES is senior lecturer in politics at Nottingham University.

PATRICK MCCARTHY teaches European Studies at SAIS, Bologna Center.

ANAND MENON teaches politics at Saint Anthony's College, Oxford.

ROGER MORGAN is a Visiting Fellow at the European Institute of the London School of Economics.

MICHAEL STÜRMER is both a distinguished academic and Chief Correspondent for *Die Welt*.

JAMES I. WALSH teaches political science at the University of North Carolina at Charlotte.

Abbreviations

BRD	*Bundesrepublic Deutschland.* See FRG
CAP	Common Agricultural Policy
CDU	Christian Democratic Union
CFSP	Common Foreign and Security Policy
CPSU	Communist Party of the Soviet Union
CSU	Christian Social Union
DDR	*Deutsche Demokratiche Republik* (German Democratic Republic)
EBRD	European Bank for Reconstruction and Development
EC	European Community
ECSC	European Coal and Steel Community
EDC	European Defense Community
EMS	European Monetary System
EMU	Economic and Monetary Union
EU	European Union
FDP	German Liberal Party
FRG	Federal Republic of Germany
GATT	General Agreement on Tariffs and Trade
GDR	see DDR
IGC	Intergovernmental Conference
IGC-EMU	Conference on Economic and Monetary Union
IGC-POL	Conference on Political Union
IMF	International Monetary Fund
NATO	North Atlantic Treaty Organization
OEEC	Organization for European Economic Cooperation
PCI	Italian Communist Party
PS	*Parti socialiste*
RPR	*Rassemblement du Peuple Républicain*
SACEUR	Supreme Allied Commander in Europe
SDI	Strategic Defense Initiative
SPD	Socialist Party of Germany
UDF	*Union de la Democracie Française*
WEU	Western European Union

Preface

After my edited volume, *France-Germany: The Struggle to Cooperate 1983–1993*, and David Calleo's *France-Germany: The European Motor* (edited with Eric Staal), one might argue that the European Studies department of the School of Advanced International Studies (SAIS), Johns Hopkins University, had two choices: to decide that it had had its say on Franco-German cooperation or that, having undertaken to chronicle this topic, it should continue. I must take responsibility for making the second choice. It seemed to me that the post-Maastricht years had been so difficult and the Franco-German relationship so turbulent that one should tackle the 1990s. The method used here is to set the decade in a broad historical context. The year 2000 provided a vantage point, albeit one whose importance should not be exaggerated.

I rounded up my collaborators from European Studies—David Calleo, who runs the program; Ulrike Guerot, Roger Morgan, and Michael Stürmer, who have taught in it; Erik Jones, who was a student in it; and Anja Dalgaard-Nielsen, who is a student in it. I was pleased to enlist two "outsiders," Anand Menon and James Walsh.

We have tried to avoid the pitfall of edited books, the absence of unity. But in this case unity emerges from the definition of conflicts. While there are no unbridled optimists or apocalyptic pessimists, there is an interesting debate between Michael Stürmer's view that France and Germany are still an "unlikely couple," via Erik Jones and Roger Morgan who see areas of both agreement and disagreement, to David Calleo who maintains that, whatever the weaknesses of the Franco-German relationship, it is a better bet than "triumphal America."

Calleo sees France and Germany in a global context just as I try in Chapter 1 to see them in a long historical context. Conversely it also seems to us that, as Erik Jones explains, cooperation is carried on more within the European Union (EU) than was formerly the case. Other countries play more of a role, which has led us to include chapters on Italy and Britain, while Spain is omitted only because of lack of space.

The domestic economy and political systems of France and Germany are being shaped by international factors to a greater degree now than in the past, but they still help "shape" the European and even the global economy and the accompanying political arrangements. For this reason, issues like the *force de frappe* and German Reunification are discussed in several chapters from several different viewpoints.

Some of these chapters began their existence as lectures or seminars at the SAIS Bologna Center. I wish to thank all the students who made suggestions, offered criticism, or sat patiently through our sometimes obsessive discussions. I also wish to thank the Director, Robert Evans, for his encouragement; the library staff for its patience and competence; and Barbara Wiza for finding the time, among many other tasks, to provide a good manuscript. Last but by no means least come my wife, Veronica, and my daughter Kate for putting up with Kohl, Mitterrand, and me.

Patrick McCarthy
Bologna, February 15, 2000

France–Germany in the
Twenty-First Century

Chapter 1

Of Richelieu, Adenauer, and Sundry Others

Patrick McCarthy

Charles de Gaulle began the second chunk of his *Mémoires* with the statement that "France comes from the depths of the ages." If it were not so pretentious, I would start this book off with a similar ringing statement about the Franco-German relationship. One cannot understand how the two countries treat each other in the year 2000 without knowing what Cardinal Richelieu's achievements were or why Friedrich of Prussia invited Voltaire to his court. But incompetence more than lack of space compels me to begin at an undefined moment in history: after the German victory at Sedan in 1870, but before the French triumphantly held firm at Verdun. This chapter is divided into three sections: the first goes from my undefined moment to the end of the Second World War; the second, which runs from 1945 to 1993, presents a problem.

These years are covered in Chapter 1 of my edited volume *France-Germany 1983–1993: The Struggle to Cooperate* (St. Martin's Press 1993), albeit in a slightly different form. Rather than repeat myself, I refer the reader to that chapter. But the matter is not so simple: much material has recently appeared on this period that looks different from the year 2000 than it did from 1993. I have tried to take account of such things in the second section of this chapter. Finally, the third section begins with François Mitterrand's speech to the Bundestag, deals all too briefly with German Reunification, and ends in the aftermath of the Maastricht Treaty.

From France's Defeat in 1870 to Hitler's Downfall

In 1914 the historian Jacques Bainville published a book entitled *Histoire de deux peuples: la France et l'Empire allemand.* Bainville was a well-known intellectual of the Action française, which was then in the period of its greatest influence. Its monarchism was no great attraction but its tough, *realpolitisch* nationalism had won over many intellectuals who might otherwise have opposed going to war against Germany. Nor was Bainville's audience limited to intellectuals: his knowledgeable, readable books about history, which rarely lack relevance to the present, were and occasionally still are to be found on the bookshelves of "ordinary" educated people.

His aim in *Histoire de deux peuples* was to present Germany as the precise opposite of France, an inevitable enemy that France must combat whether it wished to or not. Bainville's hero is Cardinal Richelieu, who understood that politics has its own logic and morality and who systematically divided Germany into tiny pieces, using religion but caring only for the security of the French state. Germany was not just a matter of foreign policy; rather, French political and economic issues must be decided in the context of resisting the neighbor from across the Rhine. Here Bainville took up his monarchist's pen and wrote the usual Action française critique of the Revolution, which had weakened France. Nor could he see much good in the mid-nineteenth century with its self-indulgent support for German nationalism. Having forgotten Richelieu's lesson that Europe can achieve harmony only when Germany has no power, France finds itself confronting a Germany united under Bismarck. The result is the defeat of 1870, which, however, solves nothing. Politics moves forward, its details unpredictable but its certainties unchanged. German power remains "the scourge of Europe," and France will have to fight its neighbor all over again.[1]

Count Harry Kessler was a francophile, although by no means uncritical of France. His *Tagebücher* show him moving easily through Parisian salons of the 1920s: Gide discusses with him his campaign for Franco-German reconciliation, and he dines with the wife of Emile Mayrich, the Luxemburg steel magnate who headed a Franco-German friendship committee. Kessler is not afraid to say that he considers Paul Valéry much overrated, and that the weight of tradition is too heavy in France. Naturally he has no use for Poincaré's obsession with making Germany pay, and he sides with Briand. In Germany he is on the left: generous toward the Spartacus uprising, he supports Stresemann and is appalled by Hitler. In June 1932, when Nazi agitation is reaching crescendo, it is Kessler whom André François-Poncet, the great French ambassador to Germany, seeks out to explain his deep-rooted belief that the "new Europe must be built on an alliance between France and Germany."[2]

Although Bainville's view of Franco-German relations seems the antithesis of François-Poncet's remark to a receptive Kessler, the two have much in common. Both were expressed in moments of crisis for Franco-German relations and indeed for France and Germany. Both presuppose that relations will be difficult but also that they are, were, and will be very important for both countries. Bainville is supposedly realistic and hence pessimistic, while François-Poncet is giving vent to a wild hope that is contradicted by everything that is happening on the German political stage. Kessler's analysis of the German character was shared by many Frenchmen, including Albert Camus.[3] Kessler argues that young Germans do not seek their greatest possible freedom but rather a doctrine that will impose discipline on them. In his view, this is a kind of death wish, which is also peculiar to Germany. The Germans may, however, not know it for they are a mystery to themselves.[4]

In France there was not much sympathy for Germany. The war leader, Georges Clémenceau, has "at last gained revenge. This is his secret, the great ambition of his life: the Germans, he hates them; they have taken two provinces from us and Clémenceau has never forgiven them. Now they are defeated and he still hates them."[5] Before 1914 a survey of French travelers to Germany shows much admiration but little liking. In the early years of the Industrial Revolution, France judged itself and found itself wanting by comparison with Britain. By contrast Germany was viewed with much sympathy and a mild contempt. Napoleon's military victories over Prussia had not been forgotten and it was considered natural that Friedrich of Prussia should write poetry in French and have Voltaire correct it. After the defeat of 1870, opinion shifted to antipathy and admiration. Travelers point out that in Germany the trains run on time, but there is much more. French Socialists are willing to learn from the German Socialist Party (SPD), experts come to examine Bismarck's social policy, which is way ahead of France in looking after the working class; and German universities are a model, especially in the domains of science and philology.

In the 1880s and later, as in the 1980s, France ran a trade deficit with Germany. Moreover, this was the period when Germany pulled ahead of France in the new chemical and electrical industries. Only culturally did France consider itself superior, and travelers were appalled to see that Germans, while paying lip service to French culture, associated France with vaudeville and cabaret. In France an argument raged about Wagner: The initial enthusiasm of Baudelaire lived on, and pilgrimages to Bayreuth were frequent, but there was criticism too; there was also admiration for the very different—and French—music of Debussy. *Pelléas et Mélisande* was a particular favorite. French writers liked Nietzsche, who ousted Schopenhauer as an influence on the generation of Gide,[6] and who was, of course, a sharp critic of German society. Culture's critical view of its society would become an issue again in the 1970s: at the moment of the founding of the EMS, the most admired German film director in France was Rainer Werner Fassbinder, whose work excoriates the Bundesrepublik.

Sympathy and antipathy toward Germany are to be found in Larbaud's brief and youthful flirtation with the country. During a 1901 visit to Berlin, where he sampled the white beer, and to the North coast, where he walked beside the wintry ocean, he constructed "his" Germany, which is not the military power that conquered Alsace-Lorraine but the land of lyric poetry—misty and melancholy. Larbaud read Heinrich Heine, whose blend of lyricism and irony won him a certain posthumous popularity in France, and briefly sought to write *Volkslieder* in French. But this Germany is also Lutheran, cursed by a puritanism that prevents the German tourists who Larbaud met in Italy from appreciating the beauty of Tuscany. Larbaud's snapshot of Germany intrigues us by its contradictions.[7]

On a popular level, the sense of "the other" as different dominated. Germans considered the French frivolous, cynical, and hard-hearted. To the French, Germans were regimented, enormous eaters and drinkers, and lived out their lives surrounded by posters proclaiming that almost everything was *verboten*.[8] French society was older and more sure of itself; Germany's emphasis on the organic barely concealed a lack of such confidence.

Relations between the two countries grew worse in the years before 1914, and many French and Germans agreed with Bainville that the war was inevitable, although they had not thought so earlier. When François Seydoux's cousin, a brilliant lawyer, was killed in 1915, his entire family considered it natural.[9] Such a view did not, however, survive the trench warfare. Moreover, now as later, France was more preoccupied with Germany than Germany was with France. One could argue convincingly that the First World War was an attempt by Germany to wrest hegemony in Europe from Britain.

The 1920s was a period of intense diplomatic activity and offers parallels and contrasts with the years after the Second World War. One difference was that German public opinion was allowed to remain embittered about the Versailles settlement and the combination of financial penalties and political isolation it imposed. Moreover, public opinion blamed the harshness of the settlement on France. Superficially France was divided between the Poincaré and Briand lines. Poincaré took a tough approach and favored the invasion of the Ruhr in 1923; Briand tried to reach agreement with Germany via Gustav Stresemann. But if this mirrors the fundamental contrast between Bainville and François-Poncet, the nuances of French diplomacy should not be forgotten. Many who supported Poincaré recognized that their neighbor from across the Rhine was not, like the United States, going to go away and that France would have to live with Germany. They simply wanted to start off from a position of strength.

The invasion of the Ruhr was also supposed to send a message to Britain, which was tending toward a more lenient view of Germany and of the need to revive the German economy if Europe were to prosper. This does not mean, however, that one should see, now or anytime before World War Two, an anti-British party that jostled with the anti-German party in France. The French middle and upper classes were anglophile: attracted by British power as well as the rituals of British life, like the London clubs. A small minority shared the views of Henri Béraud's *Faut-il réduire l'Angleterre à l'esclavage?* (Must England be reduced to slavery?)

Culturally, reconciliation won out over Bainville's view of inevitable conflict. Within the *Nouvelle Revue Française* Jacques Rivière, who edited the review until his early death in 1925 and who had been a prisoner in Germany for much of the war, first fought off an Action Française bid to take control and then joined André Gide in supporting a flexible approach to Germany.[10] German intellectuals allowed themselves to be convinced, and Ernst Robert Curtius resumed his lifelong study of France and was a regular visitor to the Pontigny seminars, although he did not forget that Paul Claudel had written about "the Lutheran hordes." The word "Europe" meant little to most French people but it too found favor among writers. The magazine *Commerce* published writers from Britain—Eliot and Sitwell—as well as from Germany—Hölderlin—in its bid to create a cultural identity called "Europe." It also went back to the Renaissance in its quest for a common European past, which may be seen as a minor parallel to Curtius's monumental *Europäische Literatur und Lateinisches Mittelalter,* an antidote to the poison that the Nazis were spreading through Europe. In France, Europeanism was suspect, for nationalists saw in it a roundabout way to stress the parallels with German culture. Maurras made a point of declaring that neither British nor German culture could inspire French writers, who must look back to their own seventeenth century or else to classical Rome.[11]

The Briand line found little popular support in its advocacy of closer ties with Germany, which remained disliked and distrusted. Briand did gain elite backing, especially after the Thoiry meeting of 1926, with the nuance that some supporters thought Stresemann dominated Briand. Yet Stresemann's death in 1929 was greeted with genuine sorrow in France.

Briand's death in 1932 seemed oddly fitting to a France that watched, as if hypnotized, the Nazis' arrival in power. The Poincaré and Briand camps agreed that Hitler was the product of bungled allied policy toward democratic Germany. If only the Allies had given Poincaré a free hand in the Ruhr, if only Briand had been able to complete his work. . . . It cannot be said that the French found the Nazi phenomenon hard to understand. The Final Solution, when the details were set out graphically after the war, provoked surprise as well as horror; but Kessler's interpretation of the German character had been proved right, as French experts on Germany knew already. One of them speaks of "a nervous sensibility, physiological even, that led Germany to extremes of violence."[12] Far from being an aberration, Hitler was an integral part of the problem of living next to Germany. That France knew this and yet took no action when Hitler was aggressive but still weak is the surprising thing, to be explained by the political weakness of the Third Republic and by the vagaries of British foreign policy.[13]

Certainly German popular support for the Nazis was partly won by Hitler's success in flouting the Versailles restrictions, and equally these were seen as a French option. The two countries agreed that they were different, and their animosity was mutual. Yet they did not ascribe to each other the same priority. Hitler was primarily interested in expanding eastward at the expense of the USSR and in exterminating the Jews, and the war in the west was a necessary means to this end. Except for a noisy fringe shouting "Better Hitler than Blum!" and a correct skepticism about the value of the alliance with the USSR, the French were united in seeing Germany as their leading foreign-policy problem. The difference between French attitudes in 1914 and in 1939 was great, but this had to do with going to war and not with Germany. To the French the "Second World War," an expression far less common in France than in Britain or the United States, was the "Third German Invasion."

The French felt quite differently about their other European enemy, Italy. In 1938 André François-Poncet was pleased to be assigned to Rome, in part because he hoped to induce Mussolini to continue playing the role of peacemaker that he had played at the Munich conference, and partly because he liked Italians and believed they liked the French. He quickly changed his mind about Mussolini, who wrote a newspaper article entitled "I Spit on France." But François-Poncet notes that the public "remained correct, pleasant and kind." By contrast he thinks the Germans had a low opinion of the Italians, who in return distrusted and disliked them.[14] François-Poncet underestimates Germany's influence on Italy—the way that Hegel penetrated Italian thought. But his view of the difference between Franco-Italian and Franco-German relations is mostly correct. This difference reemerges on the Italian side in the run-up to monetary union of the late 1990s. Italy expected French support for its candidacy and was annoyed if it was not forthcoming, whereas Italy saw in Germany a harsh taskmaster who had to be won over by good behavior.

As they were reeling from the speed of their defeat in 1940, the French were presented with a new aspect of their familiar problem. Had Germany won this war or was de Gaulle, of whom few people had ever heard, right in thinking that this was a world war and that it had barely started? If the answer was the first proposition then Pierre Laval was right and France would have to find its place in a German-dominated Europe. It did not automatically follow that Laval was right in drawing the conclusion that France should collaborate and become as much like Germany as it could. But his views were not aberrant; indeed they were logical. Just as logical was the view that many attributed to Philippe Pétain, namely, that France should accept defeat, make a show of collaborating, and wait for the fourth Franco-German war.

The Pétain and Laval viewpoints could easily be reconciled in practice, and the Pétain view was also compatible with the popular dislike of the "boches." The hard-line collaborators like Jacques Doriot, who were even more pro-Nazi than Laval, were never able to convince their compatriots that their real enemies were not the Germans "who seemed to have settled down in Paris for a long time . . . for ever,"[15] but the British. Certainly the British had gratuitously destroyed the French fleet at Mers-el-Kébir and had run away at Dunkirk, but they were not occupying France. The collaborators, however, represented a distorted version of François-Poncet's approach, whereas de Gaulle took the hostile stance of Bainville.

To join de Gaulle in London or to enter the Resistance were difficult choices, and the numbers of people who took them were small, until November 1942 when the Allies landed in North Africa and it became clearer that they were going to win the war. The Communists had entered the Resistance when Hitler invaded the Soviet Union and their publications were frenetically anti-German. The non-Communist network, Combat, was more careful to distinguish "Nazi" from "German" and its newspaper advocated a Germany divided into several parts and integrated into a united Europe. The myth of the Resistance, and the Germans' increasing cruelty as the tide of war turned against them, sharpened popular anti-German feeling; this became a barrier against Franco-German cooperation in the postwar years. The Oradour trial of SS men who had committed a massacre in a French village in 1944 helped swing the parliamentary vote against the European Defense Community in 1954.

From Adenauer and de Gaulle to Kohl and Mitterrand

Yet the war's effect on the French population was complex. Insofar as the shock of the 1940 defeat fostered a willingness to break with the past, it helped public opinion to accept experiments in Franco-German cooperation like the Coal and Steel Pool, although the Pool was not publicized until its success was assured. On the elite level, senior civil servants did not wish to repeat the mistakes made after 1918, in particular the oscillation between the Poincaré and Briand lines. Yet more important was the new international situation. Neither the Soviet Union nor the United States was going to disappear this time, so France would be dealing with Germany in quite a different context.

The Soviet Union was initially of no help. De Gaulle's visit to Moscow in 1944 demonstrated that the USSR was not interested in a privileged relationship with France in order to keep Germany weak and divided and, more discreetly, to limit the influence of the Anglo-Saxons. After the start of the Cold War in 1947 the Soviets made France's dealings with the Bundesrepublik (BRD) easier by helping to divide Germany. The BRD had all the more reason to seek France's friendship, but a hostile USSR caused France two other problems. The first, carefully nurtured by the very intelligent Konrad Adenauer, was of a "new Rapallo": the BRD, probably under a Social Democratic government, would go over to the USSR in return for reunification. The second was that the Soviet military threat made France too dependent on the United States.

The problem of the benevolent United States, which offered its lordly protection to Western Europe, had at least two dimensions. The first was military: the French might make no effort to defend themselves, instead relying on the United States which might at any time decide to pull out or to extract payment for its services by overvaluing the dollar or demanding trade concessions. The second was cultural, consisting of the threat posed to French culture by mass American culture. Much has been written about this topic in ink and in blood,[16] and all we can hope to do is to mention the most relevant points.

Far from being massively anti-American, educated Frenchmen have been more than willing to admire American high culture; this has been demonstrated by the veritable cult of Walt Whitman before 1914, the translation and appreciation of Hemingway and Faulkner in the interwar years, and the post–Second World War preference for the American cinema over better French directors like Carné or Clouzot. French intellectuals, from the young Sartre up to and including Baudrillard, have been fascinated by America, in which they have seen their own future. Whereas they have sometimes been hostile, they have rarely been indifferent. In defending their own language, the French have rendered a service to English-speakers whose mother tongue is being mutilated as it is globalized.

The French and the Germans have not been able to find common ground on this issue as the Germans have been far more willing to absorb American popular culture. With so many G.I.s living in their country, they had no choice but to absorb Elvis Presley and Johnny Ray. There is no German equivalent of the Great Coca-Cola War that ravaged France in the early 1950s. English remains the first foreign language in both countries, and only recently has the German government shown any real interest in increasing the number of foreigners who speak German. There is no German equivalent of *francophonie*.

Despite these considerable differences, the postwar situation remained one that Bainville and Kessler would have understood. Germany was there and was not going to go away. Its economy might be in ruins but it was potentially strong, thanks in large part to the coal and steel industries of the Ruhr. Its people might be cold, underfed, bewildered by the disappearance of the Reich, and made to feel guilty by the victors who showed the world the reality of Auschwitz. But they were still competent and capable of rallying behind a strong leader, as Adenauer's big majorities would demonstrate. Moreover, Europe's economy could not revive unless Germany's did. Plans for turning the country into a *grüne Wiese* (green meadow) were recognized to be absurd. Yet no one knew, least of all the Germans, where a prosperous Germany might be headed. Its own leaders continued to fear the worst right up until monetary union in 1998.

On the other side of the Rhine stood a profoundly but not obviously different France. Its weaknesses were the same as before, or so a German might think. It possessed a strong left, in the shape of a Communist Party that represented a quarter of the electorate. It was prone to strikes and to short-lived governments. The French felt they had suffered much and should be compensated. They were aggrieved that their Anglo-Saxon allies paid so little attention to their fears. Whatever guilt they might have felt about the Vichy regime was hidden by the myth of a vast Resistance and by a rather arbitrary purge in which some collaborators were executed while others escaped very lightly. The issue of French anti-Semitism was barely touched so it returned periodically to haunt the nation—the commemoration of the Vél d'hiver roundup[17] is only one recent example. Meanwhile French high culture was, as usual, the most influential in Europe: young people flocked to Saint-Germain, and Sartre's existentialism became the philosophy of a generation.

Martin Heidegger, who inspired Sartre, was regarded with grave suspicion because of his pro-Nazi sympathies, although Joseph Rovan read him ardently during the war years. Not until the first postwar voices were heard, such as Heinrich Böll's *Das Brot der frühen Jahre* (1955), did German culture gain a fresh audience. Brecht drew the admiration of many, including Roland Barthes, but he had chosen to live in the German Democratic Republic (DDR). Anyway, in 1945 Germany seemed to the British and Americans a desolate place, with its splendid cities in ruins—especially Dresden, where Bomber Harris had wreaked useless havoc. While de Gaulle tried out the Poincaré line, and France made moves toward at least the economic annexation of the Sarre, the Americans grew more worried about the USSR and the British about making their zone pay its own way.

This gave the Germans leverage and tended logically toward the creation of some kind of German entity in the west of the country. The Berlin airlift of 1948 raised the spirits of West Berliners by showing them that they still had some importance. Stalin was finally starting to play Richelieu's role! As West German politics took shape, two figures emerged in logical reaction to Anglo-Saxon intervention and to French demands. The first was Kurt Schumacher, the leader of the Social Democrats, who combined a forceful anticommunism with a distrust of the Western capitalist countries. Logically, Schumacher wanted a reunited, neutral Germany, and with equal logic neither the French nor the United States agreed with him. The second was Konrad Adenauer, who shared Schumacher's anticommunism but sought close ties with the West. Adenauer, who began the postwar German habit of conducting a trapeze act between France and the United States, has been justly acclaimed for his role in the Cold War and in the construction of a united Europe. But he should also be considered a nationalist who systematically widened the margin of freedom accorded to the fledgling German state.

As his *Erinnerungen* shows, Adenauer, who had to fight on several fronts and turn many necessities into virtues, saw that without an alliance with France there could be no viable Germany. It is worth stressing that from the outset the Franco-German couple has never just looked backward, to wars that should have been avoided. Obviously one of its goals was to substitute cooperation for what would have been the fourth conflict between the two countries in a century. But other goals included the fairest use of the coal and iron-ore belt that extends from Lorraine to the Ruhr; joint action to remedy French overproduction of agriculture and Germany's need to import food; a security arrangement that would protect both countries against a Soviet attack; and the creation of a united Europe. It is, therefore, incorrect to maintain that as the memory of the Second World War wanes, Franco-German cooperation will wither away. The photo of Mitterrand and Kohl standing hand-in-hand at Verdun is dramatic but it does not reflect the many-sided reality of the relationship.

Adenauer has been described as "the representative of a Germany purified by its ordeal."[18] He sought legitimacy for Germany by presenting it as purified and eager to become a loyal partner for the West on the international stage. His great opportunity came with the Cold War, which made the United States opt for German rearmament and, as a reward, entry into NATO.[19] On the way Adenauer had to overcome the obstacle of Geman public opinion, especially in the case of the Protestant Church and Social Democrat voters who did not wish to rearm; and to endure the humiliation of the French parliament, which in 1954 voted against the European Defense Community in which German military units would have fought alongside French or Belgian units.

French opposition was partly based on Gaullist distaste for supranationalism and anticipates the Fouchet Plan. Insofar as it was based on hostility to and fear of a new German army, it did not prevent economic cooperation. Here Jean Monnet needed access to German coal if he was to meet the targets of his industrial plan. The Poincaré line dictated that France should gain and retain as much control as possible over the Ruhr and should annex the Saar. But there would be strong opposition from France's allies, while German public opinion, as Adenauer never tired of pointing out, would not tolerate further dismembering of the country and would certainly vote him out of office. A frequent refrain of Adenauer's discourse was, "If you do not make such and such concession, then I shall be denounced as the *Kanzler der Allierten,* and replaced by some extreme nationalist."

Some version of this plaintive cry was used by most European countries in dealing with the United States: in France the danger was the communists. But Adenauer's tactic was part of his domestic policy, which was based on using "Europe" to refound a German state. That does not mean there was anything spurious about his enthusiasm for Europe, especially since German public opinion and elite opinion was pro-European and favored supranationalism. German schoolchildren were taught the virtues of Charlemagne and taken on trips to Aachen/Aix-la-Chapelle. On federalism, however, Adenauer was pragmatic: he worked well with de Gaulle, who believed in *l'Europe des patries.* In general Adenauer was an ideal partner for a France that had switched to the Briand line.

In 1950 Monnet's plan for a coal and steel pool was launched by the French foreign minister, Robert Schuman. To oversimplify, it meant that each member state gave up power over its coal and steel industry and gained a chunk of power over the coal and steel industries of other countries. Adenauer gave up the least since German coal was controlled, in theory, by an International High Commission, and, in practice, by General Lucius Clay, the American military commander. In return Adenauer gained the legitimacy of sitting as France's equal in a European organization. The Ruhr ceased to be an international zone and the Saar did not become French. Indeed after a period when it had a special status, the Saar became German again in 1957.

When de Gaulle came back to power in 1958, he took the exceptional step of inviting Adenauer to his home at Colombey-les-deux-Églises. Adenauer was duly impressed, but beyond the personal gratification he also obtained from de Gaulle two kinds of help. The first was a guarantee of support against the USSR. The immediate issue was Berlin, about which Khruschev was making threatening noises. But in general Adenauer was open to the accusation that he had no plan for reunification. In reply he maintained that a strong Bundesrepublik entrenched in a strong West would act as a magnet on the DDR, which is arguably what happened—thirty years later. To have any plausibility Adenauer had to be part of a strong Western alliance. The trouble was that the British Prime Minister Harold Macmillan cultivated ambiguity and that in 1960 the United States elected a young, inexperienced president. So de Gaulle's promises that France would hold firm on Berlin were welcome.

The second piece of help was de Gaulle's ability to win over French and German public opinion. Direct endorsement from the people was an integral part of Gaullism-Bonapartism. Until now Franco-German cooperation had remained a matter for political and bureaucratic elites. De Gaulle believed it should be rooted in popular opinion. His trip to Germany in 1962 certainly achieved that. No German politician would have dared behave in such a regal manner or could have achieved such a response from the crowds. Charlemagne himself could not have done it! Perhaps the schoolchildren had no choice, but the adults who lined the roads were free to stay at home.[20] A trip to France by Adenauer, carefully orchestrated, produced not equal but still good results. French public opinion from 1960 to Maastricht was generally, although not unfailingly, in favor of Franco-German cooperation. A substantial majority of French people declared they were in favor of German Reunification whereas the British were opposed.

Adenauer demonstrated that both the link with France and broader European unity were compatible with the strengthening of the nation-state. The BRD was born of the Cold War and nurtured by Europe, which meant chiefly a France that wanted to control Germany and also to use it as an ally against U.S. hegemony. By 1960 Adenauer was fighting another domestic battle against the supporters of Finance Minister Ludwig Erhard, who feared that Adenauer's preoccupation with France and Europe would cut the BRD off from the United States, the worldwide economy, and free trade. In the short term, Adenauer won and the Elysée Treaty he signed with de Gaulle in 1963 may be seen as crowning his life's work. From the vantage point of the year 2000 this treaty is also the basic text of Franco-German cooperation: it was used by Mitterrand and Kohl when they relaunched the relationship in the 1980s. In 1963, however, it came after de Gaulle's veto of British entry to the European Community (EC) and the failure of the Fouchet Plan. The Bundestag thought Adenauer had yielded too much to de Gaulle so it added a preamble, which stated that the treaty's provisions were subordinate to Germany's commitments to NATO and to the GATT. This made the treaty worthless in de Gaulle's eyes, and Adenauer was replaced as chancellor by Erhard not long afterward. In the short run, all that remained of the Elysée Treaty was the school-exchange program, which further helped win over public opinion in both countries to cooperation.

If we next move from Adenauer to France and reexamine the contribution of Charles de Gaulle, we must first ask whether he had any conception of cooperation that went beyond embracing Germany in order to stifle it, or making temporary use of a neighbor. The notion of the nation-state is so dominant in de Gaulle's historical imagination that it seems to leave little space to alliances or blocs like the EC. After de Gaulle's death his name was invoked by people like Philippe Séguin, who criticized the Franco-German tie in the name of the French state. One may, therefore, admit that in the de Gaulle of the "Free French" or of the "Empty Chair," there was indeed a pure nationalist.

But although Stalin denied it, de Gaulle was a complex man. The defeat of 1940 did not merely teach him that a state must be strong enough to defend its citizens. It also demonstrated that war had been globalized and that France needed allies. The United States, however, was hardly an ideal ally. It was unwilling to heed the advice or needs of its wartime partners but instead sought to dominate. In particular it arrived late in two world wars. De Gaulle never wanted the Americans to withdraw from Europe; he simply assumed that, pursuing their own self-interest, they would one day depart. One returns to Bainville's point that the Germans were not going anywhere. In 1944 de Gaulle thought Germany was the problem and the USSR part of the solution. Once the Cold War changed his mind, Germany and Russia exchanged roles. De Gaulle envisaged the EC as a European bloc, strong enough to defend itself against the USSR and to demand equal treatment from the United States.

So there is a European de Gaulle whom most of his successors have followed. Chirac invoked the nationalist de Gaulle to get himself elected president in 1995, but, once the election was over, drew on the European de Gaulle for his policies. There was, however, no supranational de Gaulle, which accounts for the guerrilla war waged against him by Monnet, Spaak, Luns, and the supporters of a federal Europe. As the Fouchet Plan reveals, de Gaulle wanted power to remain in the Council of Ministers, civil servants to be appointed to the Commission from their home countries (to which they would return), and a parliament made up of M.P.s from the national parliaments. How does this skirmish look from the year 2000? De Gaulle appears to have won: power remains with the Council of Ministers while the parliament, although elected, is weak.

One may doubt, however, whether de Gaulle anticipated the changes in the national governments. This is a vast subject, and one recent study of the agricultural negotiations in the Uruguay round of the Gatt found that the main EC actors were the French and German governments.[21] But the state can no longer distribute regional aid as it pleases and must undertake a privatization program. Its power stems more from its right to bargain with the other nation-states in its bloc than from traditional sovereignty. It is doubtful whether de Gaulle would have recognized himself in such a state.

A recent study of European unification has argued that de Gaulle was guided only by immediate economic issues.[22] Thus the veto he imposed on British entry in 1963 has nothing to do with the Polaris missile and everything to do with obtaining the best possible deal for French agriculture. This is a valuable interpretation because it works against the picture of a de Gaulle immersed in high politics and concerned only with ethereal problems like *grandeur.* Certainly de Gaulle was deeply interested in the welfare of French farmers. But to argue that he was guided only by such issues is to fly in the face of the *Mémoires* and of what his ambassadors and collaborators have said or written about him, not to mention the great weight of scholarship. It also denies de Gaulle's most interesting trait: his rich historical imagination.

From 1963 to 1969 de Gaulle neglected Germany. From 1969 to 1974 his successor, Georges Pompidou, struggled to contain the more self-confident Germany of Willi Brandt. It was not until around 1976 that cooperation began again under President Valéry Giscard d'Estaing and Chancellor Helmut Schmidt. From the viewpoint of the year 2000 these thirteen years elicit three comments. First, today when the bonds that tie the European nations together are so much tighter than in the 1960s, the Franco-German relationship could not possibly withstand thirteen years of neglect tinged with hostility. Second, it fell to Pompidou to face the troublesome fact that, with its economy rebuilt, Germany was a stronger country than France and hence the relationship was unbalanced. Pompidou tried to remedy this by a dash for growth but he ran into the oil price increase. Mitterrand, faced with German Reunification, tried the psychological approach of telling the French not to indulge in self-criticism. But the problem—which began with Brandt's *Ostpolitik,* the first independent piece of foreign policy and the mark of a more self-confident Germany proud of the *Wirtschaftswunder* and less willing to defer to other countries—has not gone away; it is revealed in the tough conditions that Germany was able to set for monetary union. Third, Edward Heath's Britain joined the EC and Pompidou tried to use Britain to counterbalance Germany, but Heath lost the next election to a Labor Party that was at best lukewarm about Europe. There is a lesson here for Prime Minister Tony Blair in the year 2000: if he wishes to turn the Franco-German couple into a troika, he must be persistent; sporadic forays into Europe are not enough.

Arguably Brandt's *Ostpolitik* had a long-term effect and helped undermine the communist regimes. But in the short term its impact was exhausted by the mid-1970s. This removed one irritant to the French, while Schmidt could also vaunt Germany's success in dealing with the oil crisis. This was a triumph for the Bundesbank rather than for the Social Democratic government: when the trade unions asked for substantial wage increases in the aftermath of the oil price increase, the government agreed but the Bundesbank, fearing inflation, raised interest rates; this led employers to lay off workers and unions to moderate their demands. From our perspective this marks the beginning of the end for government-controlled central banks, which one by one become independent in a process that culminated in the creation of an independent European central bank. It also marks the beginning of German near-hegemony in Europe ("near" because the Nazi past still forced Germany not to assert itself). In our opinion this period of near-hegemony was ended by the economic weaknesses that stemmed from reunification and that became obvious in the early 1990s. But thanks to the Bundesbank, Germany coped with the oil price increase better than any other European nation, and Schmidt was acclaimed as a leader of international stature.

His Germany was offered as a model by Giscard d'Estaing in *Démocratie française* in 1976. Giscard had to fight on two fronts: against his Gaullist allies, now led by Chirac, and against Mitterrand's Socialists, now allied with the Communists. He considered the Gaullist state too authoritarian and praised Germany as a country run by consensus. Inflation there was low because "all the social actors showed an undisguised determination to work together." The Socialists should learn from their German comrades to abandon extremism, Marxism, and the Communist alliance. Giscard had not given up hope of overtaking Germany but believed that France must first emulate its neighbor, which does not live in "a state of ideological divorce" but where "the chief political families share the same view of how society should be organized."[23] This reminds us of the pre-1914 travelers who admired German science or philology.

Giscard, who with hindsight seems an underrated president, wasted the first two years of his seven-year mandate but then appointed Raymond Barre as prime minister and backed a deflationary policy. The European Monetary System (EMS) was designed by Giscard and Schmidt to enable France to use the strength of the mark in order to strengthen the franc. It thus meshed perfectly with the Barre Plan. Giscard hoped to reduce France's oil bill, which had to be paid in dollars without relying on high interest rates to prop up the franc. Schmidt wanted to spread the gospel of disinflation, to protect intra-European trade from the vagaries of the dollar, and to end the mark's role as a de facto reserve currency by encouraging people getting out of dollars to buy francs or lire. This last hope of his remained unrealized, but the EMS marked the posthumous triumph of Stresemann and Briand and a not quite definitive defeat for Bainville and Poincaré.

When viewed retrospectively, this was also the first step toward the euro, although Giscard and Schmidt were not rewarded by the voters. They lost power in 1981 and 1982 respectively, while the EMS floundered, which proved that it could not work until governments demonstrated their willingness to make tough decisions. This moment came in 1983 when Mitterrand's Socialists, who had spent two years trying the Keynesian approach to the 1978–1979 oil price increase and had accumulated a trade deficit with Germany while remaining politically cool toward the Schmidt government, chose to stay in the EMS at the price of abandoning their attempt to inflate their way out of the recession. By demonstrating their resolution to hold the devalued franc at its new value against the mark, the Socialists also showed their desire to cooperate with the Kohl government that had taken office in 1982. Moreover, although they lost the parliamentary elections of 1986, they did better than they had feared. They had legitimized themselves as a party of government and they returned to power in 1988.

The Mitterrand-Kohl Decade

The Elysée Treaty was dusted off and cooperation concentrated on defense and the economy. The first of these issues presented a new twist: France was concerned that Germany not be soft on the Soviet Union. This was ironic since Adenauer's Germany had been virulently anticommunist, at times giving the impression that Germans could atone for their Nazi past by exemplary rejection of communism.[24] This inevitably produced in the next generation a backlash that took various forms: the Green Party, which entered parliament in 1983, was inclined toward pacifism and neutralism; the *Ostpolitik* worked in favor of continued dialogue with the Eastern bloc; desire for reunification spurred a tendency to "be nice" to the DDR; the BRD was disappointed with the waning of détente and with the Soviet invasion of Afghanistan, and reluctant to accept the need for intermediate-range NATO missiles to counterbalance the Soviet SS 20 missiles.

All this protest was less widespread and less solid than it seemed. Nor was it devoid of truth: the USSR wasted its last resources in the upsurge of hostility towards the West and then turned to Gorbachev, who tried rather desperately to improve relations with the West while undertaking domestic reform. When this proved inadequate, the Communist bloc collapsed. The German "peaceniks" were right in believing there would be no new Cold War. This did not, however, suit France. Its intellectuals had been the last to accept the reality of the Soviet threat; now they would be the last to give it up. Mitterrand had just won his party over to a Gaullist view of national security; he needed an enemy. Public opinion had long been won over to the *force de frappe* and all that it involved, like nuclear waste and uranium mining. Moreover, this was such a good stick with which to beat an economically more powerful Germany!

Jean-François Revel provides a typical French viewpoint: German public opinion is moving in the opposite direction from other Western countries. The Germans are indifferent to the Jaruzelski crackdown in Poland and they are hostile to Solidarity. The Greens are either fools or on Moscow's payroll or both. Implicit in Ravel's diatribe is the notion that Germany is pursuing some non-Western *Sonderweg,* and there is an explicit accusation that the world is witnessing the rebirth of German nationalism.[25]

Such thinking has the added merit of providing France with the excellent role of ensuring that Germany stays in the Western alliance. Mitterrand spent a delightful day in Bonn lecturing the German parliament on why it should accept the new NATO missiles. As the decade wore on, however, it became more obvious that Hans Dietrich Genscher's view of Gorbachev was correct, and so Mitterrand moved to compromise with German security policy; he took with him French public opinion, which saw no contradiction between general disarmament and France's independent deterrent. He also sought military cooperation from 1983 on via the Bold Sparrow exercises and the joint Rapid Action Force.[26] Inevitably the old problem recurred: Germany wanted to keep everything inside NATO and not irritate the United States; France wanted to create a European force tied to the EC and, if the United States disapproved, so much the worse for it.

But the end of the Cold War has brought changes in the French view of the United States, even if they did not become obvious until the right won the 1993 parliamentary elections. Since there is no longer a massive threat from the East, there is now less need for the United States to dominate the West. Conversely, Iraq and Bosnia demonstrated a new need for NATO to become a decentralized, highly mobile force capable of tackling various kinds of enemies. France can, therefore, find space for herself more easily inside NATO. A reunified Germany is also more legitimate and freer to play a security role consonant with its economic strength. This argument is generic but it indicates a possible new framework of security in the early 2000s.

It depends, of course, on U.S. willingness to give up being a global superpower and to accept this new NATO. President Bush was not willing and a December 1990 document written by Kohl and Mitterrand had to be reworked. An October 1991 version, which made more concessions to Atlanticism, was deemed acceptable.[27] But the Maastricht document of December 1991 is ambiguous: is the force to be the military arm of the European Union or the European pillar of NATO? Either way the French, Germans, and any other European participants will have to put up a lot of money for information satellites and troop-carrying planes.

On the economic front, France used the EMS to bring down inflation—2.9 percent in March 1986—and to increase the companies' share of value-added.

Business, however, remained unhappy as holding the franc's value against the mark required that interest rates be 2 or 3 percent higher than in Germany. This was the risk penalty factor, and it both reduced competitiveness and hence increased unemployment. Despite its discourse of privatization and letting market forces work, the right did no better from 1986 to 1988 and the French political class arrived at a consensus that the EMS should be reformed "to prevent one country from determining the objectives of economic and monetary policy for the group as a whole."[28]

The solution, as the French saw it, was monetary union which would give each country a say in the setting of monetary targets. German politicians were not unfavorable, provided that monetary union follow the German pattern of an independent central bank dedicated to fighting inflation. In short Germany wanted to impose *Modell Deutschland* on all Europe, whereas France sought lower interest rates and higher growth.

The communist countries prevented a thorough Franco-German debate, which might have turned into a major dispute, by choosing this moment to collapse. So German Reunification, which most Europeans had complacently relegated to the next century and also perceived as part of a general European settlement, was suddenly an immediate option. To Mitterrand's scarcely disguised horror, Kohl seized this option, ignored his European allies, and with U.S. backing struck a bargain with Gorbachev. German Reunification was an accomplished fact by March 1990.

The Franco-German relationship now faced its worst crisis since 1963: France was indeed too weak to influence Germany and it was now facing a larger, more legitimate and potentially richer Germany. French public opinion was not troubled but French elites were appalled: François-Poncet and Harry Kessler were being proved wrong. Two factors saved the relationship. Firstly, Kohl reverted, once he had achieved reunification, to the Adenauer model of a German state rooted in a uniting Europe. In my opinion there was no need for him to do this, but Kohl feared the destructive forces in the German past and he welcomed the constraints that Europe would impose. Secondly, reunification turned out to be economically more difficult than had been imagined. Some of the difficulty resulted from Kohl's mistakes: an exchange rate of one West mark for every East mark priced many DDR products out of their markets, while the decision to finance Reunification not out of taxes but by borrowing sent interest rates up across Europe.

This damaged both the French and German economies, and the deflationary effect was worsened by the Maastricht agreement. Here Germany granted monetary union but exacted tough conditions, including the independence of the European central bank. Although the agreement looks like a victory for the German view of monetary union over the French view, the role of the Ecofin (Committee of Economic and Finance Ministers) injects a political element while the troubles of the German economy have weakened the mark. Already in 1993 the deflationary effect was apparent. From the viewpoint of the year 2000, the price paid for monetary union and keeping Germany anchored to the West was high indeed—not just for the French economy but for the German and the other European economies: Italy saw its growth rate fall to 1.2 percent for 1998. Maastricht's other great innovation, the Common Foreign and Security Policy (CFSP), has been overshadowed by the euro and held back by the unanimity principle.

This historical sketch ends then with a question. Could the French and Germans avoid Bainville's gloomy view that they were doomed to be enemies? A minority of Germans were opposed to monetary union, believed that Adenauer's Germany belonged to the past, and considered the bond with France too close. The drubbing the French Socialists received in the 1993 elections resulted from their perceived failure to deal with unemployment, as well as from a subtler feeling. Nearly half of the voters rejected the Maastricht Treaty in the 1992 referendum because the French state was no longer able to protect them. They were not anti-German, but a loosening of the Franco-German tie was implicit in their view. Richelieu would have understood them. But both France and Germany had invested too much time, money, and political capital in their cooperation—and in the leading role it offered them in Europe—to abandon it now. In 1993 they needed an effort of political imagination to launch themselves and Europe again. They needed to win back that convergence of popular opinion that de Gaulle had created and that, from 1990 on, had started to ebb.

Notes

1. Jacques Bainville, *Histoire de deux peuples: la France et l'Empire allemand* (Paris: Nouvelle Librairie nationale 1914), p. 305.
2. Harry Graf Kessler, *Tagebücher 1918–1937* (Frankfurt: Insel Taschenbuch 1981, first published 1961), p. 716.
3. Albert Camus, "Lettres à un ami allemand," in *Oeuvres complètes,* Volume 2 (Paris: Pléiade 1965), pp. 219–243.
4. Today we would be more skeptical about "national character" and we might point out that Paul Claudel felt the need for discipline, which Kessler considers typically German.
5. Maurice Martin du Gard, *Les Mémorables 1918–1945* (Paris: Gallimard 1999), p. 35.
6. Here again one cannot really generalize for Gide's friend; Valery Larbaud disliked what he considered the spurious, arrogant greatness of Nietzschean man.
7. Patrick McCarthy: "The Larbaud-Ray Correspondence," *Revue de Littérature comparée* 1968/3, pp. 431–443.

8. Hélène Barbey-Say, *Le voyage de France en Allemagne de 1871 à 1914* (Presses universitaires de Nancy 1994).

9. François Seydoux, *Mémoires d'Outre-Rhin* (Paris: Grasset 1971), p. 14.

10. Patrick McCarthy, "Le dialogue de Jacques Rivière et de Valery Larbaud," *Bulletin des amis de Rivière* 1977/2, pp. 7–19.

11. See Charles Maurras, *Un débat sur le romantisme* (Paris: Flammarion 1928).

12. *Mémoires d'Outre-Rhin*, p. 95.

13. Stanley Hoffmann's "Paradoxes of the French Political Community" still seems to me the best analysis of the Third Republic. See S. Hoffmann et al., *In Search of France* (Cambridge: Harvard University Press 1968), pp. 1–118.

14. André François-Poncet, *Au Palais Farnèse* (Paris: Fayard 1961), p. 39 and p. 161.

15. *Mémoires d'Outre-Rhin*, p. 75.

16. For a balanced account see Richard Kuisel, *Seducing the French* (Berkeley: University of California Press 1993).

17. In 1942 a large number of Jews were rounded up and placed in this cycling stadium before being deported to concentration camps. Mitterrand denied that the Republic bore any responsibility but President Chirac admitted that it did.

18. *Mémoires d'Outre-Rhin*, p. 214.

19. Konrad Adenauer, *Erinnerungen 1943–1953* (Stuttgart: Deutsche Verlags-Anstalt 1963), p. 245.

20. The author is drawing on his personal memories.

21. Douglas Webber, "Agricultural Policy: The Hard Core" in his edited *The Franco-German Relationship in the European Union* (London: Routledge 1999), pp. 111–129).

22. Andrew Moravcsik, *The Choice for Europe: Social Purpose and State Power from Messina to Maastricht* (Ithaca: Cornell University Press 1998).

23. Valéry Giscard d'Estaing, *Démocratie française* (Paris: Fayard 1976), p. 123 and pp. 154–155.

24. Here again the author is drawing on personal experience.

25. Jean-François Revel, *Comment les démocraties finissent* (Paris: Grasset, Second Edition, First Edition 1983), pp. 409–419.

26. Philip Gordon, "The Franco-German Security Partnership," in Patrick Mc-Carthy, editor, *France-Germany 1983–1993* (New York: St. Martin's Press 1993), pp. 139–160.

27. George-Henri Soutou, *L'Alliance incertaine* (Paris: Fayard 1996), p. 421.

28. Edouard Balladur, "Mémorandum sur la construction monétaire européen," *Ecu* 3 (1988), p. 19.

Chapter 2

France and Germany: An Unlikely Couple

Michael Stürmer

Myths do matter, and one of the most powerful myths of modern Europe is that of *le couple franco-allemand*. Those who expect great passion between the partners are as likely to be disappointed as those who see nothing but a marriage of convenience. In the real world the myth of Franco-German togetherness can only be so powerful because it is backed by much common ground, a successful exchange program for young people, a number of elite gatherings like the industrialists' annual meeting at Evian, or the activities and publications of BILD, the umbrella group that created *Documents* and *Dokumente*. On a different level, industrial cooperation is expanding, not only in the defense sphere but also in cutting-edge life sciences (Hoechst and Rhone Poulenc merging into Aventis). There is even, in spite of the deep philosophical and strategic differences between France and Germany, enhanced military cooperation; this is all the more important as France stays aloof from NATO while Germany is at the center.

Above all, there is a shared interest in running the fate of the European Union together rather than against each other, let alone being outnumbered and outgunned by the majority of smaller countries—now and even more so in the future. Policymakers on both sides, Paris and Berlin, have a keen interest in preserving and maneuvering the balance of power in Europe. In the past, that is, before 1989, this meant Western Europe. In the future, once the widening process of the EU—the acquisition of new members—gains momentum, "Europe" will also mean what used to be called Eastern Europe.

This future began, although the participants did not realize it, the very evening the Berlin Wall came down. "Economic and Monetary Union (EMU)," drawing closer together via new institutions, "Deepening" and "Widening" are all part and parcel of the new balances that are in the making, with Germany and France the protagonists—and sometimes the antagonists. If, by and large, both countries continue to pursue largely complementary policies, the European Union can expand and flourish. If not, not.

The very openness of the EU's unwritten constitution had allowed both sides, not only at the time of Helmut Schmidt and Valéry Giscard d'Estaing but even more so at the time of François Mitterrand and Helmut Kohl, to reinforce their own national roles through sharing a European role. Inevitably, the fall of the Berlin Wall was bound to be a shock for the couple's marital bliss, as Germany seemed to win what France seemed to lose—at least in Mitterrand's history-saturated view. Would not Germany win unity and aspire to first rank in Europe while France lost her share in Four Power control over Germany and thus no longer exercised sovereignty over Berlin? Even the role of nuclear weapons, which would be easily predictable once the nuclear bipolarity of over forty years was out of fashion, would no longer be a valid entry ticket to the club running the world. *Tenir le rang* (maintaining its place) became, once again, as under de Gaulle, a vital French instinct.

In short, the fall of the Wall not only changed some of the currencies of power but also offered an X-ray view of the structures underlying every European equilibrium and disequilibrium, including the most important relationship inside the EU, that between Germany and France. Memories went back to the grand bargain that, in the early fifties, had laid to rest the demons of the past—or at least a sufficient number of them. The European Community of Coal and Steel, in conceptional terms going back to pre-1914 ideas of Walther Rathenau and to pre-1933 ideas promoted by French and German industrialists, had not only fused both countries' heavy industry but also allowed mutual control.

Ever since, enlightened politics went hand in hand with sound economics. The "Montan Union" of 1952 had become the conceptual base for the European Economic Community of 1958, opening French industrial markets to German big business and German agricultural markets to French agriculture.

But there was more to it in the original grand design: European economic integration should run parallel to integrating political destinies. What the end result would and should be, both sides left for history to decide. The compromise formula in the Rome Treaty of 1957 allowed both sides to follow incompatible dreams. For the Germans, ever closer union meant that they would transcend the prison of their unloved nation-state and become Europeans who happened to speak German. For the French it meant that they could preserve the essence of *la grande nation* through the European construction. Right from the start, however, the Franco-German community of interest was decidedly asymmetrical, once economic integration through the Coal and Steel Pool had taken off while defense integration in the EDC (European Defense Community) had crashed.

In fact, the EDC had been conceived in 1952 as an answer to American plans for the creation of a new German army and for bringing Germany into NATO. Through the EDC the French would have been in control. But they would also have had to shed a few illusions about grandeur, sovereignty, and having won the Second World War. Germany was down-and-out in military terms, while France still tried to keep the stardust of Empire together, somehow. Moreover, memories of collaboration and resistance were still fresh, and bleeding. So, while economic integration began to flourish, defense integration became a victim of an unholy alliance between Gaullists and Communists in the Assemblée Nationale one August morning in 1954. Ever since, the "ever closer union," while incorporated in the Rome Treaty only three years later, had a hollow ring; it was regarded as at best foolish, at worst dangerous to ask what it meant in the real world.

The result of the EDC's failure was inevitable. Germany found its destiny within NATO, while the "Europe of the Six"—and, subsequently, the Europe of the twelve and fifteen—developed into a hybrid plant: a political dwarf and an economic giant. The ensuing disequilibrium in the European construction, however, did not matter very much as long as the Cold War went on. It was the United States anyhow who, via NATO, offered extended deterrence against the Soviet threat, and, with or without French consent, largely determined Europe's strategic destinies.

But in the cold morning light of November 10, 1989, with the Cold War no longer the organizing principle, all bets were off. U.S. troops might withdraw, removing the linchpin from the West European construction and introducing an unwelcome moment of truth. If the Soviets really insisted and used all their negotiating power, including their influence among the left-leaning German intelligentsia, Germany might pay for unity in the currency of its NATO or European commitment—thus forcing France, once again, to seek salvation through the United States. In France even the Rapallo dossier, vintage 1922, coming from a different time and age, was reopened. There were hidden fears that, once again, France would be lost between perfidious Albion in the West, this time including the Americans, and the Germans and Russians in the East.

The nightmares from the archives came in large numbers, dating back to the aftermath of the First World War when the French system of security had fallen apart because the Americans retreated from the shores of Europe and the British turned rather pro-German. There were the ghosts of Dunkirk 1940 and of the humiliations that de Gaulle was exposed to while saving France; the loss of Empire after 1945 and the diplomatic defeat at the Suez Canal in 1956. There were sad memories of grand designs shattered. The whole of twentieth-century history was in evidence once the joyous crowds from all over Western Europe had danced on the Berlin Wall. Until that night the Iron Curtain had separated the world but, at the same time, had also kept it in a precarious balance.

Mitterrand, instead of sending Kohl (his friend of many toasts) his best wishes for the German version of the one, indivisible nation, especially in the anniversary year of France's great revolution, made it clear that he wanted a veto; as this was clearly beyond his reach, he at least wanted to be compensated. Chancellor Kohl, having forever insisted that German unity and European integration were merely "different sides of the same medal," was aware that in this game of reestablishing the balance of Europe, France could and did expect some compensation. If not, Germany would face, whether the chancellor in Bonn liked it or not, Bismarck's time-honored "nightmare of coalitions." As a consequence, Germany would risk the falling apart of the European construction, including all the benefits it offered to both countries.

Kohl and Mitterrand, whatever divided them in 1989, remembered that, ever since the Vienna Congress, Germany was too big for balance and too small for hegemony. The answer, to Kohl, was clearly to be found in strengthening NATO in order to reinforce Germany's vital American connection. But it was also to be found in readjusting the political and economic equation between Germany and France within the European Community. "Widening," or extending the legal and economic space of Europe toward Eastern Central Europe, was not yet a practical idea, with one small exception: Eastern Germany.

Jacques Delors, president of the European Commission, stated that the Germans in the GDR (German Democratic Republic) had a rightful place within the Community. In fact the Rome Treaty had conceded to the Bonn government under Adenauer that, in conformity with the *Grundgesetz* and the Paris-Bonn Treaty—also called *Deutschlandvertrag*—the other part of Germany would not be treated as a foreign country and its exports would be allowed into West Germany free of all customs, duties, and the like. This old provision took on a new meaning once the Wall had fallen and German unity came over the horizon as a practical proposition, in fact the only one.

But Delors had also paved the way for more to come: after the Single Market, his much publicized 1992 program, it was now the time of the common currency. That was what the French leader wanted, while the German chancellor was willing to discuss the difficult matter only with a vast number of "ifs and buts" attached. The Bundesbank found the project worth discussing, but certainly no more, and to stand against the Bundesbank in German public opinion was a risk no politician in his right mind would ever risk.

When Kohl pronounced his—on the whole, well-considered and, in the face of the awesome implications of the fall of the Wall, even timid—Ten Point Plan on November 28, 1989, Mitterrand reacted with shock, anger, and threats. His adviser and confidant Jacques Attali, in his three-volume *Verbatim*, describes Mitterrand's reaction, which included hints to German foreign minister Genscher that, if the Germans were to continue the great game of power politics, they might soon see themselves confronted by a Paris-London-Moscow triangle.

Kohl got a message that he took very seriously, perhaps overrating the power of the French president. Certainly he was aware of the fact that to build the future Europe on a fundamental French frustration would, by necessity, result in failure. Brinkmanship was not in his character, nor was it in the German national interest. Kohl must have seen that, if things went wrong with France, the whole Adenauer-Schuman construction could unravel within a few years. It was nightmare against nightmare, Mitterrand versus Kohl, German versus French. No amount of Grand Cru or Riesling would ever be enough to swamp the depths of history.

Indeed, the French president had not been consulted on how to proceed. He was informed only minutes before the chancellor went public on November 28, 1989, using the Bundestag's budget debate as a forum to present to the nation and the world at large how he proposed to proceed: carefully, with due respect for Four Power responsibilities—which would have to end in the end—with bilateral and multilateral consultation. The whole procedure would be based on the Grundgesetz, the Paris-Bonn Treaty of 1954, the Helsinki declaration, and the entire body of international law including the forthcoming Treaty on Conventional Stability in Europe.

Possibly, the chancellor indicated, the Germans might move from separate states to a confederate structure and from there to some kind of unity yet undefined and undefinable, and all of this not soon but in a timeframe of perhaps ten years. This was not, by any standard, the German revolution. It was no more but also no less than the German answer to the decline and fall of the great Soviet Empire. Anything short of this evolutionary concept would have cost Kohl and the CDU (Christian Democrats) their leadership in Germany and would have enhanced the international crisis, which was already at a high-water mark.

Mitterrand complained to himself and to others that Kohl's procedure and style were not in keeping with the spirit of the Elysée Treaty, renewed with much fanfare in 1983. But France, much as other NATO allies, had been in the habit of subscribing to the common NATO position that the unification of Germany as part of a wider Western system was not only desirable in theory but an objective to work for in practice. In no way did Kohl step beyond what he had said, in the Bundestag and elsewhere, many times before. But the traditional NATO vision of Germany's happy, democratic, and united future had always been platonic. Now it was the real thing. History was on the move again.

Mitterrand, for all his Florentine realism, seemed to be lost in his bitterness and frustration, and French public opinion was not a moderating force. The political class was by and large on the president's side, with French quality newspapers ruminating about the emerging "Quatrième Empire." Meanwhile the average Frenchman found that events on the other side of the Rhine warranted a feeling of relief—good riddance as far as the Russians were concerned, and best wishes for the Germans.

This time Mitterrand was led not by his instinct for reality but by the myths of history. Instead of walking triumphantly with the chancellor through the Brandenburg Gate, closed on August 13, 1961, and now opened again, Mitterrand came to see Egon Krentz, Honecker's maladroit successor. For this he went, of all places, to Leipzig where, 176 years before, Napoleon had been defeated by the united forces of Russia, Austria, and Germany. This *entrevue* was, for Krentz, a moment of illusion; for Mitterrand, a sad day of delusion.

While Mitterrand's excursion to Leipzig showed an unusual lack of judgment, the subsequent meeting with Gorbachev in Kiev would emphasize the role and weight of France in international affairs, and especially in all matters German. But apart from increasing the pressure on Kohl and Genscher it affected little in terms of French interests. And what were they, anyway? After a time adrift, the French presidency and even more so the Quai d'Orsay—helped by the then French ambassador to Germany Serge Boidevaix—collected their professional sangfroid and found that standing in the way of German unity was not only useless but positively dangerous. Russian weakness, American resolve, and the pressure of events in Germany, especially the stream of East-to-West refugees, set the real agenda. To stand in the way of the combined Americans, Germans, and Russians could not be a realistic policy for Paris.

So even the siren songs from London's Iron Lady, who entertained similar doubts to those of the master of the Elysée, went unanswered, if not unheard. Margaret Thatcher invited a group of French industrial leaders to find out whether they had a policy to offer. When she found out that the leaders of French industry kept their calm, Mrs. Thatcher, always a realist, let the Baker boys in Washington and Kohl's people in Bonn have their way. She did, however, convene an eminent historians' seminar over a spring weekend at Chequers to find an answer to the question "Have the Germans changed?" Whatever the outcome, it was to her credit that she went to listen to the oracle of history. Whether or not she liked what she heard from the professors, we do not know. But in due course she added her signature to the "Two plus Four" agreement that was to close the books on the Second World War without, of course, offering full guarantees that nothing untoward would happen to the end of time.

In 1989, nobody was obliged to join the Germans in their celebrations and share the emotional upheaval. Political leaders, including those in Bonn, found a lot to worry about. In early December 1989, Bush and Gorbachev met on huge battleships off the coast of Malta, and the ancient gods of the Mediterranean, by sending a storm, reminded them that there were forces beyond their control and that they had better retreat to firm ground. If ever there was a summit full of omens and warnings, it was this one, and the message, according to Brent Scowcroft, was not lost on the leaders.

Seeing the turmoil, both Mrs. Thatcher in London and Mitterrand in Paris were entirely justified in wanting to know what the Germans were up to this time around, and in refusing to issue a blank check to Helmut Kohl, let alone his opposite number Hans Modrow in East Berlin. The source of their concern was not so much German history of the nineteenth and twentieth centuries, as the two of them were realistic enough to understand that no replay of Wilhelmine power politics, let alone Hitler's revolution to end all revolutions, was underway.

The point was essentially one of equilibrium or rather the fear of disequilibrium. If, to the powerhouse of the Federal Republic, the vastly overrated and, in practical terms, largely ruined East German economy was added, every economic and political balance in the European Community would be overthrown. Little did the non-German leaders know that East German industry, with pitifully few exceptions, was unable to compete in world markets and, on the whole, ready for the rubbish dump. As a result of much economic data laundering by the East Germans and an unlimited willingness in the West to believe Communist fairy tales, in 1990 the prevailing view was still that the East Germans had a claim to be Comecon's California.

The Bonn government shared many of those illusions. Serious cabinet ministers were jubilant that unification would finance itself, it thus simply privatized the treasures of German Democratic Republic (GDR) industry and the lands confiscated by the Communists between 1945 and 1949. However, the moment of truth was soon to come; over 150 billion

Deutschmarks have since flown from West to East Germany annually in order to save the social balances and to reconstruct the East German infrastructure, largely state-of-the-art 1938.

In the light of reality, both the German hopes and the French fears of an economic giant emerging from the fusion of East German and West German industry proved to be far off the mark. But given the wobbliness of many German politicians on the left and the center who were willing, if necessary, to swap unity for neutralism, anxieties in London and Paris were amply warranted. Indeed it would have been a sublime irony if the Soviets, by losing their garrison state on the Elbe, had gained what they could never achieve at the time of their greatness: the neutralization of Germany.

Germany swapping NATO for unity would have meant, for the West, snatching defeat from the jaws of victory. Until Kohl received Gorbachev's assurance in the Caucasus on July 15, 1990, this was seen, in Paris and London, as a not too far-fetched possibility. Meanwhile the Americans, aware of the risk, did everything to prevent such a dangerous question from ever being put to the Germans. But from Egon Bahr to Hans Dietrich Genscher, who was, after all, the foreign minister, there were open minds.

Fortunately, from the Malta Summit in early December 1989 to the signing ceremony of the "Two plus Four" agreement one year later, the Russians never had the power nor the nerve to force the issue, and the Americans never had the slightest intention of conceding such a demand. Kohl, for one, had his priorities very clear, and it is a testimony to Western statesmanship that Germany's NATO link remained unchallenged while the country was united. What the Russians received was no more than written assurances that NATO would not station nuclear weapons in the new eastern provinces, and that, until all Russian troops had departed, no NATO-assigned troops would be stationed in the former GDR territory.

Meanwhile Mitterrand, Mrs. Thatcher, and the German left were united in wanting the negotiations on Germany's present and future status to last for a long time. On the SPD (Social Democrat) side, no less than five years were mentioned. That also happened to be the view of the international department of the Communist Party of the Soviet Union's (CPSU) Central Committee, with Valentin Falin the head, and also of parts of the Soviet foreign ministry. Instead, Messrs. Kohl, Bush, and Baker forged ahead. They shared a deep concern that the window of opportunity, opened by Gorbachev, might suddenly close; that Gorbachev might be toppled by hard-liners, which almost happened at the CPSU congress in early July 1990; or that other business might interfere—as was the case when Saddam Hussein occupied Kuwait on August 2, 1990, only days after Gorbachev and Kohl had put the final touches to the great compromise.

The 273 days from the opening of the Berlin Wall to the raising of the black, red, and gold colors all over Germany were a defining period for Germany and the Germans. But in the course of events, NATO and the European Union were also undergoing vast changes and were being largely redesigned—in fact, reinvented. By implication, relations between France and Germany were severely tested. This is clear from all the memoirs and first-hand accounts available today, including the vast body of documents from the chancellery in Bonn that were published in the summer of 1998. The key term was and continued to be *balance*.

But in the world after the Wall, there was not much balance between the United States and its European allies, or among the latter. And there was clearly not enough balance between France and Germany. So integration was to be the magic formula to overcome the new imbalances, to give reassurance and, as the somewhat strange and irritating Bonn formula said, to "bind" Germany. Moreover, U.S. Secretary of State James Baker wanted to create a security space from Vancouver to Vladivostok. He was supported by German Foreign Minister Hans Dietrich Genscher, who praised the fail-safe concept of "interlocking institutions" securing peace and prosperity like an ingenious machine, which, once invented, would be the strategic *perpetuum mobile.*

In the workshop of Franco-German relations the chancellor saw to it that the Franco-German brigade, created after the "Bold Sparrow" maneuvers, was transformed into the Euro Corps, headquartered in Strasbourg. Although both sides—and soon, also, Belgium and Spain—could not easily agree on possible deployment of the 50,000 men, the meaning was clear. It was, above all, political: to reassure the French about German military might, capped at 370,000 anyway in the process of unification, and to build a bridge between NATO-integrated German troops and non-integrated French troops.

A similar procedure was followed, with less fanfare and much more ease, when the German-Dutch, the German-British, and the German-American Corps were set up. In Kohl's view the political rationale was, once again, to reassure Germany's neighbors about its intentions and capabilities. The grim irony was that very soon NATO partners, involved in the Middle East against Iraq, would be more worried about German weakness than German strength. When sending a light division to the desert, Mitterrand let it be known to the world and especially to the Germans, who abstained, that France could not stand by while justice was raped.

Within Europe, the West European Union (WEU), once called the sleeping beauty of European security, was kissed awake. Defense planners began to understand that with the Soviet threat no longer the organizing principle of European security, the Americans might want to follow their insular instincts and leave European defense to the Europeans. While the British Defense Ministry resisted every attempt to emancipate European defense from U.S. dominance, the French presidency continued to pursue the classical Gaullist concept of European semi-independence—that is, accepting U.S. presence as a balancer from beyond the sea and U.S. intervention as a last resort.

Germany, caught in the imaginary prison of its constitution and its refusal to entertain any strategic thinking "out of area," tried to find the answer in a low-profile role for the WEU while the strategic drama would remain a NATO matter. Thus the "Petersburg tasks" were invented, in line with the modest European capabilities and the NATO-first strategy pursued by British, Dutch, Danish, and German planners. While the Euro Corps rhetoric was running high, the bottom line was clear: in strategic terms, France and Germany continued to find themselves at opposite ends of the European spectrum. The French were nation-minded, the Germans integration-minded; the French were nuclear, the Germans conventional; the French saw the United States as intruders, the Germans welcomed U.S. troops as the ultimate guarantors of security and balance in Europe, and against the residual military potential of the former Soviet Union.

It was only in the summer of 1999 when European leaders had been saved, but also humiliated, by U.S. intervention against Yugoslavia over the Kosovo atrocities, that the WEU was harnessed to the EU bandwagon. That is, the WEU should in the not-too-distant future serve as the *bras armé* of the Brussels-based merchants and bankers club. Some of the chiefs of government present at the Cologne Summit of 1998 might have believed that from then on Europe would count as a military power, that the "European Pillar" had finally been built, and that a balance between Europe and the United States had been established.

Nothing, however, would be further from the truth. While the United States turned its military around from Cold War force structures to rapid deployment forces ready to fight two different regional wars almost at the same time, the Europeans, especially the Germans, let their military run down. Military outlay in most European countries is at an all-time low. Only the French and the British have kept up their numbers and modernization somewhat in line with the United States. But none among the European powers has the technology, the means, and the will to keep pace with the U.S.-led "Revolution in Military Affairs."

Moreover, there is a serious contradiction in the intended EU-WEU merger. The WEU as such has no military muscle. At best, it can collect military forces through double-hatting or, more specifically, falling back on NATO. The same is true for state-of-the-art C3I equipment (command, control, communication, and information), wide-bodied transport aircraft, and naval transport. Without NATO and the United States there cannot be a serious effort.

Moreover, there is also a political contradiction. The EU is set to incorporate soon a number of countries in Eastern Central Europe, and by implication these countries would also be involved in the future WEU. But, as the WEU cannot function without NATO, this would amount to what the U.S. senate has always seen, and disliked, as a backdoor entry into NATO. That means that either the NATO link will be weakened or the WEU will become meaningless.

Only recently, through mergers in Britain and between French and German defense industries (DASA of Daimler Chrysler and MATRA and Aérospatiale of the Group Lagardere), industry has created the necessary critical mass. The rationale is not only military-industrial. It is also evident that the enormous investment in C3I that the Pentagon is channeling into U.S. industries will, rather sooner than later, produce a vast array of dual-use goods that will dominate markets both military and nonmilitary. Europeans can simply not afford to watch and do nothing. Governments in Paris and Berlin have been helpful in this, but have neither taken the initiative nor acted as matchmakers, let alone given assurances as to future procurement.

Those modifications in the transatlantic equation, however, are not central to European security, nor are they likely to lend substance to the Maastricht-generated Common Foreign and Security Policy (CFSP) of the EU. The idea that the latter could be the future hard core of Political Union, as stipulated at Maastricht in 1991, is far from European reality. Nor can CFSP serve as an organizing principle. Both the predominance of the United States and the resistance of national egos are too strong for this. The effort at European defense identity can, at best, add a European political element to NATO. In the foreseeable future, this will not fundamentally change the historical architecture of Europe characterized by the predominance of the economy. It was in this dimension above all that Kohl and Mitterrand all sought to reestablish the European equilibrium after 1989, or more specifically to redress the balance between France and Germany.

After the fall of the Wall the Europeans faced a choice few of them liked: to have more of Germany or more of Europe. Mrs. Thatcher found the alternative almost unacceptable but, always a realist, fell in line with U.S. and German policy without asking a price. Not so the master of the Elysée. It may well be that his initial shock reaction was genuine. But it could also be that he wanted to make it perfectly clear that, after Germany had finally said farewell to the Second World War and its inheritance, France was owed ample compensation. Helmut Kohl had won the whole of Germany. So why not ask for half the Bundesbank?

Ever since the crisis inflicted on the French franc by socialist overspending and the salvage operation by the Bundesbank and the Bonn chancellery in the spring of 1983, French monetary policy had, by and large, been run from Frankfurt. The president of the Bundesbank used to honor his French colleague by informing him by telephone before any other central banker whenever, on a Thursday afternoon, the Bundesbank council had decided what policy was good for Germany and, by implication, for the Deutschmark zone. France in fact had ceded monetary sovereignty to what *Le Monde*, in line with prevailing opinion among the political class in Paris, would call, at times, *le monstre de Francfort*.

Whereas monetary union had been seen, ever since the original Messina Conference, as the crowning finale of European economic and political integration, the sea change of 1989 turned it into the means by which to balance France and Germany. The Delors Commission had developed, together with the "Single Market," blueprints for the common currency and a European Central Bank to run it as early as 1988. The German response had always been polite refusal. The argument was that it came too soon, that policies differed widely and wildly, that inflation rates were incompatible and too high anyway, and that institutions were not in place.

The fall of the Wall changed all this overnight, literally. Kohl, pressured by Mitterrand, repeated the accepted wisdom. But he also realized that if Bonn did not make major concessions, his concept of a united Germany in an integrated Europe might suffer, and that France and Germany might in fact find themselves in deep and devastating conflict. "Two plus Four," while setting a framework for Germany's future role in NATO, was silent on EU matters. They were to be decided by an intergovernmental conference in 1991. While Mitterrand was happy to have one conference on EMU, Kohl insisted there had to be a second, and parallel, conference on Political Union. In order to save the Franco-German equilibrium he wanted a balance to be established between the political integration that he deemed essential and the monetary integration that Mitterrand insisted on. To the doubtful Germans he confirmed that without common policies there would and could not be a common currency.

After almost one year of negotiations, what emerged at the European Council at Maastricht were two dossiers: a fat one on EMU, comprising all of the *acquis communautaires,* and a thin one on Political Union. The latter mentioned, in a mere dozen words, "Common Foreign and Security Policy," and promised to study the possibility of a security and defense identity but by and large went nowhere in particular. The Germans, when asked, did have a detailed answer as to what Political Union meant beyond the current slogans. So to save appearances, the political business was shelved until, a few years later, a "Maastricht II" conference would attempt to find all the answers not yet found.

When this "Maastricht II" took place in the summer of 1997, the foreign policy "Second Pillar" remained largely unspecified, while "Third Pillar" business, comprising police and passport matters, met with stiff resistance from the nation states, not least from Germany.

In the meantime, German public opinion, while still skeptical, had slowly come to see the benefits of currency union. Industry—most notably the Bundesverband der Deutschen Industrie (Employers' Association) through its president Hans Olaf Henkel—welcomed the common currency as a means to curb politicians' spending fever, to put a damper on wages, to soften up the Deutschmark that was regarded as too strong against the U.S. dollar, and to provide a large economic space in an era of globalization. The trade unions, for their part, accepted the political bargain. While academic opinion was largely against the euro, there was hardly any substantial political debate, and no party dared to make the euro an electoral issue.

For a final verdict, the jury is still out. Banks and industry in both France and Germany are taking the common currency as a starting point. The general public is anxiously watching the poor performance of the euro in comparison with the dollar, but industry and trade unions see a bonus in precisely this fact. Political correctness has it that, in homage to Hegel: belief in the cunning of reason, the convergence of policies, generally deemed desirable, will come as an inevitable result of the use of the euro.

Meanwhile not only do the euro's long-term prospects demand the "deepening" of European institutions and policies, including the entire management modus between the Commission, the European Council, the nation-states, and the regions; but there is also the promise of "widening," issued most generously and almost indiscriminately to candidate countries to the south and east, including Turkey. Earlier on, French bureaucrats feared that in this "widening" process, Germany would win influence. But now both countries together are trying to make sure that in the future they cannot be put into a minority.

Altogether, the European project seems to have run out of imagination, power, and a sense of direction. Too much is being envisaged without the institutions catching up, let alone providing a suitable home for the visions. The Franco-German engine, while it effected the new balance in Western Europe, seems to be exhausted. The defense project lacks analysis, strategy, and serious effort. The common currency has not brought the fundamental long-term convergence that was promised. The Political Union is, in all serious matters, a house of cards. Industry and the banks are operating within the euro system but also, with even more rigor, beyond its confines.

Ten years after zero hour in Berlin, France and Germany still believe in their *destin commun*. But in daily life the marriage, after having overcome the fall of the Wall, the drama of "Two plus Four," and the ambiguities of the common currency, is once again in for some healthy routine. But the more the sole surviving superpower is otherwise engaged, the more defense matters become pressing, as does the process of widening Europe's economic and security space. This will demand much more institutional and political convergence than has been needed in the past. And for this, the couple is not well prepared.

Chapter 3 ❖

Ten Years After the Fall of the Wall: France's New View of Germany

Ulrike Guerot

Nothing Is Like It Was . . .

F rance is puzzled and lost. It has difficulties measuring and understanding the profound changes of the new *Berliner Republik*. It has problems analyzing and reacting to the new German way of "defending its own national interest" in the framework of European policy. The sense of direction within the Franco-German relationship, if not the tacit French leadership position in defining European policy, is gone. The good old days—when François Mauriac could claim that France loves Germany so much it is glad there are two of them—definitely belong to another century.

Nobody recognizes deep changes when they happen. France and Germany were both too preoccupied to understand the full extent of societal, political, and economic changes that arose in the post–1989 era. The continuity of François Mitterrand in the French presidency, Helmut Kohl in the German chancellery, and Jacques Delors at the top of the European Commission made it possible to marshal a final political effort on behalf of European integration. In 1992, the Maastricht Treaty was signed and the creation of the euro put on track. That was the last positive momentum in the history of Franco-German relations as the engine of Europe. The treaty overloaded the civil societies of both countries with repercussions on their party systems. The French party system literally collapsed under the pressure of the Maastricht debate, and European policy emerged as the real and true dividing line on the electoral landscape, replacing the traditional right/left-wing scheme. Realizing that civil society was becoming more disconnected from the project of European integration during the Maastricht process, France and Germany both submitted to electoral constraints and avoided clarification of what "European Political Union" finally should be. In this respect, the 1990s—or, more precisely, the years since 1992—have seen an accumulation of missed opportunities for the European project as well as countless misunderstandings, all covered by the tenuous rhetoric that "nothing has changed in Franco-German relations" and that everything would continue as it was.

France and Germany took ten years to realize that none of this is true. Ten years to face the fact that the former "partner" is no longer the same, that the binational engine is in trouble, and that there is no longer any clear and common Franco-German idea or vision of what Europe should be in the future. Thus, the core of the European project is missing, as the spokesman of the Christian Democratic Union/Christian Social Union (CDU/CSU) group in the German Bundestag, Karl Lamers, recently put it.[1] The countries that signed the Maastricht Treaty are no longer the same. Those having to fill the treaty with life also changed. The enlargement process of the European Union is threatening its political dimension as never before. And perhaps the former French defense minister, Jean-Pierre Chevènement, was not only right but wise in saying immediately after the events of November 1989: "Le mur de Berlin est tombé, un mort: Jacques Delors."[2]

In this contribution, we will analyze changes in French European policy after Maastricht, looking at both the external and the domestic dimensions of the treaty between 1992 and 1995 (I). We will then try to describe the Amsterdam negotiations in 1997 and how the failure of the treaty encouraged new French thinking about Germany in the years 1996 and 1997 (II). Finally, we will take a close look at the developments of the past two years, starting with the election of Gerhard Schröder as German Chancellor in October 1998 and the EU summit in Berlin in March 1999, a watershed in Franco-German relations. The outlook will touch upon the deep confusion about what happened at the EU Helsinki Summit in December 1999 and the very unclear prospects for the next intergovernmental conference, which should be concluded under the forthcoming French EU presidency in the second half of 2000 (III). Considering that this might be the last chance for the Franco-German couple to determine the path and the direction of European integration, the month preceding the EU Council in Nice in December 2000 will be historically very decisive.

I. Political Dimension and Consequences of the Maastricht Treaty

Mixing up the structure of Franco-German relations:
The undigested Treaty

The Maastricht Treaty, there is no doubt, was signed at a specifically favorable moment of history, using the dynamic of German Reunification.[3] There can also be no doubt that France and Germany signed it with very different motivations: France to lock Germany into the process of monetary union, Germany to signal its willingness to deepen European integration after its reunification. Since the time of Chancellor Adenauer, the slogan of German foreign policy has been that German and European unification are two sides of the same coin. The treaty happened to trigger a big European synergy in pushing forward and finally realizing monetary union. But until today, the political dimension of the Maastricht Treaty remains unclear and, in this sense, it is something that can be called the last "creative misunderstanding" in Franco-German relations. For moving forward in times of "creative misunderstanding" has been the guiding principle of the two countries' special relationship since the Elysée Treaty was signed in 1963. It has to be remembered that even in those days, the very political message of the Elysée Treaty remained unclear. Its principle component, cooperation in the field of security policy, was nullified with the German Bundestag's passage of a preamble that split the German political milieu into "Atlanticists" and "Gaullists" for years to come.[4] This did not prevent the treaty from being a good one, inspiring the creation of the "Franco-German Youth Agency," a reliable basis for reconciliation through the multiplication of contacts among citizens, in particular youth. Yet, in its core aim, the Elysée Treaty was an empty folder, just like the political dimension of the Maastricht Treaty. For Maastricht, while undoubtedly a success story as regards EMU, could not hide the fact that the structural asymmetry characterizing Franco-German relations since the end of the war was gone. Stanley Hofmann's *équilibre du déséquilibre*—the political strength of France compensating for the economic power of Germany—had vanished in 1989 with the completion of Germany's political restoration in the international family. All of those unspoken fundamentals of the Franco-German relationship, everything that France thought to offer Germany in the period up to 1989 and spelled out in de Gaulle's memoirs,[5] were fading away: France's assistance for Germany to regain international legitimacy; France's offer to be an additional element of security against the Soviet threat; France's willingness to help Germany achieve reunification. (These were the basic points that de Gaulle offered to Adenauer at his residence in Colombey-les-deux-Eglises where the two leaders prepared the Elysée Treaty. In return de Gaulle asked Adenauer for financial aid for

French agriculture and for a strong Franco-German partnership against Great Britain.) The Germany of post–1989 no longer needed any of those French offers. Would Germany continue to need France at all? Would it need and continue European integration in the way it did before? When France looked at Germany between 1989 and 1992, these were the dominant concerns, and the behavior of Mitterrand—analyzed elsewhere[6]—speaks volumes about this. The Maastricht Treaty was said to be the answer. But in retrospect, leaving EMU momentarily aside, it was more the closing chapter of Franco-German relations and European integration between 1957 and 1989, than the blueprint for Europe's future.[7] The following years are nothing but the restless search for new goals for the Franco-German engine, and for the project of European integration as a whole. But the quest for this "new finality" of European integration grew increasingly difficult in a changing domestic and electoral landscape, first in France, then in Germany.

Mixing up the societies: The domestic consequences of Maastricht in the period 1992–1995

Since the referendum on the Maastricht Treaty, the French political and electoral system is out of step. The very narrow vote in favor in ratification—only some 51 percent voted yes—literally split French society, including most of the parties, into two parts. The "enemies" of Maastricht could be found in both parts of the political spectrum. Philippe Séguin, president of the National Assembly, and Charles Pasqua, former Minister of the Interior, organized the anti-Maastricht wing within the Gaullist party.[8] The focus of the argument was the abdication of national sovereignty to Europe in the fields of monetary, interior, and security policies. Séguin often invoked the spirit of the French Republic as autonomous and undivided. The fundamental inseparability of the French republic and "the nation" expressed in the famous concept of "nation-state" meant to him and his supporters that the signature of Maastricht would eviscerate France as a country. As an alternative, Seguin formulated a "counter-concept" to what he called "Maastricht Europe" in a speech on December 1, 1993, entitled "For the refounding of the great Europe," thereby setting the tone for the next European elections in June 1994.[9] Within the Gaullist establishment and electorate, he easily could refer to de Gaulle's ideas of "The Europe of Independent Nations" extending from the Atlantic to the Urals. The manifest cleavage within the Gaullist party along the dividing line between a "supranational" Europe (Maastricht) and an "intergovernmental" Europe—only five Rassemblement du Peuple Républicain (RPR) deputies in the National Assembly voted in favor of the ratification, all the others abstained—rapidly became a burden for the party itself and the governing center-right coalition. The Union de la Démocratie Française (UDF), the center-right coalition partner led by Valéry Giscard d'Estaing, had strongly supported the Maastricht policy of Mitterrand. The exception was Philippe de Villiers, an outsider belonging to the Parti Républicain (PR), a subfraction of the UDF. Villiers led an "anti-Maastricht party" in the European elections but obtained a mere 4.5 percent of the votes in the polls.[10] The decisive question was thus not Villiers' party list in itself, but how to manage a combined RPR/UDF list based on the lowest common denominator on European integration. The center-right coalition of UDF and RPR, in power since the general elections of 1993, had the difficult task in the 1994 European elections of satisfying pro-European UDF voters without repelling more skeptical Gaullist voters. On the left side, there has been the same phenomenon. Bernard Tapis, a former minister during the Mitterrand presidency, decided to run his own popular-left wing and slightly anti-European list for the elections. Jean-Pierre Chevènement decided to leave the party for the same "republican" reasons that Philippe Séguin had spelled out for the right. The result was a disastrous decomposition of the French party system during the European elections of June 1994, in which the traditional parties on the right and the left[11] could only get some 30 percent of the votes, all the others being "protest votes."[12]

But it was not only the feeling that Maastricht was threatening the very identity of the French Republic. It was also the way the policy of EMU was pushed that troubled the political landscape in France. From the very beginning, as regards EMU, France felt subjugated by German pressure. After the distortions of the European Monetary System (EMS) in consequence of German Reunification—when Germany raised its interest rates and France had to follow the movement, the French franc being bound to the German Deutschemark via the exchange rate—France was stumbling into enormous economic difficulties that were also aggravated by the 1992–1993 recession. Suddenly it found itself with a deficit amounting to 6 percent of the GDP and had to drastically cut public spending to fulfill the criteria of the Maastricht Treaty, allowing only a 3 percent ratio. The austerity policy of the French government of Edouard Balladur after the 1993 elections had undeniably bad repercussions in terms of unemployment. This quickly brought up the slogan in France that "Maastricht is killing employment." During the presidential election of 1995, Jacques Chirac was torn between sticking to the necessary austerity policy and promising new elements of social policy and measures against unemployment. Chirac won the elections with this doubled-sided campaign. In the first few months of his presidency, he started a policy of public spending; but then, together with his prime minister, Alain Juppé, he administered a U-turn in pushing forward major reforms in the social security system thus going back to an austerity policy. The result was the longest general strike in French history since 1968. As a consequence, the left picked up the unemployment question and campaigned against austerity and for more social policy in the 1997 general elections.[13] Lionel Jospin, the leader of the Parti Socialiste (PS), made it pretty clear that he would be against a Europe that would completely neglect the social questions. He won, and the French political landscape saw another policy reversal within a few months. But it is important to note that the left basically won the elections, because the leader of the Front National, Jean-Marie Le Pen, asked his voters after the first round to shift to the left in the second round, sharing the anti-austerity course of the left. In the 1997 general elections, one can observe that the FN was able to maintain 133 candidates in the second round,[14] competing either in a *triangulaire* situation against two other candidates, one from the PS and one from the traditional center-right, RPR/UDF, or in a duel directly against the left-wing candidate of the PS.[15] The FN succeeded in shifting most of its voters toward the PS candidates rather then to the RPR/UDF candidate in those constituencies that had a *triangulaire* situation. As a result, the FN was the kingmaker in some 47 constituencies in favor of the left-wing candidate, and it was with exactly this small majority that the left came into power. The new left-wing government started to condition the signature of the "stability pact"[16]—a German proposal seeking sustainable deficit consolidation after entering EMU—with a parallel agreement on a "European Pact against unemployment." But Germany expressed deep concerns about all kinds of unemployment policies on the European level. As a result, there were enormous tensions between France and Germany on the eve of the Amsterdam Treaty, causing a clash at the bilateral Franco-German Summit in Poitiers on June 17 and 18, 1997. France simply announced that it would not sign the "stability pact" if the Amsterdam Treaty did not contain a chapter on unemployment policies. The relationship was at its worst!

Yet the institutional strength of Franco-German relations finally brought a compromise. France signed the stability pact and Germany did not oppose a chapter on unemployment policies in the Amsterdam Treaty. But relationships had suffered a lot; in particular, the struggle about how to realize and implement EMU—with or without flanking policies—left an unacknowledged but bitter taste in France of being dominated by the German view of EMU. After the summer crisis of 1997, the new left-wing government of Lionel Jospin also turned to a policy focusing on price stability and sustainable public finances. But it did it more eloquently than its predecessor, communicating to the French citizens that their new government took into consideration their social fears.

3. Political instability versus concepts of European integration

What France experienced over the past seven years, moving from one election to the next while steadily changing the government and the economic policy, was simply that there is no clear majority for any European project in political terms. As both political camps have to bridge a major dissent over the European question—the *droite bourgeoise* as well as the *gauche plurielle*—electoral constraints prevent both sides from clarifying the political concept of Europe. As a consequence, the changing administrations have been more than reluctant. The strike against Maastricht has profoundly paralyzed the European elites in France, and the European debate seems to be a down-to-earth issue these days. Since the introduction of the euro, this is no longer a mere technical debate about institutions. Thus, the traditional "top-down" method of the Franco-German engine—that is, pushing integration forward through "joint letters" to the Council Presidency—is no longer functioning. Among the population at large the discussion about Europe is more about agricultural subsidies, unemployment, and beef hormones than about the political finality of Europe. The electoral system in France, with a two-tiered majority voting on the one hand and focus on the directly elected president on the other, reacts more to the population's irritation with Europe than it solves the citizens' concrete problems. Not only has the Front national, as we have seen, become the "kingmaker" in this electoral situation, but the French administration was *ex ipso* incapable of pushing forward major European plans. This pattern also applies to the current situation, in which France is preparing to conclude the Intergovernmental Conference at the end of 2000, while preparing for the next presidential elections of 2002.

Until recently the more consensual Germany party system, combining the direct election of candidates with proportional representation and producing stable coalitions, has been more robust in coping with the increasing distance, if not to say hostility, of the citizens to European issues. But the financial scandals of the German Christian Democrats might break up the German party system. And nothing is less sure, in this case, than the capability and willingness of at least some German parties to pursue a true and convincing European policy leading to a political union.

4. Repercussions of the French domestic situation on the Franco-German relationship

French domestic and electoral difficulties over European policy rapidly brought a deterioration of the Franco-German relationship in the years 1994, 1995, and after. France felt pressured to respond to several German proposals for deepening the European Union before the 1995 enlargement that would include Sweden, Finland, and Austria. Germany and France simply were not in step, politically and electorally, and the Franco-German engine for Europe suffered as a result. To be sure, Chancellor Helmut Kohl's reelection in 1994 had been by a narrow majority, but the victory and the stability of the German party system allowed the governing CDU to pursue a coherent European policy and demand steps toward political union: for example, institutional reforms and progress on Common Foreign and Security Policy (CFSP). The domestic German debate on European policy was dominated by the completion of political union, which was considered to be necessary for a successful monetary union—the latter considered nothing more than the "crown" of the former. And the German SPD, although tempted momentarily to open an "anti-Maastricht" flank in the domestic debate, had to realize that, even though the German population was massively against the euro, there was no space for a clear anti-European stance in Germany.[17] German CDU politicians thus confronted France with several papers, among which the most famous was the "Schäuble-Lamers" paper on a "core-Europe"[18] that was published on September 1, 1994. The message of the paper was clear: France and Germany would have to oversee the deepening of the integration process, including institutional reforms, prior to the 1995 enlargement. A core-Europe of countries could be set up that would be *able* and *willing* to push forward a politically closer union. For the first time the idea was published that those countries slowing down the path of European integration should not prevent the others from moving ahead. The paper also called for a Franco-German initiative in the direction of clearly politicizing the European Commission, which was to be shaped more and more like a European government.

Yet France was unable to respond to these far-reaching proposals. France had just been through the quixotic 1994 European elections, and the forthcoming presidential elections of May 1995 were even more unpredictable given the unprecedented situation of two candidates from the Gaullist RPR but none from the UDF. The country was in no situation to fix a clear stance in favor of European political union. Nothing illustrated the situation better than the European cleavage within the governing moderate right, with Eduard Balladur leading the pro-Maastricht wing and Jacques Chirac more vague. The French political milieu thus reacted with several ineffective attempts to "answer" the German proposal, with articles in the press that picked up some German ideas and refused others. Most such articles, however, mainly transformed or confused the key idea of the German paper, which was that Europe needs a core, and that the core of the core is the Franco-German partnership. Eduard Balladur spoke of "concentric circles;"[19] European Minister Alain Lamassoure tried to redefine "*géometrie variable*"[20]; Jacques Chirac pleaded for a Franco-German "*renouveau*"[21]; and finally Valéry Giscard d'Estaing, head of the UDF, published his ideas of "*Europe puissance—Europe espace,*"[22] which, in fact, came quite close to the German ideas. However, secret talks[23] between the UDF and the CDU on how to implement the idea of a core Europe failed, mainly because of the UDF's weakness. In spring 1995, the European Parliament ratified the EU enlargement and thus buried the last Franco-German attempt to deepen the Union. The last hope of some Europeans had been that the Parliament would reject the enlargement, and indeed there were some rumors going in this direction. With this window of opportunity closed, the negotiation of the Amsterdam Treaty in 1996 and the reform of the EU institutions quickly took on the bitter taste of a Greek tragedy.

Amsterdam: The Second Chance

1. The unemployment chapter as a secondary theater

The result of the Amsterdam Treaty was, as a French member of the European Parliament, Jean-Louis Bourlanges, once put it, the work of a group of people who were asked to paint a sheep but instead painted a cow. The treaty had some positive results like introducing the subject of human rights and a chapter on unemployment policies. France demanded the latter to compensate for tough budget reduction and price-stability policies, and to provide some window-dressing formulations to pacify the increasing anti-European, anti-EMU, and anti-Maastricht mood in France. Needless to say, the unemployment chapter remained vague and ineffective, owing basically to Germany's preference for keeping unemployment policies on the national level. The chapter's contents entail comparing the so-called "best-practices" of unemployment policies in the member states and do not allow for the effective coordination of macroeconomic policy, as France had wanted. Basically, the unemployment chapter opened a useful secondary theater next to the fundamental questions of institutional reforms—reducing the number of commissioners, redistributing votes in the Council, expanding majority voting—and thus diverted Franco-German energy. The only Franco-German initiative in institutional terms was the common proposal[24] to introduce the so-called "flexibility clause," taking up the basic idea that some countries should be allowed to move forward without the permission of the others. The proposal was coupled with some ideas on how to move forward on CFSP, which were welcomed as "a revolutionary jump forward"[25] but quickly revealed themselves to be no more than an intelligent résumé of existing Franco-German and European security policy: old wine in new bottles. Yet the new flexibility clause was not supposed to be applied to CFSP issues, where it would have been a quite useful tool, and it did not really break with the veto right of one or more members over the "strengthened cooperation" of other members. The very important institutional questions have thus not been solved. They were nicknamed "the leftovers of Amsterdam," and are haunting the discussion of Europe's future to this day.

2. Germany's withdrawal

Once again, and unfortunately for the history of European integration, France and Germany were not in step. This time, an ambitious France was puzzled by a reluctant Germany. France's domestic situation had calmed down with the new Socialist government. The cohabitation between Jacques Chirac and the left-wing coalition of Lionel Jospin stabilized the political climate and brought back, if not a consensus, at least an equilibrium in economic and budgetary policy with regard to preparations for EMU. There were no elections in view. On the opposite side, Germany was in domestic trouble. Later than in France, but with the same vehemence, the politics of budget consolidation showed very negative effects on unemployment in Germany. This situation was coupled with the fact that the Deutschemark was temporarily overvalued in 1995 and 1996, partly a result of the German campaign for the euro to be as strong as its own currency. In April 1997, two months before the Amsterdam Treaty was signed, the number of unemployed persons jumped over the psychological barrier of five million and thus fed the argument—even in Germany—that "the Euro is killing jobs."[26] With the new "left-wing" criticism of the euro and the traditional, more conservative criticism that "the euro won't be as strong as the D-mark," for one second of history it was touch-and-go whether Germany would finally implement the euro. In addition, the European Commission had just published for the first time economic data forecasts according to which Italy would be a starting member of the EMU—a fact that Germany had quietly and massively tried to torpedo.[27] The consequence of this was that German nerves were shot and its energy for political union was lacking, be it for institutional reforms, CFSP, or the third-pillar issues of justice and home affairs. Anticipating deadlock on institutional reforms and CFSP, Germany had pushed for negotiations on third-pillar issues at the beginning of the negotiations in order to have a policy field in which substantial progress could be made. Now, however, there was little energy for progress on the third pillar. Something, at least, had to be presented to the German public both as a symbol of the political union that Amsterdam should achieve and as the missing political counterpart for EMU. Yet the irony of the Amsterdam negotiations was that exactly the country that had most intensively called for political union and criticized French reluctance was now neither able nor willing to step forward on behalf of its own initiative. It was Germany that prevented the establishment of majority voting in the Third Pillar. The reason for this was basically that a large share of the stream of refugees from the former Yugoslavia had settled in Bavaria. Germany feared being outvoted in the voting on EU quotas for refugees. Meanwhile Germany had reformed the "European article" in its constitution (Article 23), giving more power to the minister presidents of the German Bundesländer.[28] Thus, even an outspoken pro-European chancellor like Helmut Kohl joined hands with two of the minister presidents, Edmund Stoiber from Bavaria and Johannes Rau from Northrhine-Westphalia, in the Amsterdam EU Council meeting to resist majority voting on third pillar-issues.

As a result, France voted together with Italy and Belgium for a protocol to the Amsterdam Treaty to address the question of institutional reform before the next enlargement, adding Central and Eastern European countries, which was already on track. Yet France, looking at Germany at this moment, was puzzled like never before. The shadow of a new Germany appeared: Germany simply could *not* be pro-European. That had never happened before in the history of European integration, apart from some small battles on milk quotas in the 1980s. But never had Germany allowed itself to slow down the integration process so openly! After Amsterdam, at the EU Summit of Cardiff in summer 1998, France and Germany undertook a last attempt to renew the tradition of "common letters" in preparing the outcome of a EU Summit. But this time the outcome was a very poor one, as the "Cardiff letter" focused exclusively on the principle of subsidiarity, thus was not going specifically in the direction of deeper integration. The contents and tone of this letter were striking and revealed that both France and Germany had reached the maximum of what they could administer in European policy, given their domestic situations.

In sum, between 1994 and 1998, France and Germany repeatedly failed to join hands to push forward European integration. Like acrobats on a trapeze, each kept missing the hands of the other. When Germany—in domestic terms—was able and willing, France was not, and vice versa. Unfortunately Europe had no safety net. Appeasing rhetoric or not, the engine was broken.

The New Legacy: The Schröder Government

1. The new persons:
Gerhard Schröder, Joschka Fischer, and Oskar Lafontaine

If France had had to vote in the German elections of October 1998, it would have voted for Kohl. The farewell of this chancellor, symbolizing above all stability and continuity as well as a pro-French and a pro-European stance, was difficult for the French. When they looked at the new leaders who would govern the important neighbor, Gerhard Schröder, the new chancellor, raised severe concerns. Already in 1995, Schröder had expressed in the columns of *Der Spiegel*[29] that he would not stick to the conception of a European policy like that of Helmut Schmidt, which "basically consisted of paying a high net-contribution to the EU budget for realizing the European idea." His generation, Schröder continued, would no longer be in the same position, "as it is, for the first time, confronted with a big problem of legitimacy when abandoning the D-mark for the euro," which would be a price "of another dimension." In summer 1997, Schröder took the French review *Politique Internationale* as the appropriate forum to raise the question "whether Europe should not wait for a better business cycle to launch the euro"[30]; he declared on March 28, 1998, that "the euro is a premature birth." Apart from these statements, Schröder was a dark horse in terms of foreign and European policy and was said not to have a coherent conception of either. Admittedly, he succeeded in a reversal of his position on the euro shortly before he got elected. He chose again, probably not by chance, *Politique Internationale*[31] to rectify his euro-hostility and to calm down French concerns. At the same time, he published "Twenty-six letters for a modern Germany" for the German public, in which he asks his readers "to consider the chances of the euro more than the risks" and even adds that the euro is "an option for the future" that necessarily requires a political union.[32] In his first governmental declaration of November 10, the references to European policy were neither overwhelming nor enthusiastic, but "politically correct": "European integration is of capital importance for German policy."[33] From the very beginning, Schröder's stance on European policy tried to achieve two goals: to place himself and his new government in a certain continuity as regards the European engagement of Germany, while emphasizing slightly more the "defense of national interest" in European affairs. In addition, three other aspects puzzled the French perception of Schröder's European policy plans. First, France was skeptical of Schröder's commitment to strengthen relations with Great Britain and to shift bilateral Franco-German initiatives in the direction of a more triangular relationship involving Britain. Second, his obvious intention, with the appointment of Oskar Lafontaine as the new Minister of Finance, to create room for economic voluntarism in the fight against unemployment was perceived with mixed feelings. The French left had just accepted the rhetoric of price stability and a sound and sustainable budget policy. Finally, France was indifferent to Schröder's open intention to slow down the process of the eastern enlargement of the EU, which had never been a French priority.

Confronted with this ambivalent picture, French president Jacques Chirac tried to pretend that business was as usual in Franco-German relations. Three weeks before the elections, he published an article pledging "a new chance" in the relationship.[34] But in the beginning, Schröder's behavior, lacking any sense of foreign policy continuity—for example, his refusal to participate at the memorial celebration of the end of World War One—surprised and disappointed France.

By contrast, French European elites were more than happy to find in Joschka Fischer a kind of young and modern reincarnation of Helmut Kohl, at least as regards his convictions on European policy. Fischer had long made the effort to express determined pro-European convictions—for example, on the euro, the successive transfer of sovereignty in important policy areas, and the idea of political union.[35] He was the real element of continuity in European policy, in French eyes, and was soon highly regarded.

Oskar Lafontaine was the third of the new leaders who raised concerns. Doubtlessly, he was the "strongest" person in the government and his unhidden rivalry with the chancellor has been at the center of French political debate. There were two reasons for French concern about Lafontaine. First, compared to the other members of the government—many of whom were more or less unknown and came from the German Länder—Oskar Lafontaine was the *one* person who had a reputation in France and was highly appreciated for establishing contacts between the PS and the SDP. Secondly, Lafontaine's Keynesian thinking sounded familiar to most of the left-wing French elites. For the French, there was some hope and expectation to work out a more decisive economic policy on the European level together with the new German government, but this hope was an ambivalent one.

2. The goal of an "Economic government": New oil for the Franco-German engine?

Schröder had done everything to underline the fact that the question of unemployment would be central to the policy of the new government, and that Germany would now be willing to reconsider the question of an "unemployment pact"[36] at the European level. This corresponded exactly to what France had wished for over the years, ever since Amsterdam. Would a new Franco-German engine find a common will to create an "economic government," and in so doing also find a political union? Yet, contrary to what might have been expected, France distanced itself from the way the new German government pushed this topic, and especially from the way Oskar Lafontaine flanked this U-turn in economic policy with excessive declarations on the franc and the role of monetary policy in reducing unemployment.[37] But France had struggled internally for years to reeducate its elites on the politics of price stability and the independence of the Central Bank, and could not reasonably go beyond a certain economic and monetary rhetoric that it had since acquired, and of which it was proud. Thus, Lafontaine's intensive, exaggerated, repeated demands that the Bundesbank should cut interest rates annoyed even Dominique Strauss-Kahn, the French finance minister. To some extent, France and Germany talked past each other on this matter because they were not domestically in step, and Germany failed to strike a balanced tone. At the informal meeting of the EU heads of state and government in the Austrian town of Pörtschach, on November 3, 1998, the situation boiled over.

After unofficial declarations on the necessity of interest rate cuts, the Spanish, Portuguese, and Swedish central banks cut their rates. These developments were coupled with some incautious remarks by Hans-Jürgen Krupp, member of the board of the Bundesbank, in a German newspaper on November 4. Krupp declared that on the basis of Article 105 of the Maastricht Treaty, "monetary policy has to contribute to solving the problem of unemployment as long price stability is not compromised."[38] It was clear that Lafontaine would have to leave the government. As a result, the Franco-German economic and monetary policy rapprochement failed. The attempt to construct EMU flanking policies as a component of political union à la Jean Monnet's idea of creating "spill-over effects" from economic to political integration, could not be worked out. What followed was simply that Germany, with a new and more sober finance minister in Hans Eichel, turned to Great Britain to look for the famous "third way" of economic policy. With less accent on the organization and structure of flanking EMU, Germany tried to shift to an economic policy of the "New Center," focusing on tax reduction and flexibility and more individual responsibility. Bodo Hombach, Schröder's principal advisor, laid out the new economic stance of the German government in his book *Aufbruch: Die Politik der neuen Mitte,*[39] which had few things in common with the initial governmental declarations of November 1998. Shortly thereafter, Gerhard Schröder and Tony Blair signed their common paper on "Europe's new Third way"[40] without consulting France. Looking at this British-German initiative, France was not shocked, but disappointed. The promising new left-wing government in Germany was not ashamed to spread the word, through newspapers and opinion-makers, that French socialism was outdated and that Great Britain and Germany would be the *avant garde* of a new social-democrat economy. Key points in the analysis of the Schröder-Blair paper—for example, that unemployment is essentially structural and that tax reduction and other supply-side measures are needed—did not correspond to French ideas about the need for fiscal harmony in Europe to avoid "tax dumping."[41]

Under these conditions, French efforts to use the EU Cologne Summit on June 3 and 4, 1998, to elaborate on the "Unemployment Chapter" of the Amsterdam Treaty could only fail. France suggested EU measures to reduce working hours, establish quantitative employment goals, and provide funding for so-called "*Grands Travaux*"—big infrastructure projects such as construction and long-distance trains. The Cologne Summit merely resulted in the release of 1.5 million euros through the EBRD for capital investment in small and medium-sized companies and for high technology research. But the biggest questions, such as taxes—ranging from establishing harmony on the VAT, or value added tax, which was between 15 and 25 percent in the EU, to taxes on enterprises—remained unsolved. Thus it is true for institutional reforms as well as economic policy that if France and Germany collaborate, Europe moves forward; and if not, nothing happens. As a reaction, France, more precisely French prime minister Lionel Jospin, decided later in November 1999 to publish a kind of counter-paper to the Schröder-Blair paper, entitled "Vers un monde plus juste,"[42] calling for an end to the "neoliberal" offensive. The "human costs" of capitalism were much too high and the relationship between the state and the market would have to be redefined. The paper was hastily written by Jospin's European minister, Pierre Moscovici, and picked up the main ideas Moscovici had published beforehand in a book.[43]

The very irony in this particular case of economic cooperation between France and Germany is that, in spite of the Keynesian rhetoric of the French left-wing government and the neoliberal or "Third-Way"-tones of the German one, the economy is performing better in France than in Germany. France had an average growth rate between 1997 and 1999 of 4.7 percent against Germany's 2.2 percent. France has since 1997 consistently reduced unemployment—by more than 600,000 between 1997 and 1999—and it is reducing its budget deficit.[44] Germany speaks the neoliberal rhetoric but is bound in its corporatism and rigidities and fails to pass reforms. France speaks the left-wing rhetoric, but has a superior economic record lately. The two talk past each other, instead of facing the economic realities. And when France looks at Germany now, it does so with more self-confidence. France no longer needs Germany as an economic role model. The fearful discourse on the "big and economically powerful" Germany that dominated French discussion at the beginning of the 1990s has dissipated, but Germany has failed to take notice of a modern and emancipated France.

3. The Berlin Summit: Unknown watershed for Franco-German relations

The EU Summit in Berlin on March 23 and 24, 1999, was meant to solve the financial problems of the EU (budget, agricultural policies, structural policies) in the so-called "Agenda 2000." Agenda 2000 ushered in a major change in Franco-German relations. The German demand for reducing its net budgetary contribution, coupled with the idea of shifting more of the burden for financing in the Common Agricultural Policy (CAP) to recipient member states, touched a raw nerve in France. Germany, already using a much more national tone in European politics, went into the negotiation with very high expectations. This demand of "cash back" was just a translation of the fact that "for Germany also, the period in which European integration has been a goal in itself"[45] had come to an end. Schröder thus pledged that "a federal structure of Europe would be the only guarantee for solidarity and progress,"[46] and wanted a new equilibrium in the structural funds and the financial burden for the member states. Germany, which in 1999 accounted for 60 percent of total EU contributions at some 11.4 billion euro, made its thankless role as the paymaster of Europe the central theme of the German presidency. By comparison, France's net contribution, due to the agricultural backflows, was a mere 1.7 billion euro. Germany's new defense of "national interests" apparently came down to money, and the tone and the roughness of Schröder's statements surprised not only France: "We are not going to buy any longer the *bienveillance* of our neighbors via direct transfers to the Union which are unsupportable for the national budget."[47] The German proposal to solve the problem was quite simple and based on mainly three elements. First, drastic reforms of the CAP in the sense that European subsidies for agriculture would be, to a large extent, replaced by national subsidies ("cofinancing"). This measure would mainly affect France as the country that benefits the most from the CAP. Second, the structural funds would be cut back to 213 billion euro. Third, the taboo of the British rebate, accorded since 1984, would have to be broken. The expected gains of these measures altogether have been calculated to represent some 3 billion euro; the CDU opposition even demanded a reduction of 7 billion euro. But France bluntly opposed the cofinancing system of the CAP, which represented in French eyes the very solidarity of the EU system and the *"just return."* Introducing cofinancing would thus empty the sense of the Union.

The final conclusion to Agenda 2000 takes the GDP into greater consideration as a basis for calculations, and not the VAT income that had been introduced as the fourth EU budget resource in the late 1980s. The calculated result will be a de facto gain for Germany of some 700 million euro from 2001 to 2006, much less than the three or seven billion euro that the government and CDU opposition had sought. In the very end, Schröder was criticized by the German press for the "concessions" he made[48] to France on the CAP and to Spain on the structural funds. The new Schröder government learned two important lessons from the Berlin Summit. First, Germany could not simply and easily move toward a "defense of its national interests." And secondly, perhaps more important, Germany could not count on France for budgetary reforms, despite France's superior economic performance. The agricultural lobby in France, and especially President Chirac's dependence on the rural vote for the next presidential election, prevented France from agreeing to a fundamental restructuring of EU financial policies. As in 1957 or 1967 when France's "empty chair" policy in the European Council was provoked by a dispute over the CAP, in 1999 France still held to the conviction that the EU must take into account its own agricultural needs as a major "national interest." Schröder succeeded in binding together the difficult "Agenda 2000" in part because the war in Kosovo diverted attention from the financial problems of the Union. After the summit he changed his tone. In the German government's declaration, he placed "German interest" on the same level as "European interests," spelling out "that the overall goal of the EU was to strengthen cohesion."[49] But the summit deeply blemished Franco-German relations not only at the highest levels, but also among the staff in several departments of the German Auswärtiges Amt (Foreign Office), many of whom resigned. Like an engine running low on fuel, the energy of the people tackling Franco-German relations on a daily basis had vanished. In this sense, the governmental change in Germany, including the turnover of staff, contributed to the deterioration of Franco-German relations. It is true that in the ministries of the *Berliner Republik* there is less unconditional and unquestioned *francophilia* than in those of the *Bonner Republik*.

Outlook and conclusion

Yet new efforts and repeated symbolic gestures were not lacking, even in recent times. On November 30, 1999, Schröder was the first chancellor to address the French National Assembly on the occasion of the 74th bilateral Franco-German Summit since the Elysée Treaty. The main topic of his address was European security and defense policy and preparations for the EU Summit in Helsinki. A day later, Schröder published in the Frankfurter Allgemeine Zeitung an article, *"Europe puissance"* (Powerful Europe), in which he tried to renew the dynamics of the Franco-German engine: "Nothing has been achieved in Europe, when France and Germany did not agree."[50] But rather than calm French fears about the new Germany, the article raised more concern and did not make any clear proposals for the Helsinki Summit or the future of Europe. The article in itself exemplifies the new lack of communication between France and Germany, each looking back with a certain nostalgia to what once was, but unable to draft in common a new design for Europe. A major reason for this breakdown is a new, subtle but undeniable mood of reciprocal distrust after several Franco-German disputes over the nominations for leading positions in the EU and other international institutions. In Spring 1998 France pushed for Jean-Claude Trichet, rather than Wim Duisenberg, to head the European Central Bank. More recently, France refused to support the German candidate Cajo Koch-Weser as a successor to Michel Camdessus at the IMF. Such minor disputes have caused more damage than substantive disagreements over EU policies, adversely affecting the tone that each country takes with the other.

Of course the Helsinki Summit of December 1999 brought some major steps forward in regard to CFSP with the decision to build up a European intervention force of some 60,000 soldiers. This decision had been possible after some progress in the field of European Security and Defense Identity (ESDI) with the St. Malo Declaration[51] of December 1998, in which Great Britain basically changed its view on ESDI and moved to a less Atlanticist and more European position. Without mentioning more details about progress in the field of ESDI and CFSP, it is important to note that these proposals were based on a Franco-British and not a Franco-German initiative. Germany, during 1999, was simply jumping on the bandwagon.

The Helsinki Summit began another era in the history of European integration by deciding to open enlargement negotiations with another six Eastern European Countries[52] and according Turkey the status of an official candidate. Without resolving the problems of institutional and financial reforms—Agenda 2000 had papered over the financial prerequisites for enlargement—the EU will take steps toward enlargement on the basis of the so-called Copenhagen criteria (such as democracy, market economy, and human rights) and is now more likely to develop in the direction of a "stability zone" than anything else.[53] There may even be a question about whether the Single Market with all its regulation can be extended to this zone, let alone the traditional EU agricultural and structural policies.

Thus, anything that was associated with European integration until 1989—such as political union and federal structure—belongs to the past, unless at least some countries reactivate the idea of a "core Europe" including new and specific institutional structures.[54] Yet even France and Germany, from which one would expect such an initiative during this very decisive time in European integration, are struggling with the three "leftovers of Amsterdam"[55] in the current Intergovernmental Conference set to conclude at the EU Summit in Nice in December 2000. Even if this happens, it will not be enough. The eventual shape of Europe is less clear than ever, and it is up to France and Germany to give it that shape. But neither is ready to do so for the moment.

Notes

1. Karl Lamers, "Interview," in *Handelsblatt,* February 3, 2000.

2. Radio interview on "Europe 1," November 12, 1989 ("The Berlin Wall came down. One dead person: Jacques Delors").

3. Olaf Sievert, "Der Maastrichter Vertrag wurde in einer historisch einmalig günstigen Gelegenheit ausgearbeitet," *Die Zeit* August 26, 1997.

4. Reiner Marcowitz, "Option für Paris. Unionsparteien, SPD und Charles de Gaulle 1958 bis 1969," *Studien zur Zeitgeschichte,* Oldenbourg 1996, pp. 109–132.

5. Cf. *Akten zur Auswärtigen Politik der Bundesrepublik Deutschland 1963,* Volume I, January 1963–May 1963, edited by the Auswärtiges Amt and the Institut für Zeitgeschichte, Oldenbourg 1996, Document no. 37, pp. 111–123: Gespräch des Bundeskanzlers Adenauer mit Staatspräsident de Gaulle in Paris, January 21, 1963.

6. François Mitterrand, *De l'Allemagne, de la France* (Paris: Odile Jacob 1996), p. 58; Hubert Védrine, *Les mondes de François Mitterrand. A l'Elysée 1981–1995* (Paris: Fayard), p. 423 and following, p. 551 and following; Pierre Favier and Michel Martin-Roland, *La décennie Mitterrand,* Volume 3: "Les défis" (Paris: Seuil 1996), pp. 159–237.

7. Cf. Daniel Vernet, "Un destin commun sans vision partagée," in *Le Monde* September 23, 1995.

8. See speech, Philippe Séguin in the National Assembly, May 5, 1992, in *Discours pour la France* (Paris: Grasset 1992).

9. "Pour la réfonte de la grande Europe," *Le Figaro,* December 2, 1993.

10. Cf. *Le Monde,* May 2, 1994.

11. The list of Michel Rocard for the PS was getting some 15 percent; the UDF/RPR list of Dominique Baudis got a similar result.

12. See Ulrike Guerot, "Frankreich nach den Europawahlen," in *Dokumente,* August 1994, Jahrgang 49, pp. 169–175.

13. The general elections had been advanced a year. The center-right coalition feared even worse results in 1998 when the deficit would have necessitated an enhanced austerity course. Advancing the elections a year was intended to escape the scenario of campaigning in a very bad economic environment.

14. Every candidate who gets more than 12.5 percent of the electorate in the first round can go into the second round.

15. Out of the 133 candidates of the FN that maintained themselves in the second round, 79 were in a "triangulaire" position; 54 had duels with the PS candidate.

16. The stability pact was signed in December 1996 under mainly German pressure. Germany made it pretty clear that the start of EMU would depend on signing the "stability pact." See for more details: Ulrike Guerot, "L'Allemagne et l'UEM. Essai d'analyse," Groupement d'Etudes et de Recherche Notre Europe, No. 1, Paris, March 1997.

17. Over the whole period of implementing the euro, opinion polls showed some 80 percent of Germans against the euro. On the other hand, the SPD got its worst electoral result in Baden-Würtemberg in March 1996 after having campaigned openly against the euro, dropping from roughly 36 percent

down to 28 percent. See for more details: Ulrike Guerot, "Deutschland, Frankreich und die Währungsunion. Über Diskussion und Metadiskussion," in *Frankreich-Jahrbuch* 1997, pp. 223–240, (Opladen: Leske und Budrich 1997) pp. 223–240.

18. Reflections on European Policy, CDU/CSU group of the German Bundestag, September 1, 1994.

19. See *Le Monde,* October 18, 1994.

20. See *Le Monde,* November 23, 1994.

21. See *Le Monde,* December 12, 1994.

22. *Le Figaro,* January 10, 1995.

23. In January 1995, Schäuble and Lamers met Valéry Giscard d'Estaing and other influential people of the UDF in Paris.

24. Presented in one of those legendary "common letters" by Helmut Kohl and Jacques Chirac in December 1996, during the IGC negotiation. See *Le Monde,* December 12, 1996.

25. See *Le Monde,* December 12, 1996 ("Nürnberger Erklärung").

26. That is, the German Trade Unions started to become very critical of EMU.

27. See Ulrike Guerot, "Le débat sur l'UEM en Allemagne. Essai d'analyse," Groupement d'Etudes et de Recherche, Série, Problématiques Européennes, No. 1, Paris, March 1997, p. 22 and following.

28. Martin Kreile, "Federalism Doomed? Institutional Implications of EU Enlargement," discussion paper (unpublished), Humboldt University, Berlin 1999.

29. *Der Spiegel,* December 25, 1995.

30. *Politique Internationale* 76, Summer 1997.

31. *Politique Internationale* 81, Fall 1998.

32. Gerhard Schröder, "Und weil wir unser Land verbessern . . ." *26 Briefe für ein modernes Deutschland* (Hamburg: Hofmann & Campe 1998), pp. 100–101.

33. Presse- und Informationsamt der Bundesregierung, Bulletin 74, November 11, 1998.

34. Jacques Chirac, "La France et l'Allemagne, une nouvelle chance," *Le Figaro* September 29, 1998.

35. See Joschka Fischer, *Risiko Deutschland. Krise und Zukunft der deutschen Politik* (Cologne: Kiepenheuer & Witsch 1994), p. 223; Joschka Fischer: *Für einen neuen Gesellschaftvertrag. Eine politische Antwort auf die globale Revolution,* (Cologne: Kiepenheuer & Witsch 1998), pp. 269–270.

36. See Bulletin der Bundesregierung, Presse- und Informationsamt, No. 74, November 11, 1998, p. 907, 913; Bulletin No. 79, December 10, 1998, p. 961; Bulletin No. 80, December 14, 1998, p. 967.

37. See Bulletin No. 80, op. cit., p. 967; *International Herald Tribune,* November 10, 1998 (Declaration of Heiner Flassbeck).

38. *Die Welt,* November 4, 1998.

39. Bodo Hombach, *Departure: The Politics of the New Middle* (Düsseldorf: Econ 1998), see in particular p. 14 and following.

40. Tony Blair and Gerhard Schröder, *Europe: "The Third Way"* (London/Bonn: June 8, 1999).

41. For this see the speech by Lionel Jospin at the Milan Meeting of European Socialists on May 1, 1999, and the adopted memorandum.

42. "For a world with more justice," see *Le Monde* and *FAZ* of October 6, 1999.

43. See Pierre Moscovici, *Au Coeur de l'Europe, Entretiens avec Henri de Bresson* (Paris: Le Pré aux Clercs 1999).

44. See *Le Monde*, February 11, 2000, "Les recettes fiscales sont exédentaires de 66 milliardes de francs en 1999."

45. See Christian Hacke, *Die Außenpolitik der Bundesrepublik Deutschland. Weltmacht wider Wilen* (Frankfurt/Main, Berlin: Ullstein 1997), pp. 535–536.

46. See Presse-und Informationsamt der Bundesregierung, Bulletin No. 74, November 11, 1998, p. 914.

47. See Bulletin No. 80, December 14, p. 967.

48. See *Der Spiegel*, March 29, 1999, and *Süddeutsche Zeitung*, April 27, 1999. Spain, in particular, had refused to consider any reduction of the structural funds that initially was to be shifted to the new members.

49. Presse-und Informationsamt der Bundesregierung, Bulletin 13, March 29, 1999, p. 162.

50. See December 1, 1999, p. 8: Gerhard Schröder, "Europe puissance als gemeinsames Ziel. Die Verantwortung Frankreichs und Deutschlands für die Zukunft Europas," *FAZ*, December 1, 1999.

51. Franco-British Declaration on ESDI, as outcome of bilateral Franco-British talks in December 1998.

52. Rumania, Bulgaria, Latvia, Lithuania, Slovakia, and Malta, in addition to the six Central and Eastern European countries with which enlargement negotiations had already been opened after the EU Summit of Luxembourg in December 1997—Poland, the Czech Republic, Slovenia, Estonia, Hungary, and Cyprus.

53. These criteria were voted at the EU Summit of Copenhagen in 1992 as basic conditions for accession to the EU.

54. See "Interview with Jacques Delors," *Le Monde*, January 19, 2000; Werner Weidenfeld, "Die Achillesferse Europas," *FAZ*, January 31, 2000.

55. Reduction of the number of commissioners, new way of calculating of the votes within the EU Council, and extension of majority voting.

Chapter 4 ❧

Franco-German Economic Relations: From Exchange and Convergence to Collective Action

Erik Jones

In the early twenty-first century, the Franco-German relationship remains at the center of European integration but it is Germany, without France, that lies at the center of Europe's economic and monetary union (EMU). It is Germany's monetary institutions that provide the template for those bestowed on Europe; Germany's constitutional court that underscored the essential importance of European price stability; and Germany's Ministry of Finance that elevated fiscal rectitude above other concerns such as growth or employment.[1] This predominance of Germany in EMU poses a problem for the future of the Franco-German relationship. As EMU becomes more important for Europe, will France become less important for Germany? Put another way, does economic integration continue to provide a common basis for Franco-German reconciliation?

The record of economic cooperation between France and Germany in the 1990s is unimpressive. So too is the record of French and German economic performance. Although both countries succeeded in constructing (and joining) Europe's monetary union, they did so only with great difficulty, against a background of controversy, and to initially mixed reviews. Meanwhile, France and Germany ended the decade with slow growth, high unemployment, and the promise of only a gradual recovery. The contrast with the economic accomplishments of the late 1980s, and the tight pattern of bilateral cooperation underwriting the Maastricht Treaty negotiations, could not be more striking. Economic relations, it would seem, are no longer a Franco-German forte.

The principal argument in this chapter is that economic issues continue to serve as a focal point for relations between France and Germany, and that Franco-German economic relations remain important for European integration. Nevertheless, the emphasis within the economic relations of France and Germany has changed fundamentally in the aftermath of the Cold War. Whereas France and Germany might once have focused on the importance of bilateral exchanges or patterns of convergence, now Franco-German economic relations are rooted more completely and intentionally in processes of collective action. European integration may not be an objective in its own right, but it is much more than a by-product of the Franco-German relationship.

This argument is not entirely unique in the broader literature on recent developments in Western Europe. Among others, Simon Bulmer, Peter Katzenstein, and Jeffrey Anderson have made a similar point about the growing importance of Europe in "taming" German power after unification.[2] Broadly, their claim is that the complex web of institutions, rules, and procedures in Europe have so defined, divided, and restrained German interests that the increase in power resulting from unification could have only a transitory effect on the pattern of German relations. In other words, Germany has become so entangled in Europe that self-extraction is no longer an option. The low points of the 1990s derive from German assertiveness or recalcitrance, the high points from German acceptance of multilateral identities and constraints.

The "tamed power" argument has considerable merit. Nevertheless, the emphasis is misplaced when applied to economic relations between France and Germany. It can explain some of the excesses of German behavior but not those of the French. Therefore a secondary purpose of this chapter is to provide a different perspective on recent analysis of German power. Specifically, I argue that the stability of the Franco-German relationship derives not simply from the fact that European institutions constrain actors or reshape their preferences, but also from the reality that institution-building and institutionalized collective action are mechanisms for generating and exercising national power.[3] Despite (the supposed) French resistance to multilayered identities and federal arrangements, France is also "tamed" because it is also empowered. Put another way, and borrowing from Patrick McCarthy's introduction in chapter 1, both France and Germany have put too much into their relationship—and stand to gain too much from it—to give up on it now.

This change in emphasis has important implications for the role of the Franco-German couple in Europe. The roots of Franco-German antagonism may stretch back to the dawn of time, but now cooperation between the two countries is the norm and not the exception.[4] Hence, the old emphasis on how European integration has helped to facilitate Franco-German reconciliation should be replaced with a new emphasis on how France and Germany cooperate to achieve a range of objectives both at home and abroad.[5] Paraphrasing Julius Friend, the question is not whether France is as important as Germany or whether France has anything to offer Germany directly, but whether either France or Germany can manage Europe alone. No matter how central Germany is within EMU, France and Germany remain central to each other and to both countries' strategies in Europe.[6]

The chapter has five sections. The first surveys Franco-German economic relations in the 1990s. The second examines the evidence that France and Germany have less in common—at least from the broad statistical perspective—in the aftermath of German unification. The third analyzes the pattern of Franco-German economic relations in terms of changes in German power, and the fourth reinterprets those relations in terms of collective action. The fifth section offers a conclusion.

Those Troubled Nineties

The record for French and German macroeconomic performance is poor–particularly in comparison with the United States, but also relative to the United Kingdom. Both France and Germany experienced a prolonged slowdown in real economic growth (overall and per capita), rising levels of unemployment, and creeping public debts. Meanwhile, the two countries did succeed in mastering inflation and lowering long-term real interest rates, but not much more impressively than did the Anglo-Saxons. Finally, where available, early predictions suggest that any improvements in the year 2000 will be gradual (see table 4.1).

This mixed bag of macroeconomic performance carried a high price in terms of Franco-German efforts to form a monetary union. The relative exchange rate stability of the late 1980s was lost; the institutional structure of the European Monetary System had to be changed; the first deadline to form EMU was missed; and speculation that France and Germany would themselves fail to meet the criteria for entry continued right up until the end. In any event, both France and Germany were accused of fudging their national data in order to ensure that they could join.[7] If only in symbolic terms, the appearance of incompetence and impropriety was costly.

Allegations of impropriety were not the only failings of France, Germany, or the Franco-German relationship. In addition, the poor record for macroeconomic performance of the French and German economies has been punctuated by a series of economic-related conflicts. Differences between

Table 4.1 Macroeconomic Performance in France and Germany Compared

	1986–1990	1991–1996	1996–1999	2000
Unemployment (percent labor force)				
West Germany (unified Germany)	5.9	5.6 (7.3)	9.2	8.7
France	9.7	11.1	11.8	11.0
United Kingdom	9.0	9.5	6.9	6.6
United States	5.9	6.6	4.9	5.1
Real GDP Growth (annual percentage change)				
West Germany (unified Germany)	3.3	1.5 (1.2)	1.7	2.3
France	3.2	1.1	2.3	2.7
United Kingdom	3.3	1.6	2.3	2.3
United States	2.8	2.0	3.4	2.1
Real GDP per Capita Growth (annual percentage change)				
West Germany (unified Germany)	2.6	0.2 (0.7)	1.9	2.4
France	2.6	0.6	1.9	2.2
United Kingdom	2.9	1.2	2.0	2.0
United States	1.9	0.9	2.7	1.3
Price Deflator, Private Consumption (annual percentage change)				
West Germany (unified Germany)	1.5	3.5 (3.3)	1.3	1.3
France	2.9	2.3	1.0	1.0
United Kingdom	5.3	4.2	2.4	2.0
United States	4.1	2.9	1.6	2.3
Real Long-term Interest Rates (deflated by private consumption)				
West Germany (unified Germany)	5.2	3.7 (3.5)	3.7	n/a
France	6.0	5.4	4.1	n/a
United Kingdom	4.2	4.1	3.7	n/a
United States	4.2	4.0	4.0	n/a
Public Debt (percentage GDP)				
West Germany (unified Germany)	43.8*	44.7 (48.0)	61.1	61.2
France	33.8	44.5	58.2	59.2
United Kingdom		45.9	49.7	45.7

Note: Data for 2000 are estimates; all German data post–1996 are unified Germany.
*1990, only.
Source: European Commission.

France and Germany emerged repeatedly during the 1990s and covered the gamut of core European issues from agricultural policy to interest rates, enlargement, fiscal balances, employment, and the relationship between politics and economics. In summary form, these controversies can be grouped around three questions: Who pays for Europe (coupled with what does Europe pay for)? What are the priorities for economic adjustment? How should the broad guidelines for European economic policy be set?

The question about who pays for Europe touches on a range of issues that emerged at the end of the Cold War about the enlargement of the European Union and about the reform of the Common Agricultural Policy (CAP). In reduced form, it concerns the parity of net contributions to EU coffers across member states on the one hand, versus the depth and breadth of European outlays on the other hand. The French position has been that the existing distribution of burdens is roughly equitable, and that European support mechanisms should be deep but narrow. In other words, the French believe that net contributions should remain much as they have been, and so should the CAP; meanwhile, any enlargement of the EU should be supported only to the extent to which it does not disrupt existing financial arrangements. By contrast, the German position has been that the distribution of burdens needs to be rebalanced, and that European support mechanisms should be less generous but more widely spread. In this view, the level of German net contributions should be decreased both through an increase in gross benefits and through a decrease in outlays to Europe. Moreover, the financial arrangements of the EU should be made more realistic, phasing out excessive programs (such as the CAP) in order to facilitate European enlargement.

The contrast between these French and German positions is considerable. As a result, France and Germany came into repeated conflict over enlargement, CAP reform, and budgetary reform more generally. The record of outcomes is mixed. France was unable to delay enlargement to Austria, Finland, and Sweden, and has been signally unsuccessful in postponing an eastward expansion of the EU for the "decades and decades" anticipated by François Mitterrand in June 1991.[8] However, France was able to moderate—but not to prevent—a succession of CAP reforms, first during the Uruguay Round of GATT negotiations, and later during the financial planning surrounding the Commission's Agenda 2000 program for enlargement.[9] For its part, Germany was able to push for an accelerated enlargement and to place a cap on its contributions to Europe. In essence both sides achieved their objectives by shunting the burdens onto third parties—principally the applicant countries in Central and Eastern Europe but also, and to a far lesser extent, the so-called "cohesion" countries whose structural and regional funds are most subject to reform. France and Germany were able to agree on the notion that enlargement should not be allowed to undermine existing financial relations within Europe. Hence while the scope of Europe increases, the benefits of European support mechanisms will become ever more focused.[10]

The question about the priorities for economic adjustment concerns an equally broad set of issues relating to labor market performance and fiscal balances. In a nutshell, the question is whether there is a necessary trade-off between efforts to reduce unemployment and to stabilize fiscal balances. The French position has been that there is: No matter what the merits of fiscal austerity for price stability, the cost is high in terms of employment. Therefore, on the margin at least, governments should be allowed some flexibility on the fiscal side to pursue nonmonetary objectives. The German position is that the causes of unemployment lie principally in the institutions of the labor market—including the relations between employers and trade unions—rather than in the relative austerity of the government's fiscal stance. Indeed, any observable relationship between employment (or unemployment) and fiscal balances operates only over the short term. Over the long term, fiscal imbalances threaten employment prospects through (*inter alia*) their effects on price stability. Therefore any excess flexibility on the fiscal side is likely to worsen, rather than benefit, the functioning of the labor market.

Here again the conflicts have been numerous and the outcomes mixed. For its part, Germany succeeded not only in enforcing the criteria for fiscal performance established in the Maastricht Treaty but also in getting the member states to accept a code of fiscal conduct—called the "Stability Pact"—that is even more restrictive. Meanwhile, France was able to push employment issues closer to the center of the European agenda by adding an "employment chapter" during the treaty revision process at Amsterdam. Finally, both parties were able to secure important elements of compromise. France diluted the procedures and sanctions to be applied in enforcing the Stability Pact, and Germany prevented France from tabling an even more ambitious proposal for the financing of job creation.[11] In this area, as in the previous one, the French and the Germans were able to find sufficient common basis for ameliorating their differences.

Such relative success was less available with regard to conflict over the political direction of European economic policy. In institutional terms, what is at stake is whether European macroeconomic policy should be guided by rules or discretion. Moreover, the basis for disagreement is predictable, at least in light of the disagreement concerning the relationship between fiscal austerity and unemployment just discussed. The Germans prefer rules and the French would rather see more scope for discretion. The problem is that the dichotomy between rules and discretion is not symmetrical in terms of the symbolic exercise of political influence. If the choice is for discretion, then all parties can exercise influence both at the moment of choice and during any exercise of discretion. In symbolic terms, the actor who prefers rules loses only once but remains in the game as an equal participant. If the choice is for rules, the parties can exercise influence only over the constitution of the rules. Once the rules are in place, the opportunity for political influence is lost and the actor who prefers rules seems to predominate. From the French perspective, what this means is that the choice is not one of rules versus discretion but rather of equality versus subordination. And the only way out of this symbolic trap is to find some way to be seen as managing the rules.

The conflicts that have emerged around the political direction of European economic policy have been bitter. On an institutional level, France has repeatedly insisted that the European Central Bank (ECB) take some form of guidance from the European Council, the Council of Economic and Finance Ministers (Ecofin), or even a consultative body comprising the Ecofin delegates of those member states participating in EMU. Equally often, the Germans have insisted that the ECB must retain its political independence in order to pursue a rule of absolute price stability. The compromise between these two positions is relatively easy to anticipate. The Ecofin delegates of EMU member states do coordinate their positions in a separate group (called the Euro–11), but this group neither issues instructions to Ecofin nor does it issue guidance to the ECB. Put another way, no political discretion is permitted to interfere with the functioning of the price stability rule.[12]

On a symbolic level, the conflict between France and Germany over the political direction of European economic policy is much harder to reconcile. Thus during the launch of EMU in the spring of 1998, France attempted to place its own candidate, Jean-Claude Trichet, at the head of the ECB. However, the job had already been promised to a Dutch candidate, Wim Duisenberg, who enjoyed considerable German support. Neither France nor Germany could afford to back down because doing so would suggest either that France had lost power or that the ECB was subject to political influence. Even the compromise ultimately reached—that the two candidates will split the eight year term—is symbolically unsatisfactory because it taints both parties. France is still weak and the ECB is still subject to influence. As a result, this conflict is generally regarded as a low point in Franco-German cooperation.[13]

Drifting Apart While Standing Still

These recurrent ups and downs in Franco-German economic relations look decidedly different from the close cooperation in the mid-to-late 1980s. One possible explanation is that the formula that bound the two countries together before German unification has somehow ceased to apply. The difficulty lies in sorting out what exactly that formula was or is. Obviously a huge range of factors should be taken into account, including common interests, identities, history, shared experiences, and personalities. However, arranging these factors into a framework for analysis is complicated, to say the least. Rather than trying to reinvent the wheel, perhaps it is best to start where others have gone before.

From the 1950s through the early 1990s, two perspectives on the Franco-German relationship have predominated. In one, the relationship is based on patterns of exchange: France wants something from Germany, and Germany wants something from France. In the other, the relationship is based on patterns of convergence: France and Germany each want to become more like the other. These perspectives are not necessarily symmetrical and neither are they mutually exclusive. France can give more or less than Germany, and France can move more or less toward Germany than the other way around. Moreover, the two perspectives can complement each other. France can give something to Germany and, in return, Germany can facilitate the process of French convergence.

As a set of analytic tools, notions of exchange and convergence necessarily restrict the scope of the argument. Nevertheless, they can help explain many of the most important developments in the Franco-German relationship. Hence, for F. Roy Willis, the founding of the European Coal and Steel Community represents an exchange of German sovereignty for French economic benefits. For Haig Simonian, the European Monetary System represents a convergence of French macroeconomic preferences on the German model. And for Patrick McCarthy, the welter of events surrounding the hardening of the European Monetary System and the relaunching of Europe after 1983 represents a complex combination of exchange and convergence. Implicitly in each case, the stability of the development derives from the terms of the exchange and from the commitment to convergence. So long as these are fair and firm, the Franco-German relationship will remain stable.[14]

Notions of exchange and convergence can also help to locate sources of change. What will happen to the Franco-German relationship if one day France and Germany have less to offer one another, and little or no desire to become more alike? Within the context of the argument, the answer is in many ways more obvious than the question. If, for whatever reason, France and Germany had little to exchange, or if they no longer sought to converge, then the ardor of their relationship should be expected to cool. Correspondingly, the stimulus for further integration in Europe should weaken. However, economic integration is not assumed to work that way. Countries become *more* dependent upon one another and not less. Moreover, in the fire of global competition, both macroeconomic strategies and market structures should be expected to look more and more alike.

Europe's economic and monetary union represents a good starting point for analyzing this problem because it combines many of the classic perspectives on the Franco-German relationship: It is almost wholly Franco-German in origin, it builds on some form of exchange between France and Germany, and it involves a process of convergence with the effect of making the two countries more alike. In characterized form, the origins of EMU can be stated as follows: France was pursuing closer monetary integration with Germany as a means to bring more symmetry into the economic relations of the two countries, but with limited success. Once the Berlin Wall fell, however, EMU became an essential part of the French strategy for binding Germany to the West. Hence, France agreed to support German unification in return for German acceptance of EMU. This exchange was insufficient to persuade Germany to abandon the Deutschmark, and it was inadequate to ensure that the EMU created would function according to German norms. Therefore, France agreed to embed EMU within a larger reform of the political institutions of the EU, and to construct the monetary union around a framework of predominantly German-looking institutions. According to this characterization of events, EMU represents both an attempt to integrate the French and German economies more deeply and to encourage their convergence.

This characterization of EMU is not an accurate reconstruction of historical events, nor is it meant to be. Indeed, according to at least one account, the events are simply too detailed and complicated to permit easy characterization.[15] That said, characterizations are both useful and used. Despite its obvious simplification, this hackneyed telling of the origins of EMU accurately reflects the thumbnail sketches that appear throughout the literature. What it fails to reflect is the actual development of Franco-German economic relations during the run-up to monetary union. And that is precisely the point.

The broad statistical data suggests that France and Germany have grown less dependent upon one another—at least in terms of the trade in goods and services. In the 1990s, France and Germany have tended to trade less with one another than they have with everyone else. German exports to France have accounted for only a decreasing proportion of total German exports. By the same token, French imports from Germany have accounted for a decreasing share of total French imports. The story with respect to French exports to Germany is much the same. Although French exporters have sent an increasing share of their output to Germany, German importers have come to rely increasingly on suppliers elsewhere.[16] These data can be found in table 4.2, which gives the averages for bilateral imports and exports as a

Table 4.2 Trade Dependence between France and Germany

	1984–1990	1991–1998
German Exports to France		
Percent total German exports	12.4	11.8
Percent total French imports	18.4	17.6
French Exports to Germany		
Percent total French exports	15.4	16.9
Percent total German imports	11.4	11.2

Source: International Monetary Fund.

Table 4.3 Import Penetration in France and Germany

	1984–1990	1991–1998
Imports from Within Europe		
France	11.8	11.4
Germany	13.3	11.5
Imports from Outside Europe		
France	7.3	6.9
Germany	9.3	8.8

Note: Percentage gross domestic product.
Source: European Commission.

percentage of the total for the periods from 1984–1990 and from 1991–1998, which is to say roughly the period from the relaunching of Europe to German unification, and from the signing of the Maastricht Treaty to the start of EMU.

Of course there is some scope to argue that these data are the result of the general downturn in economic activity across Europe. France and Germany trade less with one another because they trade less, period. In such an event, the expectation is that—all things being equal—the country with the sharpest decline in imports will also show the sharpest decrease in import penetration. Hence we should expect French import markets to have contracted more than German ones, if only with respect to Europe and perhaps not everywhere else. In fact, the opposite is the case. While French and German import markets do contract in relation to their extra-European partners by roughly equivalent amounts, German import markets contract by considerably more in relation to Europe. At the same time, while German imports into France have declined, the volume of French imports overall has remained much the same (see table 4.3).

Another possible explanation is that everything has not remained the same from the 1980s to the 1990s. Specifically, German unification has forced a number of dramatic changes on the German economy and, in particular, on German trade patterns. With the incorporation of the five new *Länder*, Germany also acquired substantial market relations with the countries of Central and Eastern Europe. As a result, Germany trades considerably more with those countries—and, by implication, marginally less with France. The data here are supportive. Between 1991 and 1997, the share of German exports going to the non-EU countries of Europe increased from 8.0 percent to 12.1 percent, while the share of German imports coming from that region increased from 7.4 percent to 11.3 percent. The same figures for France show a much lower expansion, at least in absolute terms if not in proportional terms. Between 1991 and 1997, the share of French exports going to non-EU Europe increased from 2.8 percent to 4.9 percent, while the share of imports increased from 2.9 percent to 3.8 percent.[17]

The prospect that trade between France and Germany has been displaced by trade between Germany and the countries of Central and Eastern Europe represents a significant challenge to any conception of the Franco-German relationship based on a binding notion of exchange. Accepting for a moment that one purpose of the Maastricht Treaty—and specifically of EMU—*was* to bind Germany to the West, the effectiveness of that strategy is open to question: Germany's economic center of gravity appears to have shifted nonetheless. Moreover, the prospect that this movement has not been reflected in a change in Germany's basic approach to commercial policy, and that the driving force for accessing eastern markets originates in the old western *Länder*, is more problematic still.[18] Despite the best of intentions, the possibility exists that whatever France has to offer Germany is not as attractive as that which can be found elsewhere.

Then again, the decreasing intensity of trading relations between France and Germany could signal the success of Franco-German convergence rather than the failure of some pre-existing exchange. As France and Germany become more alike, it is only natural that they should look elsewhere for trading partners. Of course some division of labor would continue to operate between French and German manufacturing—particularly on the level of intraindustry trade—and yet both countries will have to find trading partners specializing in other parts of the product cycle. For Germany these partners are to the east, and for France to the south. From 1991 to 1997, the share of French imports originating in Italy, Spain, and Portugal increased slightly from 17.1 percent to 17.4 percent, while the share of German imports originating in these countries decreased from 12.9 percent to 12.3 percent.[19]

The problem is that there is little evidence either that France and Germany are still converging on common institutional arrangements, market structures, or levels of productivity, or that they are converging on a common set of preferences—whether microeconomic or macroeconomic—about how the economy should function. There was some convergence during the 1970s and 1980s, but not after. During the 1990s, French and German macroeconomic *performance* has "converged"—at least as measured according to the criteria for participation in EMU—but the two economies have remained characteristically French and German. Following the logic of this claim, any dispute over the political direction of economic policy is necessarily exacerbated by disputes over how the economy should function.

Evidence of persistent structural differences between France and Germany is relatively plentiful. For example, trade union density declined in both countries by approximately 6 percent during the period from 1990 to 1995. Nevertheless, the level of trade union activity in Germany remains three times that in France. German trade union confederations are larger, more centralized, and more diverse in their membership. French trade union confederations are more numerous, more decentralized, and far more heavily represented in the public sector than anywhere else.[20] Similarly persistent differences are evident in terms of the distribution of employment across different branches of the economy. During the 1990s, both France and Germany experienced a shift away from agriculture and manufacturing and toward service-sector employment. Within that broad movement, however, the relative importance of French agriculture and of German manufacturing remains apparent (see table 4.4).

The broader panoply of institutions and policies that constitute the French and German economies is harder to characterize. Nevertheless, a recent study by Andrea Boltho (1996) seems to encapsulate the consensus view: Although the French have made much discussion of adopting Germany as an economic model, French successes at developing German-style institutions or practices has been limited.[21] Indeed, in microeconomic or institutional terms, France appears to be moving more toward the market liberalism of the United States than toward the organized market economy in Germany.

The lack of structural or institutional convergence between France and Germany makes any meaningful convergence of macroeconomic preferences unlikely. Despite the obvious comparisons of macroeconomic indicators such as those for inflation, interest rates, and fiscal balances, the mechanisms at work behind that macroeconomic performance are bound to differ from one country to another. For example, it is one thing to explain that large German trade unions make their wage-bargaining claims in anticipation of stable monetary conditions, and out of respect for the capacity of German monetary authorities to create unemployment damaging to German union members. This is, in essence, the classic explanation for German wage moderation—and it relies precisely on those characteristic

Table 4.4 Sectoral Composition of German and French Employment

	1980–1985	*1986–1990*	*1991–1997*
Agriculture			
West Germany	4.9	3.9	2.9
Unified Germany			3.1
France	7.8	6.3	4.8
Construction			
West Germany	7.5	6.7	6.7
Unified Germany			8.1
France	8.1	7.3	6.8
Services			
West Germany	53.2	56.0	60.6
Unified Germany			60.5
France	59.4	64.3	68.7
Industry (excluding construction)			
West Germany	34.4	33.3	29.8
Unified Germany			28.2
France	24.8	22.1	19.7
Manufacturing			
West Germany	32.5	31.6	28.3
Unified Germany			26.6
France	23.5	20.9	18.6

Note: Period averages, percentage total employment. Industry and Manufacturing are two different aggregations of similar data.
Source: European Commission.

features of German trade unions, their density, diversity, and centralization, that distinguish them from the French.[22] There is no analogous explanation for French wage moderation. That it happened is apparent in the data. *Why* it happened is not.[23]

Finally, without a common set of mechanisms to underwrite macroeconomic performance, the meaningful expression of similar macroeconomic preferences is surely open to question. That France and Germany both claim to value sound money and stable finances cannot be taken to mean that they hold these values for the same reasons and with the same intensity. Indeed, this has been a concern of German monetary policymakers throughout the process of monetary integration, and it explains to a large extent their desire for a "political union" to complement Europe's monetary union. As Bundesbank president Hans Tietmeyer explains: "A momentary similarity of interests without a lasting political connection hardly forms a sufficient basis for a monetary union."[24] By implication, the mixed record of Franco-German economic relations in the 1990s is a symptom that their "momentary similarity of interests" may be coming to an end.

The Riddle of German Power

At this point it is necessary to arrest the discussion from falling into extreme pessimism. The economic basis for cooperation between France and Germany may have deteriorated, but that is no reason to write off the Franco-German relationship altogether. For example, relations in other areas—such as defense and foreign policy—could strengthen to pick up the slack.[25] The objective of the argument so far has been simply to establish that something has changed, and to begin to explain why. And the answer is still only partial. By itself, the decline in the old formulas for the Franco-German relationship is insufficient to explain the mixed record of performance and conflict during the 1990s. It can help to establish the basis for disagreement, but not the motivation for continued good relations.

One possible solution is to change the emphasis in the argument from exchange and convergence to state power. For example, analysts of Germany have tended to assign any blame for the deterioration of Franco-German relations to the change in Germany's power potential, which was a result of unification. With the end of the Cold War, Germany both regained its sovereignty and acquired a host of new political interests. Germany also became manifestly the largest member of the EU. It is only natural, therefore, that Germany would become more assertive even if such assertiveness brings it into conflict with France (and Europe). Again, what is important to note is that this transformation has not sparked a complete collapse in Franco-German (or Euro-German) relations. This continued cooperation despite the change in German power and interests is attributed both to the country's robust institutional structures and to the Germans' "exaggerated multilateralism."[26]

The argument from German power provides a different perspective on the above thumbnail sketch of the origins of EMU than do the arguments about exchange and convergence. In this telling of the story, the economic changes were inevitable. Germany was manifestly going to gravitate toward the east no matter what the institutional configuration of Europe. The "binding" characteristic of the Maastricht Treaty refers to the institutional links that force Germany to dialogue with France (and the rest of Europe) *despite* the change in its economic center of gravity. From the power perspective, unified Germany is Europe's Ulysses, strapped to the single currency and the other EU institutions while struggling not to succumb to the siren calls of nationalism or narrowly defined national self-interest.

The strength of this interpretation lies in the attention it draws to the domestic determinants of Germany's policies in Europe. If Germany is becoming more assertive after unification, then it is relevant to ask what it is that Germany wants as well as who is pushing the agenda. Its weakness derives from its reliance on a peculiar notion of German exceptionalism in order to explain cooperation. Continuity, Jeffrey Anderson suggests, is "testament to the resilience of [the] core political values [of the Federal Republic of Germany in Europe] and the national framework of institutions that uphold them."[27] The problem with focusing on changes in German power, interests, and behavior is that it makes it necessary to consider France in the same way. And, once the comparative basis is established, the shortcomings of the argument from German power are apparent: Germany is not so strong, the domestic determinants of German European policy are not so unique, and the institutions of Europe are not so beneficent. Put another way, if unified Germany is even potentially as strong, self-obsessed, and dangerous as it is made out to be, why are the French so eager—and why does Europe provide so many opportunities—to goad the beast?

The claim that Germany is not so strong in comparative terms is the most easily demonstrated of the three. Looking at a range of indicators suggested by Stephen Krasner as proxies for measuring the economic power potential of states, it is clear that the changes brought about by German unification are undramatic, even if still significant.[28] The incorporation of the five new *Länder* did increase Germany's size both in terms of population and gross domestic product (GDP), but a substantial part of such advances served only to compensate for West Germany's relative decline since the late 1960s. Moreover, the impact of unification on Germany's share of world trade—both including and excluding the European Union—was marginal. By the same token, Germany's relative per capita GDP declined. In essence, then, unification made Germany bigger, but not necessarily more important and at the cost of taking on substantial socioeconomic differences (see table 4.5). These findings are confirmed through an anecdotal and institutional analysis of Germany's role in Europe and are broadly accepted by those who argue from the position of German power.[29]

Germany's new assertiveness derives not from any increase in its aggregate economic power potential, but from a combination of four factors—two of which have changed as a result of unification and two of which have remained the same. The factors that have changed are the status of German sovereignty and the diversity of German interests. In contrast with West Germany, unified Germany is fully sovereign but, as mentioned, contains a much wider diversity of socioeconomic interests. Moreover, this diversity of economic and social conditions was remarkably persistent.[30]

The factors that have remained the same are Germany's economic reputation and its domestic institutional arrangements. Whether or not France and Germany are actually converging, Germany remains attractive as an

Table 4.5 German Economic Power Potential in a European Context

| | Share in EU 12 (percent) | | World Trade Share (percent) | | GDP p/c* |
	Population	Real GDP	Including EU	Excluding EU	EU 12 = 100
1960–1969					
West Germany	20.1	25.6	8.3	6.1	128
France	16.7	19.2	5.0	3.8	115
Italy	17.4	14.8	3.7	3.1	83
United Kingdom	18.7	21.5	6.8	7.3	116
1970–1979					
West Germany	19.9	24.9	10.8	6.1	126
France	16.9	20.3	6.6	3.7	120
Italy	17.5	15.6	4.7	2.9	88
United Kingdom	18.1	18.7	6.4	4.9	104
1980–1989					
West Germany	19.1	24.3	9.5	5.1	127
France	17.2	20.7	5.8	3.2	120
Italy	17.5	16.7	4.5	2.7	95
United Kingdom	17.7	18.0	5.6	3.4	102
1991–1999					
Germany	23.5	28.2	9.7	5.4	115
France	16.7	18.7	5.6	2.7	117
Italy	16.5	15.3	4.4	2.3	95
United Kingdom	16.9	15.7	5.2	3.1	101

Note: *This data series has been temporarily discontinued by the Commission—the final panel is 1990–1996.
Source: European Commission.

economic model at least in rhetorical terms.[31] Germany also remains a federal state, with strong elements of decentralization and powerful institutional checks on the exercise of state power. Taken together, these factors suggest that—on economic grounds at least—not only is it attractive for Europe to strive to become more like Germany, but it is difficult for the German government to make concessions to Europe. In this sense, "internal weakness may thus be a source of external strength."[32]

From this standpoint, the argument from German power looks different from that sketched above. Germany is not necessarily stronger as a result of unification, it is just more problematic. But how is this any different from France? If the claim is that unified Germany is now just as problematic as France ever was, then the argument from German power does not actually tell us very much. It can explain why France and Germany would come to loggerheads—for example, because the French state is held in sway by the powerful farm lobby and because the German government has little leverage over the Bundesbank. But it cannot explain why either country would be willing to back down, or why they retain their special relationship in the first place.

The influence of European institutions might fill the gap in the argument, but only if it is possible to accept that such institutions can impose restraints and influence identities without incurring costs or provoking antagonisms. Of course no one is arguing that Europe is cost-free or uncontroversial. Equally, however, few are willing to admit that the costs of Europe could come to overpower its beneficial restraints. Nevertheless, the forces are much more balanced than one-sided, and the momentum occasionally shifts.

A specific example of this "clash of institutions"—European versus domestic—relates to what has earlier been referred to as the classic argument for German wage moderation. Because they are large and centralized, trade unions in Germany tend to moderate their wage claims in order to stave off unemployment. In turn, this wage moderation plays an important role in underwriting Germany's capacity to reconcile economic growth and price stability. The paradox is that while the institutions for EMU are patterned on those found in Germany, and guided by a German-inspired absolute price-stability rule, the replacement of German institutions with European ones may inadvertently undermine trade union support for wage moderation. Far from establishing German economic norms, EMU may weaken German economic performance and even ignite a conflict between labor and capital in Germany.[33] The point here is not to say that this will happen, but only that it could—which is sufficient to establish the potential of European institutions to generate contradictory economic effects.

A further set of examples can be found in the relationship between rising unemployment and the shift from center-right to center-left in France and

Germany. Here the clash between national and European institutions can be understood on two levels. To begin with, European institutions can exacerbate differences between the two countries. Thus, while Germany is decentralized, France is not. By implication, it is relatively easier for German politicians to segment responsibility for macroeconomic instruments and objectives than it is for the French. The German public may be content to hold the Bundesbank responsible for price stability, the minister of finance responsible for government balances, and the minister of the economy responsible for employment. However, the French hold their president and prime minister responsible for all of these things. Thus, in the 1995 French presidential election, Jacques Chirac campaigned on a platform that economic policy should focus on the objective of reducing unemployment even though this brought him into conflict with many of the German-inspired macroeconomic policy norms embedded in EMU.[34] The German response was to propose the Stability Pact as a mechanism for strengthening the fiscal requirements for membership. That Chirac recanted, and pledged his support for EMU, certainly contributed to the December 1995 protests in France and may have helped to undermine the position of the right in the 1997 legislative elections as well.

At another level, the impact of European institutions can be to exacerbate differences within countries even as it forges partial alliances between them. Here the example focuses on tension within the post–1998 center-left government in Germany between the newly elected prime minister, Gerhard Schröder, and his finance minister, Oskar Lafontaine. The conflict between the two men was both personal and ideological. The personal conflict is relevant only as a motivational factor. The ideological conflict was more threatening, both to Schröder and to the German-inspired constitution for EMU. Specifically, Lafontaine argued for increasing political coordination of macroeconomic policymaking as well as more strenuous efforts to target macroeconomic instruments to the reduction of unemployment. This stand put Lafontaine into conflict both with the Bundesbank and with the newly launched European Central Bank (ECB). However, it put him into alliance with French interests in general and with the French minister of finance, Dominique Strauss-Kahn, in particular. For a while it seemed that Lafontaine "had emerged as the most powerful player in Bonn" and that the emphasis in German economic policy would change accordingly.[35] In any event, Schröder was able to wrestle away control over his own government and Lafontaine resigned. Importantly, not only was Lafontaine able to gain leverage from his opposition to a particular institutional configuration in Europe, but he was able to block the functioning of European institutions as well. Faced with the prospect of being perceived as under

German political influence, the ECB held off making an important interest rate reduction until after Lafontaine had left.[36]

European institutions may have played a role in taming German power but they have had a range of other and potentially less desirable influences as well. Moreover, the impact of European institutions is much the same for France as well. As a result, our ability to explain the ups and downs of Franco-German cooperation in the 1990s through this particular form of institutional sociology is limited. We can gain some insight on Germany's problematic nature as a "normal" European power, and possibly some purchase on why France and Germany prefer some institutional arrangements over others. Nevertheless, the continuity of Franco-German economic relations as a special relationship remains relatively unexplored.

Power Restored:
The Ins and Outs of the Franco-German Coalition

The solution to explaining the Franco-German economic relationship in the 1990s is institutional empowerment as well as institutional constraint. The argument is that France and Germany cooperate in Europe to achieve a range of objectives that are held both separately and in common. Within this argument, the observation that France and Germany continue to cooperate is simply a function of the fact that their objectives remain to be achieved, and that their continued cooperation is necessary to achieve them. For example, without France and Germany there can be no EMU, and without EMU Europe cannot improve the functioning of the single market. What is novel is not the basis for cooperation, but the recognition that power emanates from the Franco-German *relationship* rather than from France or Germany *per se*.

This notion of power is borrowed from Michel Crozier's 1973 study of French society in the late 1960s and early 1970s, as well as from the larger corpus of his sociology.[37] Essentially, it has three characteristics: All power derives from social relations; within social relations, the distribution of power is a function of each agent's control over the sources of uncertainty in achieving their common purpose; and any exercise of power is either within the accepted norms of the relationship (control) or contrary to those norms (blackmail). A strength of this notion is that it encompasses both the traditional formula for the Franco-German relationship and the argument about the restraining influence of institutions. As Crozier says, "Any relationship between two parties requires a measure of exchange and mutual adjustment," the terms of which "create compulsory hurdles and opportunities for manipulation for the players, and therefore determine their strategy."[38] Crucially, for collective action to arrive at its desired outcome, the behavior of the participants must be made predictable and transparent.

The notion of predictability is a recurrent theme in Crozier's identification of power within social relations. To the extent to which predictability can be equated with the process of institution-building, Crozier's conception of power can help to explain why France and Germany cooperate within Europe, and indeed rely on Europe as a focus for their economic cooperation. Nevertheless, saying that France and Germany create institutions for common purpose does not help in understanding the dynamics of the relationship—at least beyond the *European Rescue of the Nation-State* type of argument advanced by Alan Milward.[39] Therefore it is necessary to focus attention on three further aspects of Crozier's theory of power: control, blackmail, and integration.

For Crozier, the exercise of control and the resort to blackmail both represent a manipulation of uncertainty. They correspond to agents exercising power. However, where control is relatively easily translated into institution-building, blackmail must first be accepted as legitimate. Only once it is accepted within the rules for collective action, can blackmail be relied upon as the basis for institution-building. In the parlance of European integration, the "empty chair" crisis was blackmail. However, the Luxembourg compromise legitimized national vetoes and so institutionalized unanimous voting procedures in the Council.

In turn, successive rounds of institution-building constitute integration. Moreover, as more and more different (and different types) of agents come into contact with one another, power tends to become more diffuse, and the institutional requirements for transparency and predictability tend to increase. In other words, so far Crozier's theory of power tends to conform to the patterns of relations in Europe today—starting perhaps with a narrow focus on Franco-German reconciliation, but soon broadening and deepening to engage a much wider range of member states and subnational interests.

What Crozier adds to our understanding of the Franco-German relationship is the notion that control and blackmail both play a role in national strategies for collective action. The ups and downs do not signal a flaw in the Franco-German relationship. They *are* the Franco-German relationship in the sense that they reflect the ins and outs of French and German strategies within that relationship. This point can be made formally through Michael Winkler's observation that players can maximize their voting power by starting from within the winning coalition.[40] It can also be made anecdotally: both the conflict over CAP reform at the start of the 1990s and the conflict over the ECB president at the end of the 1990s originated in a French defection from a common Franco-German position. In the first case, the French strategy was successful. In the second it was not. The point is simply that such defections cannot signal a desire to end the Franco-German relationship because, as a strategy, they could not function without the relationship.

Prospects for the Future

Franco-German economic relations have progressed from exchange and convergence to collective action. In doing so, they have become embedded in institutions that both empower and constrain that relationship. France and Germany approach their relationship with strategies of cooperation and defection designed best to pursue their national interest. In turn those strategies are informed by national actors who make use of domestic institutions and relationships to further their own agendas. Where these actors can leapfrog their own member states to appeal either to Europe or to the other half of the Franco-German couple, that is to be expected. Blackmail is not the sole purview of the nation-state, and neither is the exercise of power under the nation-state's monopoly control. Moreover, while it is possible that France and Germany have succeeded in ruling the political manipulation of macroeconomic instruments to be beyond the bounds of good behavior, the rule of thumb remains that some rules are made to be broken. Whatever the case, the point to note is that no matter how complicated the pattern of European integration becomes, Franco-German economic relations will continue to lie at the center.

Notes

1. Three excellent books have recently been published surveying Germany's monetary role in Europe: Dorothee Heisenberg, *The Mark of the Bundesbank: Germany's Role in European Monetary Cooperation* (Boulder: Lynne Rienner Publishers, 1999); Karl Kaltenthaler, *Germany and the Politics of Europe's Money* (Durham: Duke University Press, 1998); and Peter Henning Loedel, *Deutsche Mark Politics: Germany in the European Monetary System* (Boulder: Lynne Rienner Publishers, 1999).
2. See Simon Bulmer, "Germany and European Integration: Toward Economic and Political Dominance?" in Carl F. Lankowski, ed., *Germany and the European Community: Beyond Hegemony and Containment?* (New York: St. Martin's Press, 1993), pp. 73–99; Simon Bulmer, "Shaping the Rules? The Constitutive Politics of the European Union and German Power," in Peter J. Katzenstein, ed., *Tamed Power: Germany in Europe* (Ithaca: Cornell University Press, 1997), pp. 49–79.; Peter J. Katzenstein, "United Germany in an Integrating Europe," in Katzenstein, *Tamed Power,* pp. 1–48.; Jeffrey Anderson, "Hard Interests, Soft Power, and Germany's Changing Role in Europe," in Katzenstein, *Tamed Power,* pp. 80–107; and Jeffrey Anderson,

German Unification and the Union of Europe (Cambridge: Cambridge University Press, 1999). The notion of "tamed power" appears most prominently in the title of Katzenstein's book, but also emerges in the final sentence of Bulmer's 1993 essay. For a generalized version of the argument, see Paul Pierson, "The Path to European Integration: A Historical Institutionalist Analysis," *Comparative Political Studies* 29:2 (April 1996) pp. 123–163.

3. Peter Katzenstein omits France from his collection of essays, *Tamed Power,* and instead focuses attention on relations between Germany and the smaller countries. Nevertheless, he seems to be pushing the argument in the direction of empowerment when he states that: "Only when we move institutional power to center stage can we hope to understand why Germany is willing to give up its new sovereign power or why institutional inefficiency has not stopped European integration (p. 3)." He returns to this theme again to claim that: "The answers this book offers derive from the premise that we can adequately understand the world of power and interest in Europe only when we see power and interest not simply as attributes of distinctive actors, Germany *and* Europe, but as aspects of relationships that place Germany *in* Europe, through institutions that tame power (p. 6)." However, the rest of the introduction focuses on the role of Europe in constituting, shaping, and constraining national interests.

4. Patrick McCarthy makes much the same point somewhat differently in suggesting that "today, the French and the Germans take conflict for granted . . ." See, Patrick McCarthy, "The Grand Bargain: A New Book Demystifies European Integration," *Foreign Affairs* 78:5 (September/October 1999) pp. 150–157.

5. This argument parallels the conclusions made by Andrea Szukala and Wolfgang Wessels, but from a different basis. See, Andrea Szukala and Wolfgang Wessels, "The Franco-German Tandem," in Geoffrey Edwards and Alfred Pijpers, eds., *The Politics of European Treaty Reform: The 1996 Intergovernmental Conference and Beyond* (London: Pinter, 1997), pp. 74–95.

6. Julius W. Friend, "The Linchpin: French-German Relations, 1950–1990," *The Washington Papers, No. 154* (New York: Praeger for CSIS, 1991), p. 98.

7. Christopher Pierson, Anthony Forster, and Erik Jones, "Changing the Guard in the European Union: In with the New, out with the Old?" *Industrial Relations Journal: European Annual Review 1998* 30:4 (December 1999) pp. 277–290.

8. Françoise De la Serre and Christian Lequesne, "France and the European Union," in Alan W. Cafruny and Glenda G. Rosenthal, eds., *The State of the European Community Vol. 2: The Maastricht Debates and Beyond* (Boulder: Lynne Rienner, 1993), p. 156.

9. Douglas Webber, "Franco-German Bilateralism and Agricultural Politics in the European Union: The Neglected Level," *West European Politics* 22:1 (January 1999) pp. 45–67; Geoffrey Edwards and Georg Wiessala, "Editorial: *Plus ça changes . . . ?*" in Geoffrey Edwards and Georg Wies-

sala, eds., *The European Union Annual Review 1998/1999* (Oxford: Blackwell, 1999) pp. 1–8.

10. Patrick H. O'Neill, "Politics, Finance, and European Union Enlargement Eastward," in James Sperling, ed., *Two Tiers or Two Speeds? The European Security Order and the Enlargement of the European Union and NATO* (Manchester: Manchester University Press, 1999) pp. 81–99; David Galloway, "*Agenda 2000*–Packaging the Deal," in Edwards and Wiessala, *The European Union Annual Review 1998/1999*, pp. 9–35.

11. Christopher Pierson, Anthony Forster, and Erik Jones, "The Politics of Europe: (Un)Employment Ambivalence," in Brian Towers and Michael Terry, eds. *Industrial Relations Journal: European Annual Review, 1997* (Oxford: Blackwell, 1998), pp. 5–22.

12. Pierson et al., "Changing the Guard."

13. Desmond Dinan, "Governance and Institutions: A Transitional Year," in Edwards and Wiessala, *The European Union Annual Review 1998/1999*, pp. 37–61.

14. F. Roy Willis, *France, Germany, and the New Europe: 1945–1963* (Stanford: Stanford University Press, 1965); Haig Simonian, *The Privileged Partnership: Franco-German Relations in the European Community, 1969–1984* (Oxford: Clarendon Press, 1985); Patrick McCarthy, "France Faces Reality: *Rigueur* and the Germans," in David P. Calleo and Claudia Morgenstern, eds., *Recasting Europe's Economies: National Strategies in the 1980s* (Lanham: University Press of America, 1990) pp. 25–78. Here it is useful to note that while Andrew Moravcsik takes issue with McCarthy about the structure of the exchange underwriting the 1983 turnaround in France, he does not challenge the presumption that some exchange was necessary to support the relaunching of Europe. Andrew Moravcsik, *The Choice for Europe: Social Purpose and State Power from Messina to Maastricht* (Ithaca: Cornell University Press, 1998) p. 232. See also McCarthy, "The Grand Bargain."

15. Kenneth Dyson and Kevin Featherstone, *The Road to Maastricht: Negotiating Economic and Monetary Union* (Oxford: Oxford University Press, 1999).

16. The period averages do not reveal the full extent of the trend. Thus, for example, the share of French exports to German peaks in 1991 at just over 18 percent of total French exports and then declines for five of the next seven years.

17. These data are from the Direction of Trade Statistics of the IMF.

18. Anderson, *German Unification*, pp. 72–73.

19. These data are from the Direction of Trade Statistics of the IMF.

20. Jelle Visser, "European Trade Unions in the Mid-1990s," in Towers and Terry, *Industrial Relations Journal: European Annual Review, 1997*, pp. 113–130.

21. Andrea Boltho, "Has France Converged on Germany? Policies and Institutions Since 1958," in Suzanne Berger and Ronald Dore, eds., *National Diversity and Global Capitalism* (Ithaca: Cornell University Press, 1996) pp. 89–104.

22. Peter A. Hall, "Central Bank Independence and Coordinated Wage Bargaining: Their Interaction in Germany and Europe," *German Politics and Society* 31 (Spring 1994) pp. 1–23.

23. Stephen Bazen and Eric Girardin, "France and the Maastricht Criteria: Fiscal Retrenchment and Labor Market Adjustment," in David Cobham and George Zis, eds., *From EMS to EMU: 1979 to 1999 and Beyond* (London: Macmillan, 1999) pp. 95–128.

24. Hans Tietmeyer, "Europäische Währungsunion und politische Union–das Modell mehrerer Geschwindigkeiten." *Europa Archiv* 49:16 (25 August 1994) pp. 458.

25. This appears to be the assessment of Edwards and Wiessala although Menon's contribution to this volume suggests that such aspirations are likely to be disappointed. See Edwards and Wiessala, "Editorial," pp. 3–4.

26. Anderson, "Hard Interests," p. 104.

27. Anderson, *German Unification,* p. 192.

28. Stephen D. Krasner, "State Power and the Structure of International Trade," *World Politics* 28 (April 1976) pp. 317–347.

29. Simon Bulmer and William E. Patterson, "Germany in the European Union: Gentle Giant or Emergent Leader?" *International Affairs* 72:1 (1996), pp. 9–32.

30. Alun Jones, *The New Germany: A Human Geography* (Chichester: John Wiley and Sons, 1994).

31. Kenneth Dyson, "The Franco-German Relationship and Economic and Monetary Union: Using Europe to 'Bind Leviathan'," *West European Politics* 22:1 (January 1999) pp. 25–44.

32. Bulmer and Patterson, "Germany in the European Union," p. 31.

33. Kathleen McNamara and Erik Jones, "The Clash of Institutions: Germany in European Monetary Affairs," *German Politics and Society* 14:3 (Fall 1996) pp. 5–30; Peter A. Hall and Robert J. Franzese, Jr., "Mixed Signals: Central Bank Independence, Coordinated Wage Bargaining, and European Monetary Union," *International Organization* 52:3 (Summer 1998) pp. 505–535.

34. Jean Pisani-Ferry, "France and EMU: Economic and Political Economy Issues," in Jean Pisani-Ferry, Carsten Hefeker, and A.J. Hughes Hallett, *The Political Economy of EMU: France, Germany, and the UK* (Brussels: Centre for European Policy Studies, CEPS Paper No. 69, 1997) pp. 5–38.

35. Kenneth Dyson, "Benign or Malevolent Leviathan? Social Democratic Governments in a Neo-Liberal Euro Area," *The Political Quarterly* 70:2 (April-June 1999) p. 205.

36. Miriam Campanella, "The Battle between Ecofin 11 and the European Central Bank: A Rational Choice Perspective," in Maria Green Cowles and Michael Smith, eds., *State of the European Union: Risks, Reforms, Resistance, and Revival, Vol. 5* (Oxford: Oxford University Press, in press).

37. Michel Crozier, *The Stalled Society* (New York: The Viking Press, 1973); Michel Crozier and Erhard Friedberg, *L'acteur et le système* (Paris: Éditions du Seuil, 1977).

38. Crozier, *The Stalled Society,* pp. 25, 27.
39. Alan Milward, *The European Rescue of the Nation-State* (London: Routledge, 1992).
40. G. Michael Winkler, "Coalition-Sensitive Voting Power in the Council of Ministers: The Case of Eastern Enlargement," *Journal of Common Market Studies* 36:3 (September 1998) pp. 391–404.

Chapter 5 ✥

The Franco-German Partnership and the European Union

Roger Morgan

Introduction

In 1993, as the Maastricht Treaty on European Union was coming into force, an assessment of the Franco-German partnership, and of its success in leading the EU toward closer unity, noted that the two nations had many divergences of interest and attitude, especially after the strains arising from Germany's rapid unification. Yet despite this, Paris and Bonn were continuing to work systematically to overcome these differences, and making an essential and irreplaceable contribution to the progress of European integration.[1]

What are the prospects in the year 2000, following the further EU treaty revisions agreed upon in Amsterdam in 1997, the shaky start of the common currency stage of Economic and Monetary Union (EMU) in 1998–1999, and the commitment to press ahead with further eastward enlargement of the EU (and southeastward, in principle including Turkey) in the early years of the twenty-first century? More concretely, what role can we expect the EU's Franco-German "engine" to play during the Inter-Governmental Conference (IGC) scheduled for the year 2000, which is expected to produce major institutional and other reforms to be agreed upon at the summit meeting of the European Council in December under France's presidency? It is still a widespread view, in 2000 as in 1990 (or indeed in 1950), that progress in European integration depends essentially on consensus and cooperation between these two countries. An experienced German diplomat, Klaus-Peter Klaiber, has argued that "talking about Europe is impossible without looking at the Franco-German couple. . . . No two other countries in the world have developed such close cooperation as Germany and France."[2] Other observers have said of France and Germany that "the functioning of this relationship remains now as always the essential precondition of any significant integration initiative in the EU"[3]; or, as Patrick McCarthy put it when the list of member-states to be admitted to the common currency was about to be decided: "The two countries will have to provide leadership because the sound and fury that accompany monetary union will grow more, rather than less violent after the first group of countries is formed in spring 1998."[4]

Of course, the Franco-German relationship has many different aspects, not the least of which is this: Not only is the bilateral partnership a positive factor for the EU, but the EU itself provides a positive environment for the bilateral relationship (and indeed for the national interests of each of the two partners). In pointing this out, Douglas Webber has underlined the importance attached to the relationship by the political elites of the two countries:

> In the case of France, the dominant analysis . . . is that . . . the European integration process and the special relationship with Germany are as much, if not more, in the interests of France as they were before 1990. . . . In the case of Germany . . . no relevant political force yet questions . . . the indispensability of the Franco-German partnership.[5]

In assessing the performance of this partnership, the present chapter will start by analyzing the underlying interests of France and Germany, from the time of the Maastricht Treaty to the present, in relation to the central issues contained therein. It will consider to what extent the 1990s have seen the achievement of these French and German objectives; and it will ask in conclusion, in the light of the balance between agreement and disagreement between the two partners, what the prospects are of further progress in the years ahead.

In summary, if we examine French and German interests in relation to what have been called the two main "pillars" of European policy enshrined in the Maastricht Treaty, we can see a clear pattern of dissimilar priorities between the two countries. Regarding Maastricht's "first pillar"—the area of economic integration whose centerpiece was the development of Economic and Monetary Union (EMU)—we can say that while both France and Germany were committed to the same overall objective, Germany had a more concrete program for action, and more specific requirements. By 1998–1999, as we shall see, the EU's very considerable progress in fulfilling these German requirements meant that the form eventually taken by EMU represented a success for Germany. (This success, of course, reflected the fact that the German point of view was accepted, for whatever reasons, by the majority of the EU's member-states.)

In the second major "pillar" of the Maastricht construction, the program for progress toward the loosely defined concept of "Political Union," it could again be said that in the early 1990s it was Germany rather than France that had specific wishes and proposals for change and reform. Here, however, the course of events during the ensuing decade resulted only in relatively modest changes in the institutions and practices of the EU (including the treaty's much-heralded "Common Foreign and Security Policy" or CFSP), and this relative lack of innovation reflected, broadly, success for the position adopted by France in 1990–1991. (As with Germany's success over EMU, this signified that the cautious French position on the issues of institutional reform and foreign policy reflected a kind of consensus among the EU's more influential member-states. As we shall see, even Germany's enthusiasm for "Political Union" was to weaken in the course of the 1990s.)

By the year 1999, then, the position was that the first major Maastricht project, the development of EMU with its common currency, had made decisive progress, essentially in a form desired by Germany. On the other central project, the "Political Union" one of institutional strengthening and a formally structured CFSP, it was the French preference for cautious and limited change that had prevailed.[6] As the EU entered the year 2000 and faced the pressing problem of how to manage its extensive eastward enlargement (to which its leaders had emphatically committed at their Helsinki summit in December 1999), the unfinished business of institutional reform (unfinished at Maastricht in 1991, side-stepped at Amsterdam in 1997) presented itself to France, Germany, and their European partners with a new urgency.

Back in the early 1990s, the reactions to these challenges by Paris and Bonn (after September 1999, Berlin) had reflected—as they continued to reflect—long-standing national attitudes. Simplifying greatly, we could say that the fundamental motives of France and Germany in seeking to "construct Europe" were geopolitical: for France, the wish to build a Europe strong enough to contain the power of Germany in collective institutions; and for Germany, the wish for a Europe in which Germany's unavoidable strength and influence could develop without alarming its neighbors. The roots of these partly irreconcilable purposes lie far back in history, notably in the 1920s, when the first systematic Franco-German attempts at building European institutions were made.[7] There were naturally many other considerations. France, from the 1950s to the 1990s, has wanted to create a "European identity" strong enough to stand up to the United States in world affairs; it has also been inclined to make Europe's institutions the basis for economic planning of the kind practiced in postwar France, as well as striving for monetary union in order to give France the benefits of close links with the strong D-Mark.

Somewhat paradoxically, France has tried, ever since the presidency of Charles de Gaulle (1958–1969), to combine these strongly European policies with an institutional approach that favored the EC's individual member-states, upgrading such "intergovernmental" institutions as the Council of (national) Ministers or the European Council of top political leaders at the expense of the "supranational" Commission and European Parliament. This French view of the EC or EU as a combination of nation-states—although it has been shared by Britain, Denmark, and others—is in sharp contrast to the prevailing view in postwar Germany. Germans have certainly shared France's wish to use "Europe" to control Germany, but they have normally gone further, in wanting Europe's institutions to be placed on a formal constitutional basis, extending Germany's own federal system to the European level. In economic policy, Germans have preferred market concepts to French ideas of planning, and they have also wished to see the EC or EU occupying an ever-wider area of Europe, making it a region safe for German trade and investment. Externally, Germany has supported a less protectionist trade policy than France, and has worked for the EC's Common Foreign and Security Policy (known from 1970 to 1993 as "European Political Cooperation" or EPC), which has helped Germany's world-wide influence to grow. As a close ally of the United States, Germany has tried to combine an "Atlanticist" with a "European" dimension in its foreign policy.[8]

These differing French and German perspectives marked the arduous negotiations that led to the Maastricht Treaty. The project of establishing a common currency, debated since the 1960s and confirmed in detail at Maastricht, was directly stimulated by the plan to liberalize the EC's internal market. The agreement that embodied this plan, the Single European Act of 1986, provided for the "four freedoms"—free movement of goods, capital, employees, and services—to become a reality by the end of 1992, and this gave new impetus to the integration process, including the idea of a common currency. This progression from a (developing) single market to a (controversial) common currency marked a shift in emphasis from German to French thinking. Whereas the idea of a single European market for goods and services appealed to more interests in Germany than in France, that of linking the national currencies irrevocably together appealed more to French interests. The French approach to Economic and Monetary Union (EMU) came to be classified as "monetarist," since it argued that the fixing of monetary parities would in itself induce closer economic integration; the German approach—that monetary unification could be attempted only after considerable economic convergence had already been achieved—became known as "economist."[9]

These Franco-German differences explain why, in the debates on EMU in the years preceding German unification, France argued that the "1992 program" for a single market should logically be followed by the early introduction of a common currency, while Germany insisted that this step could only come after a period of convergence between the national economies involved. This situation was changed by the unexpected achievement of German unity in 1990. While Mitterrand increased his pressure for movement toward monetary integration, Kohl changed the German position; and by the end of 1991, at Maastricht, he had accepted that a common currency would become a reality, perhaps as early as 1997. Kohl seems to have calculated that German acceptance of monetary union would calm French fears about the prospect of German unification. In any case, the idea of monetary union was by now supported, for economic reasons, by substantial interest groups in Germany.[10] Germany thus took a decisive step on EMU in 1990, though it was later, as we shall see, to impose strict conditions for its implementation.

The unification of Germany, accompanied as it was by considerable economic and political difficulties, weighed heavily on the negotiations leading to the Maastricht Treaty. The negotiations were carried on, throughout most of 1991, in two distinct Inter-Governmental Conferences (IGCs), both meeting in Brussels. One of them was concerned with EMU (the theme that was to be embodied in the "first pillar" of the Treaty's architecture), and the other with the institutional, political, and legal questions that were to be incorporated in the Treaty's second and third "pillars." The roles of France and Germany in the two IGCs, and in what followed, will be discussed in the next two sections of this chapter.[11]

EMU and the Birth of the Euro

Once the fundamental decision had been taken in 1990 that the European governments would negotiate seriously about EMU, the IGC devoted to this subject went relatively smoothly, and agreement was reached by late 1991. This was partly because the objective was clear, the ground had been well prepared, and many of the expert negotiators involved had been dealing with the issue for years. It also helped that Germany's partners, including France, were ready to accept the German viewpoint on many important questions. These included the timetable for the establishment of the new European Central Bank (ECB), and the locking-together and subsequent unification of the currencies it was to manage. The original French "monetarist" view that this should be done within five years or so was modified in deference to Germany's "economist" insistence that Europe's national economies would need longer to achieve the necessary degree of convergence.

A second French concession concerned the degree of autonomy to be granted to the ECB. Whereas France believed that a central bank should act in conformity with the macroeconomic policies of the political authorities (like the Banque de France), Germans were deeply convinced that financial stability required the independence of the bank from governmental control (as with, in principle, the Bundesbank). Again, German views were accepted, and the ECB was given a status similar to that of the Bundesbank. As we shall see, France continued to press the idea that the ECB should be counterbalanced by a European "economic government" of some kind, but the basic principle was to remain the German one of the ECB's independence. Germany's partners further agreed that all of their (national) central banks should be freed from governmental control, and given a status like that of the Bundesbank, by the time they joined the ECB system.[12]

German influence was apparent not only in these formal arrangements, but also in the substance of the criteria for assessing convergence between the states aspiring to join the EMU. All members had to satisfy the following criteria:

- Their annual inflation rate must not exceed the average rate of the three best-performing members of the system by more than 1.5 percent.
- Their long-term interest rates must not exceed those of the three lowest-interest members by more than 2 percent.
- Their budget deficits must not exceed 3 percent of their GDP.
- Their total public debt must not exceed 60 percent of their GDP.
- They may have only limited fluctuations in their exchange rates.

The Maastricht timetable for applying these criteria originally provided for the assessments to be carried out in 1996, with a view to the locking of parities at the start of 1997. However, as the difficulties faced by many states in meeting the criteria became apparent, the timing was postponed—again in line with German wishes—until 1998–1999. As we shall see, it was even then a matter of controversy whether or not some member-states truly complied with the criteria.

As for the leaders of France and Germany, the deep commitment of both Kohl and Mitterrand to the EMU project can be measured by the hard battles they fought and won before they could get the Maastricht Treaty accepted and ratified within their national political systems. In France, where a referendum was necessary, Mitterrand and his supporters had to campaign long and hard; despite all their efforts the French voters, in September 1992, accepted the Treaty by only the smallest of margins. In Germany, where Kohl resolutely rejected any idea of a referendum, there was widespread hostility to the Treaty, and it was only ratified, after extended political and legal wrangles, late in 1993.

The nature of the opposition in both countries is worth considering, as its arguments influenced the policies pursued by the two governments in the years that followed. In Germany, there was predictable emphasis on the argument that the solid and reliable D-Mark (older by one year than the Federal Republic itself, and arguably a stronger symbol of national identity) must not be abandoned in favor of a currency that one of Kohl's critics, a leading Bavarian politician, called "Esperanto-money." Wide sections of the German press, from the mass-circulation *Bild Zeitung* to the influential weekly *Der Spiegel,* attacked the abandonment of the D-Mark; and groups of dissident politicians, professional economists, and others mounted assaults on EMU that included a legal challenge to its constitutionality, brought by one of these groups before Germany's Constitutional Court.

In France, criticism of EMU was less directly linked to the currency question itself; the criticism was more broadly political, and often specifically directed against Germany. On the left, Mitterrand's former defense minister Jean-Pierre Chevenement denounced the project for putting France under German domination. On the right, Gaullists including Jacques Chirac and Philippe Seguin accused Mitterrand of sacrificing France's national independence, and some press articles compared his actions with French collaboration with the occupying Germans of the Second World War.[13]

While the argument about EMU was raging, tensions between Germany and many of its European partners (including France) was also heightened by the economic consequences of German unification. In order to pay the immense cost of rehabilitating Eastern Germany without increasing taxes (as Kohl had promised in his successful election campaign of 1990, and wanted to promise again in 1994), Germany covered these costs essentially by raising public loans; this led in turn to repeated rises in interest rates, which went up six times during a brief period. This upward pressure on German interest rates led to complaints from Germany's partners that its high rates were sucking investment away from their own economies, and preventing them from making the cuts in interest rates that most of them needed. Most of Europe was at this time suffering from acute recession, and there were great difficulties in maintaining the currency parities in force in the existing European Monetary System, even before the attempt was made to move toward the more stringent rules required by the projected EMU. It was at this stage (in September 1992) that the United Kingdom and Italy were forced to drop out of the European Monetary System's exchange rate mechanism, and France also experienced grave difficulties. Fortunately for the future of the European Union, the French and German governments continued to act in concert: in 1992–1993 the Bundesbank gave essential support to the

French franc, and in August 1993 the rules governing exchange-rate varia-tions in the European Monetary System were made more flexible. On the French side, the conviction grew stronger that France would be better off under a single European monetary authority, as projected in the EMU, than in a state of dependence on the autonomous decisions and actions of the Bundesbank.[14]

The adjustment of national economic policies that was needed to allow the states to meet the Maastricht criteria by the target date of 1997 did not, of course, take place in a vacuum. In addition to the economic conse-quences of German unification and of Europe's general recession, the French and German governments—and their partners—had to count the prospective costs of enlarging the EU into Central and Eastern Europe. The inclusion of the former German Democratic Republic, completed by the end of 1990 with German unification, had been costly but manageable, and the planned addition of the affluent countries of the European Free Trade Area (Austria, Sweden, and others) would clearly improve the EU's budgetary situation, not harm it; but it was reckoned that to incorporate the Central European states of the "Visigrad Group," Poland, Hungary, and the Czech and Slovak Republics, would add 50 percent to the EU's annual budget, unless current policies were radically changed. However, the prospect of major cuts in the EU's Common Agricultural Policy raised po-litical difficulties both in France and Germany, and it is not surprising that both of them faced the issue of the EU's enlargement with considerable caution. At the Union's Copenhagen summit in 1993, when the question was concretely discussed, France was particularly reluctant to support a process of eastward enlargement that would leave France financially worse off and geopolitically marginalized. Germany, despite its prospective eco-nomic and other gains from acquiring "Western neighbors to the east," was hesitant about adding further financial burdens to those already carried by Germany as the EU's largest net contributor.[15]

For the last two years of François Mitterrand's presidency, from the leg-islative elections of June 1993 until his retirement in 1995, France was ruled by a government of "cohabitation" between the left-wing president and a prime minister of the center-right, Edouard Balladur. This partnership func-tioned fairly well, especially in relation to European issues, where the two leaders held similar views, but at the same time they had to avoid any im-pression of making concessions on any of France's vital interests. The ultra-nationalist National Front party, led by Jean-Marie Le Pen, had won 14 percent of the votes in the 1993 elections; Mitterrand and Balladur also had to be wary of the looming figure of Jacques Chirac, the president of the Gaullist party, who was likely to exploit any apparent weakness on the French government's part in his bid to win the presidential election in 1995.

This revival of nationalist sentiment in France was paralleled to a certain extent in Germany, where the far-right Republican Party gained 11 percent of the votes in a state election in Baden-Wurttemberg in 1993. This situation added a degree of bitterness to current disputes between France and Germany, to which various aspects of EU policy had given rise. These included the apparently minor issue of international trade in bananas, in which Germany was inclined to side with the United States in wishing to open up the EU market to imports of "dollar bananas" from Latin America, while France sided with Britain in wishing to retain preferential treatment for banana imports from former Caribbean colonies. There were also such issues as the possible regulation of television programming by the EU (the French preference to impose the screening of a high quota of European-made films, in conflict with the more market-oriented German approach); and the perennial problem of farm subsidies and the difficulties they created in the EU's relations with external trading partners, especially the United States. On this last point, as on others, France's basically protectionist stance was in conflict with Germany's generally more free-trading approach. At this stage, in 1993–1994, compromise agreements were reached on these points, which on the whole involved concessions by Germany; but on other major issues requiring a decision, the German position was harder.

In particular, with regard to decisions affecting the development of EMU, German views prevailed over those of France and some other member-states. Under strong pressure from Germany, it was agreed late in 1993 that the new European Monetary Institute—designed to be transformed in time into the European Central Bank—would be located in Frankfurt. (Kohl had argued that the new institution would look more reassuring, to Germans and others, if it was in the same city as the Bundesbank.) It was also agreed that Europe's new common currency would be known as the "euro," and not as the "ecu": This last point was important to Germany since the ecu, the accounting unit used by the European Monetary System since its foundation at the end of the 1970s, had consistently dropped in value against the D-Mark, as well as having a name that sounded much better in French than in German.[16]

The European Monetary Institute accordingly began work in Frankfurt late in 1994, under its Belgian director Alexandre Lamfalussy, and in due course began to issue its assessments of the progress made by the national economies toward meeting the convergence criteria laid down in the Maastricht Treaty. At the same time France and Germany, together with their EU partners, were adjusting to being in the enlarged European Economic Area. This structure, which came into being in January 1994, associated the member-states of the long-established European Free Trade Association (Austria, Finland, Liechtenstein, Norway, Sweden, and Switzerland) in a single trading market with the EU, which most of them were expected to join as full members within a year or two. The prospect of this enlargement (to be followed in time by the addition of the new democracies of Central and Eastern Europe) led to anxious speculation throughout Europe about how the institutions of the EU, originally designed in the 1950s for a homogenous group of a half-dozen states, could continue to function in a union comprising something between twenty and thirty. How could the system work if every one of these member-states still had the right to nominate one member of the Commission? How could the system of majority voting be fair both to a large number of small member-states and to a small number of large ones? And should the whole European Union try to proceed with economic and political integration at a uniform pace, or should different groupings of states within this now very diverse ensemble go ahead with making progress at the speed that suited their own requirements? Basic questions of this kind had been due for consideration and perhaps for resolution in the Inter-Governmental Conferences leading up to the Maastricht Treaty of 1991, but the more difficult institutional reform proposals had been postponed, as so often, for further discussion.

Of the many responses provoked by these questions in the mid-1990s, as the need for some decisions became more urgent, there was one response in particular that had a sharp impact on French-German relations as the two countries prepared for the EU's next steps forward, the 'deepening' represented by EMU and the "widening" signified by enlargement to the east. This response was the so-called "Lamers paper," written by Karl Lamers and another influential member of Helmut Kohl's Christian Democratic Union and published in December 1994. Among the arguments advanced by this paper, the one that enraged French opinion was its rationale for creating a "hard core" within the EU, a "strong center" of states willing to proceed faster than the others on such critical issues as EMU, fiscal and social policy, and foreign and security policy. To be sure, France was to be included in this "hard core" (along with Germany and the Benelux counties, but not Italy or Spain—to their indignation). However, the reason given for France's inclusion in the "strong circle" was that this would

> counteract the centrifugal forces generated by constant enlargement and, thereby . . . prevent a South-West grouping, more inclined to protectionism and headed in a certain sense by France, drifting apart from a North-East grouping, more in favor of free trade and headed in a certain sense by Germany.[17]

There were other controversial aspects of this German paper (including the whole idea that a limited "core" of the EU's member-states should go ahead at a faster rate than the consensus of the whole membership), but its main political result was that many in France felt insulted at being publicly criticized in a document that was widely assumed to have Chancellor Kohl's personal support. Observers of Franco-German relations at this time could indeed detect many sources of strain, alongside such outward manifestations of harmony as the grandiose celebration in January 1993 of the thirtieth anniversary of the Elysée Treaty, and the now traditional joint Franco-German messages addressed to the member-state holding the EU's presidency, in advance of meetings of the summit-level European Council. On the negative side, there was obviously French resentment at the way the EU was becoming more Germanic through the imminent accession of Austria, Sweden, and Finland. As one observer put it, the French were also "musing aloud about how much more they had in common with Britain than with Germany, both in defense issues and in the desire to avert a federal European polity of the kind Kohl seemed to want."[18] In budgetary matters, France voiced an increasingly strong wish that the EU should devote more resources to stabilization and development in North Africa, the "backyard" of France, as well as to Germany's backyard in Central Europe. Moreover, France's position in the EU's institutions appeared to be weakening, thanks to the departure of Jacques Delors after ten years as president of the Commission, and to the strong German influence in the staffing and practices of the new European Monetary Institute in Frankfurt. When the Lamers paper sharply criticized France because "it often hesitates in taking concrete steps" toward European unification, and when Germany's foreign minister Klaus Kinkel declared that "the time has come . . . when our interests and those of France do not necessarily coincide,"[19] France's leaders had to realize that they were dealing with a new and more assertive German partner.

In practice, as we have noted, German pressure on France and on others had essentially been exerted in connection with the formulation and implementation of the Maastricht decisions on EMU, but there had also been the occasion in 1991 when Germany had pressed hard for European recognition of Croatia and Slovenia. More generally, the Lamers paper had given a clear message that if France and others went on giving priority to short-term national interests rather than long-term European ones, the result might well be a more anarchical Europe, in which the economic and political weight of Germany would give it the upper hand. It may even be that this message was designed and delivered in part to warn Jacques Chirac, the leading right-wing candidate to succeed François Mitterrand as president in 1995, that he should think hard before persisting in the nationally oriented Euro-skepticism that had always been one of his trademarks. If this was indeed one of the motives underlying the Lamers paper, it would appear to have been successful, as we shall see.

Meanwhile, on the practical level of European cooperation, German and French officials succeeded in playing down many of the underlying tensions between their two countries, and in managing current decision-making in a cooperative way. They used their consecutive presidencies of the EU (Germany's in the second half of 1994, France's in the first half of 1995) to coordinate long-term policies on a range of important issues; these included the eastward enlargement that Germany now actively wanted, the engagement in North Africa sought by France, and the financial adjustments necessary for these and other purposes.

By 1995, as the original 1997 deadline for assessing national compliance with the Maastricht criteria drew near, renewed arguments about the dangers of premature monetary integration were heard in Germany. The Constitutional Court had decided in 1993 that the Maastricht Treaty had carried the transfer of power from the national government to EU institutions as far as this could constitutionally be allowed: that is to say, any further transfer of competences to the EU would have to be accompanied by further development of its institutions, and specifically by a reduction of its by now notorious "democratic deficit," by strengthening either the powers of the European Parliament or the capacity of the member-states' national parliaments to exercise democratic control over the EU's activities. There was also a wave of skeptical comment about the risks of giving up the D-Mark from some of the powerful leaders of Germany's federal states, notably Edmund Stoiber of Bavaria, Kurt Biedenkopf of Saxony, and Gerhard Schröder of Lower Saxony. The federal states had been given a greater say in the EU's policymaking (at the expense of the Federal Government in Bonn) as a condition for their consent to the Maastricht Treaty, and their leaders did not hesitate to speak up against the possible risks to the economies of their regions if the EMU project went ahead. In the end, only Kurt Biedenkopf (a rival and victim of Helmut Kohl in the Christian Democratic Union's internal battles) voted in the Bundesrat against the EMU project, but the pressure on the Kohl administration could not be ignored.

Faced with these political pressures, and the persistent skepticism of the Bundesbank, Kohl proceeded to extract further concessions from Germany's European partners when the next steps toward the common currency were debated at the Madrid meeting of the European Council in December 1995. It was here that the name "euro" was formally adopted for the new currency, on Germany's demand. In addition, the start of EMU's third stage, the date for the pegging-together of national currencies, was postponed for two years, as the German government wished, to January 1999. The German government, responding to pressure from its regional authorities (who insisted that the regional banking systems would need a fairly long period to adapt), obtained agreement on a further three-stage transition period for implementation, to occur after 1999. Germany and France also differed on the timetable for Europe's governments to begin issuing nonnegotiable debts denominated in euros. France pressed for this to be introduced as soon as the euro-zone's parities were set in January 1999, and although this was agreed on at the Madrid meeting, Germany obtained in exchange an agreement that these debts could continue to be denominated in national currencies as well. As Jonathan Story puts it, this

> was tantamount to keeping an option open for the whole project to start not as one money, but as a common currency, thereby preserving the DM. In other words, if Germany secured no satisfaction on fiscal probity, the DM would survive, in competition with the euro.[20]

These Franco-German differences relating to the management of Europe's economy were to be resolved before 1999, as we shall see, but not without further hard bargaining. The issue of "fiscal probity," and other aspects of the Maastricht criteria, led to a series of running arguments between the two countries. In Germany, the Bundesbank's president Hans Tietmeyer and Finance Minister Theo Waigel were united in insisting on the strictest possible interpretation of the criteria: No EU member-state with a budget deficit even slightly above 3 percent should be admitted; moreover, the measurements to be applied (upon the critical date of spring 1998) should be the objective ones of actual economic performance in 1997, rather than mere forecasts for the near future. An interesting difference between the Bundesbank and the Federal Government concerned the speed of introduction of the new euro (the bank now argued that this should be rapid) and also the volume of transactions, which should be conducted in the new currency once it was introduced. On this latter point the Bundesbank, by arguing that the euro should, early in its life, be used for as much as 90 percent of all transactions, appeared to side with the French government's position rather than the German one.

On the other hand, when it came to insisting on strict observance of the Maastricht criteria, the Bundesbank and the German government were at one. France, in contrast, argued for a more flexible interpretation of the Maastricht rules; this was partly in order to safeguard some room for budgetary maneuver in dealing with France's worsening employment situation, and partly to ensure that Spain and Italy, whose situations were more marginal in relation to the criteria, would be admitted to the common currency group in the first wave. (France's motives included both the hope that Spain and Italy, once inside the Euro club, would support French flexibility against German rigor, and also the fear that if Spain and Italy were excluded, their currency devaluations would create damaging competition for France.)

A very acute Franco-German disagreement arose during preparations for the Madrid Summit, when the German government, strongly backed by German industrial and financial interests, demanded that the countries joining the common currency should adopt a stringent "stability pact." This pact, designed to ensure responsible financial behavior by all member states after monetary union came into effect, as well as before, was to enforce strict disciplinary measures on any member-state that, having met the criteria and been admitted to the monetary union, then relapsed into inflationary ways and thus endangered the whole project. The sanctions proposed by Germany for such cases, which included automatic fines on member-states developing excessive budget deficits, appeared so Draconian that they aroused suspicions in some quarters that Bonn now wished to prevent the EMU project from going forward at all.[21]

Discussion of the controversial stability pact was postponed, as it was obvious that French and German views were very far apart. Meanwhile, public attention was focused on the EU's new Inter-Governmental Conference, which opened in March 1996 and ended with a summit conference and a new treaty in Amsterdam in May of the following year. This attempt to move forward from the institutional and other arrangements agreed upon in Maastricht over five years earlier, and in particular to ensure that the EU was financially and organizationally capable of welcoming new members from Central and Eastern Europe, produced disappointing results. As we shall see, the goals of political union and a common foreign and security policy appeared scarcely nearer in 1997 than in 1991, despite some organizational tinkering. On the other hand, the concrete matter of making a reality of the next stage of EMU by 1999—an issue of towering importance, which did not figure on the agenda at Amsterdam because it was already being actively dealt with—was of increasingly pressing concern for France and Germany, as for the other states involved.

Many questions were still in dispute, not least the degree of independence to be enjoyed by the new European Central Bank and the form that the proposed "stability pact" should take. However, the pressure of the approaching deadline helped to force the participants to reach agreement. Another important factor was the upturn in the European economy in 1996–1997, which made it appear more likely that the majority of candidates would meet the criteria required to join the common currency. In this connection, there were now arguments of an increasingly technical character: whether, for instance, the gold reserves held by the Bundesbank, or the debts owed by German hospitals, should be counted as assets or liabilities in assessing whether Germany met the 3 percent limit on public debt. There were other issues that led much more directly to clashes between France and Germany. In the case of the controversial stability pact, a compromise was reached whereby the agreement was renamed "Stability and Growth Pact," and the automatic fines on delinquent states, which Germany had demanded, were introduced on a less stringent basis, subject to decisions to be taken by the EU's Council of Ministers.[22]

Another Franco-German conflict developed in late 1997, when President Jacques Chirac suddenly demanded that the first Governor of the European Central Bank should be not the Dutchman Wim Duisenberg (who was strongly backed by Germany, and had been regarded as the agreed-upon nominee) but Jean-Claude Trichet, of the Banque de France. A threatened deadlock, and a period of high tension, were broken by an informal understanding that Duisenberg, although formally appointed for the whole of the prescribed eight-year term (this long-term appointment having been regarded as an essential guarantee of the Bank's independence), could in practice be expected to hand over the post to Trichet after four years. This deal obviously raised the broader issue of how far the ECB could really operate in a fully autonomous way—or, at the very least, as autonomously as the Bundesbank. Although Trichet was reputed to be personally as strictly committed to financial orthodoxy as Duisenberg (or indeed the chiefs of the Bundesbank), the manner of his appointment led to complaints in Germany that the independence and thus the credibility of the new ECB were being compromised. On the broader issue of whether the ECB, with its autonomous responsibility for monetary policy, should be counterbalanced by some form of political authority responsible for overseeing and coordinating Europe's macroeconomic policy, France and Germany still remained divided. France continued to press for the establishment of a formal Council of Finance Ministers of the EMU's member-states, which would be charged with laying down the parameters of the fiscal and monetary policy within which the ECB would have to work. By the time the common currency was launched in January 1999, Germany had agreed to the establishment of such a council, or rather a structure of interlocking ones: the Economic and Financial Affairs Council (known as "Ecofin") for the whole European Union, and the informal "Euro–11" ministerial group for the eleven member-states linked in the common currency, both groups underpinned and serviced by the Economic and Financial Committee consisting of officials from the national finance ministries. However, in a characteristic Franco-German compromise, it was agreed that the powers of these bodies vis-à-vis the ECB would be strictly limited. Despite this apparent resolution of the issue, as of summer 2000 the dispute continued between the French view that the ECB should be subject to an "economic government" of some kind, and the German view that a central bank, whether national or European, should be essentially autonomous.[23]

The story of how the EMU project was conceived and carried forward, from Maastricht to the introduction of the euro, has rightly been characterized as one of "conflicts and partial accords" between the dominant partners in the project, France and Germany. It is also the story of a determined effort to overcome these conflicts for the sake of the broader objective of European unification, to which Paris and Bonn were both committed. This fundamental area of policy, as suggested above, was one in which Germany, after initial hesitation about the whole project, yielded to France's insistence on carrying it forward; and then, in the process, successfully made one demand after another to the point where the product finally launched in 1999 reflected German views much more than French ones. Even though, finally, the Maastricht criteria were interpreted liberally enough to admit some states with excessive national debt burdens, it is significant that Jonathan Story is able to quote a German negotiator as saying, during the process, "We have de facto exported German monetary order to Europe."[24]

"Political Union" and Foreign Policy

A judgment like the one just quoted could certainly not have been made about the other major issues negotiated at Maastricht, those of political union and foreign policy. Indeed, as recorded in the Maastricht Treaty on European Union, the decisions on these matters were distinctly meager. They may be said to have corresponded to some extent to the minimalist position represented by France (as well as the United Kingdom and others), but they certainly did not reflect the ambitious objectives with which Germany, at least in its declaratory policy, had entered on the IGC process.

As noted above, the "political" projects tabled and discussed in preparation for the Maastricht summit meeting were handled separately from the preparations for the development of EMU. Whereas the latter were the subject of systematic negotiations throughout 1991 by an Inter-Governmental Conference on EMU (known as "IGC-EMU"), the issues designated as "political" were debated in a separate operation known as "IGC-POL." The negotiators for IGC-POL were diplomatic personnel from the foreign ministries of the member-states. This division reflected the well-established division of labor between finance ministries and foreign ministries (the two departments of government most comprehensively concerned with European integration), and also the very different subject matter and procedures of the two IGCs. While the IGC-EMU worked systematically through a concrete and orderly agenda prepared for by years of preliminary studies, the IGC-POL was faced with an extremely disparate array of questions all loosely "political." First, there were institutional questions: Should the powers of the European Parliament be increased, and if so, how far? As the membership of the EU continued to expand, should each member-state continue to have the right to nominate one member of the Commission (and the bigger states two)? In decision-making in the Council of Ministers, should the principle of unanimity give way to majority voting in order to prevent deadlock on big policy issues? Since the new member-states likely to join the European Union were mostly small ones, should the "weighting" given to larger states in votes in the Council be increased to prevent their being outvoted? What should be the functions and composition of the EU's "Committee of the Regions," a newly created body designed to give a greater voice in European affairs to the subnational regional bodies in some of the EU's member-states (not least the component *Länder* of the Federal Republic)? Should the idea of granting some kind of "EU citizenship" to the people of Europe be expressed by appointing an EU ombudsman to deal with citizens' complaints, and by allowing voters from one member-state to vote in elections in another, if they resided there? The IGC also faced the big question of how the EC's existing system of diplomatic coordination (known rather confusingly as "European Political Cooperation" or EPC) should be developed into something more effective and substantial, perhaps to be called a "Common Foreign and Security Policy," and possibly even deserving this grand title. If this projected CFSP was to include a serious military element (the draft treaty under discussion talked of the possible development of the common "security policy" into a "common defense"), then the relationship between the developing EU and the Western European Union would have to be defined, and the defense ministries as well as the foreign ministries of Europe would have to be drawn into EU policymaking.

The IGC-POL also had to consider a difficult range of issues connected with attempts to create a common European policy on immigration, the treatment of asylum-seekers, anti-crime cooperation among national police forces, and greater cooperation among Europe's national legal and judicial systems.

In view of the complexity of the issues, and the wide differences between national positions on many of them, it is not surprising that the different component parts of the Maastricht Treaty—which came to be described as the "three pillars" of its architecture—took on very different forms. The Treaty's "first pillar," the one concerned with EMU, embodied a set of extremely precise commitments and a timetable for the advance toward a common currency; the second and third pillars, respectively concerned with the projected CFSP and with cooperation in justice and internal security affairs, remained comparatively general and, in practice, noncommittal.

Among all these issues, and in relation to the institutional reforms contained in the Treaty's introduction, it is possible to identify many issues on which France and Germany, the central partners in the negotiating process, were in agreement. On the other hand, in relation to the institutional questions, there was a distinct difference between the two governments. Chancellor Kohl, who saw the question of firmly binding the newly unified Germany into Western Europe as essentially political, argued strongly that the link between EMU on the one hand and more effective political institutions on the other was "of fundamental significance." As he put it, EMU would be condemned to "remain only a torso if we did not achieve political union at the same time."[25] Kohl's enthusiasm for an institutional strengthening of the EU came not only from his wish to demonstrate (to France and others) that the new Germany saw itself as still committed in every way to Western Europe. He was also aware that, in terms of domestic politics, he could more easily persuade Germans to give up the D-mark if the package of changes included the incorporation of Germany in a politically strong Europe of a federal kind: a sort of Federal Republic at the European level, or what he sometimes referred to as a "United States of Europe." In pursuit of this political objective, German negotiators before and during the Maastricht conference put forward proposals for a strengthened role for the European Parliament, a significant share of influence for the new Committee of the Regions, and other measures designed to bring "Europe" nearer to the citizens. Bonn was even ready to let certain major decisions in relation to the proposed Common Foreign and Security Policy be subject to majority vote, whereas France (like Britain and other member-states) insisted on the principle of unanimity.

In general, the French approach to institutional reform, during the crucial year 1991, concentrated on strengthening those parts of Europe's institutional machinery in which the member-states played the decisive role, notably the European Council of top national leaders. France also made proposals for a European "Senate" of delegates from national parliaments to oversee the existing European Parliament, and produced a plan to give the Union stronger leadership by replacing the rotating presidency with a president elected directly by the citizens of Europe, to serve—like the French president—for a term of several years. Such suggestions did not appeal to France's partners—in Germany, for example, the idea of a directly elected president carried unpleasant echoes of President Hindenburg's position before 1933; and they left no traces in the text finally agreed upon in Maastricht. Thus the progress recorded in the "political" parts of the Treaty remained much less significant than the progress represented by the first pillar, the one concerned with EMU. (The Common Foreign and Security Policy, the substance of the second pillar, forms a partial exception to this judgment; it will be considered separately in what follows.)

In the case of EMU, as we saw earlier, France and Germany agreed in 1990–1991 on the general objectives, and during the 1990s Germany was able to ensure that its own specific views on what should be done were adopted at almost every stage of the process. With political union, the position was different. At Maastricht itself, Germany's proposals for substantial institutional reform were blocked by the reluctance of France and others to follow this path, and during the ensuing decade Germany's continued efforts to revive projects for reform met with only limited success. Indeed, as we shall see, midway through the1990s Kohl himself explicitly modified some of his key institutional demands, and even insisted on unanimous voting being retained for certain important policy areas. Paradoxically, this move coincided with some relaxation of the French attitude on this point, and this partial coming-together of the EU's two leading powers indicated the start of a new period in their relationship as the IGC scheduled for 2000 approached.

Although Helmut Kohl had insisted during the pre-Maastricht negotiations that it would be unthinkable for Europe to launch the EMU without corresponding progress on political–institutional matters, he adapted to the new situation created by the uneven outcome of Maastricht. Although he continued, to some extent, to press France and other partners not to forget the need for the institutional "deepening" of the EU, he sometimes seemed to do so in ways that suggested he was now less confident of a positive outcome. The "Lamers paper" of 1994, discussed earlier, was an example of a more troubled debate than in earlier years. As we noted in discussing the progress of the EMU project, France and Germany maintained a close dialogue on European affairs, and gave a number of public manifestations of their commitment to cooperation. They certainly reached agreement on a number of issues: one example was France's acceptance that the number of Germany's Members of the European Parliament should rise from 81 to 99 at the time of the 1994 elections. There were also encouraging signs that the military defense policies of the two countries might be significantly converging when France resumed participation in NATO ministerial meetings after an absence dating from the 1960s.

These signs of rapprochement were, however, to be sent into reverse—especially in the area of defense—by the election of the Gaullist leader Jacques Chirac as president of France in June 1995. Chirac, a noted Euroskeptic, began his presidential term with some disturbing surprises for Germany and other EU partners. He drastically reduced France's ground forces in Germany, as part of a program to abolish compulsory military service in France, and then (again without any consultation with allies) unilaterally resumed the testing of French nuclear weapons at a time when a revised test ban treaty was being negotiated. Kohl loyally supported Chirac, at least to the extent of abstaining from the chorus of criticism of France by other EU states, but the Franco-German relationship suffered a shock. Matters improved as France's new president made it clear (as his predecessor Mitterrand had done in 1983) that he basically accepted German policies of free-market competition and strict budgetary discipline as the way forward for Europe's economy. He even toned down his Gaullist rhetoric about the need for the EU to be "a Europe of fatherlands."[26]

It was at about this time that Kohl also took a significant step, loosening the links between economic and political union on which he had insisted so long and so strenuously, and began to reduce his urgent demands for progress on the latter point. He seems to have concluded that, since EMU now appeared to be firmly on track in its own right, and was clearly taking a form that incorporated a number of Germany's key demands, there was less urgency for him to continue his demands for progress in the EU's institutional strengthening, especially since this had never appealed to France as it had to Germany. Indeed as early as 1993, Kohl had said he would no longer use Winston Churchill's old expression, "United States of Europe," to describe his long-term goal, since it gave rise to "misunderstandings." He also dropped his demands for increased powers for the European Parliament.[27]

There was thus a considerable contrast between the "maximalist" spirit in which Kohl had approached the 1991 IGC (or IGCs) before Maastricht, and his attitude toward the next IGC of 1996–1997, which represented the EU's renewed attempt at institutional reform and would produce the Amsterdam Treaty of 1997. In the run-up to this event, Kohl and his foreign minister Klaus Kinkel carefully adopted a low-key position; Kinkel even argued, in a virtually Gaullist or "British" way, that the EU should remain essentially an intergovernmental structure, in which the last word should remain with the governments of the member-states.

As Elizabeth Pond has shown, the trend in German thinking was unmistakable: By 1995 or so, Bonn no longer regarded a federal Europe as a realistic goal, and preferred a pragmatic "step by step" approach toward whatever institutional set-up the EU consensus would support.[28] This, of course, brought German views closer to French ones (just as in the economic field France was coming nearer to Germany), and meant that the two countries were in general agreement as the IGC of 1996–1997 followed its low-key way to very modest institutional conclusions. Indeed, one of the more striking moments of the Amsterdam summit conference came when Kohl himself broke with a longstanding tradition of German policy by insisting on Germany's right to retain the veto in an important policy area, that of immigration.[29] This was in a way characteristic of the Amsterdam summit, which postponed decisions on the big institutional issues facing the EU until the next IGC, that of 2000.

While the Franco-German partnership appeared to be united in pursuing an active policy on EMU and a passive one on institutional reform, in the specific area of Common Foreign and Security Policy—the "second pillar" of Maastricht—Paris and Bonn/Berlin showed themselves ready for at least a serious effort to move forward. This important area of European policy, essentially a system of consultation and coordination on foreign policy issues among the foreign ministries of the member-states, had from its inception in 1970 been kept strictly separate from the areas of EC policy governed by the Treaty of Rome; in the latter the supranational institutions, the Commission, and the European Parliament had significant roles, and the Council's voting procedures were precisely laid down. Foreign policy or "political" cooperation, on the contrary, involved foreign ministers and their senior officials in a strictly intergovernmental consultative process that did not necessarily lead to action.[30] This method, although still preserved in its essentials when EPC became CFSP at Maastricht, had by then undergone some modifications, and was to evolve further. The Single European Act of 1986, largely the result of a Franco-German initiative, had given EPC a formal position directly under the European Council of governmental leaders, and also a small permanent secretariat to enhance its effectiveness. By this time, the EPC system had proved effective in representing Western Europe's joint interests in the East-West "Helsinki Process" of the 1970s, and also in relation to the Middle East and other areas. Maastricht went further by giving the EU's diplomatic system a new range of potentially important instruments, including common strategies and "joint actions" (to be undertaken following unanimous decisions by the European Council); and by associating the Commission, and thus the EU's economic resources, directly with the common foreign policy. Maastricht also gave the CFSP the prospect of a military dimension, although its language on this was particularly opaque and non-committal.[31]

As we have seen, French and German attitudes to foreign policy since 1945 had been very different. It was difficult to see how a common European foreign policy could easily combine the nationally centered French approach (including national nuclear forces, the permanent Security Council seat, and systematic mistrust of the United States) with the "Atlanticist" approach of Germany (the loyal NATO ally without nuclear pretensions, the "civilian power" that until the 1990s limited the use of its military forces exclusively to European defense). France and Germany (along with Britain) did set the pace of diplomatic cooperation among the European states; but in regard to the military (the "security" part of the CFSP), there were great obstacles to effective cooperation. Even though France and Germany developed bilateral collaboration in conventional ground forces, it was hard for them to bring together their conflicting attitudes to NATO and other military groupings. For instance the Western European Union, potentially a significant agency, was condemned to relative impotence because of the conflict over whether it should remain essentially a West European adjunct to NATO (as Germany on the whole wished) or should be developed into a military arm of the EU (the French view).[32]

The intensive debates on these questions at Maastricht only codified the prevailing ambiguities. In 1997 in Amsterdam any thought of the EU's developing any serious military capacity—which France and Germany agreed to try to promote—was vitiated by the strong insistence of Tony Blair, Britain's new prime minister, that a "European Security and Defense Identity" would dangerously undermine NATO. By the end of the decade, however, the attitude of Britain and other countries had changed (partly because of the revelation of Europe's military impotence in the Balkans). In its 1999 summit meetings (in Cologne in June, Helsinki in December), the EU, with France, Germany and Britain in the lead, decided to appoint a (Spanish) High Representative to head the CFSP, and to merge WEU's functions into the Union, while planning for it to have a military intervention force under European command.[33]

Conclusion

This account of the Franco-German partnership in the 1990s, in the context of the European Union, has devoted more attention to the development of EMU than to other issues, partly because it has without doubt been the EU's most significant undertaking during this period. Attention has also focused on illustrating the difficulties of bringing together the viewpoints and interests of two nation-states and two national societies, even when their leaders are deeply committed to common action, in circumstances when really fundamental questions of national interest, national autonomy, and national identity are at stake. From the perspective of the year 2000, it can be said that the member-states of EMU, led by France and Germany, have invested so much in the project—in every sense—that they are very unlikely to let it fail.

It is another question whether France and Germany will be able to lead Europe forward to overcome the next major challenge: that of completing the revolution of 1989—the liberation of Central and Eastern Europe from Russian domination—by incorporating the new democracies of that region into the EU. If they do succeed—and again, much has been invested in success—they are likely to solve some of their own problems as well as contributing to stability in the east. As indicated above, further enlargement of the EU will make it imperative for the organization to find solutions to some of the problems that France, Germany, and the other member-states have been unwilling to face so far: those of financial priorities, organizational structure, and policy-making procedures. The chances of effective solutions should be increased by the urgency of the problems involved, and by the very fact that the European Union—or at least most of it—has in fact embarked on the great venture of EMU, which will draw the members together in intensified cooperation in essential areas of policymaking.

France and Germany both have new governments. Whereas they are unlikely to experience a revival of the kind of close personal relationships that existed between Giscard d'Estaing and Schmidt, or between Mitterrand and Kohl, there appears to be enough common ground between the Schröder and Jospin governments to offer a prospect of effective cooperation. The German government's new coordinator for Franco-German relations, Professor Rudolf von Thadden, aroused controversy with a provocative statement that "the dialogue between Britain and Germany, America and Germany, Russia and Germany, is as important as the dialogue between France and Germany."[34] However, insofar as the context of the EU is concerned, the Franco-German dialogue does have a unique importance, both for the two parties themselves and for the future of the EU as a whole.

Notes

1. See Roger Morgan, "France and Germany as Partners in the European Community," in Patrick McCarthy, ed., *France-Germany, 1983–1993. The Struggle to Cooperate* (New York: St. Martin's Press 1993), esp. pp. 93–96 and 109–110.
2. Klaus-Peter Klaiber in David P. Calleo and Eric R. Staal, eds., *Europe's Franco-German Engine* (Washington, DC. 1998), p. 38.
3. William E. Paterson and Charlie Jefferey, "Deutschland, Frankreich—und Grossbritannien?" in *Internationale Politik*, Vol. 53, No.11 (November 1999), p. 19.
4. McCarthy in Calleo and Staal, op. cit., p. 133.
5. Douglas Webber, ed., *The Franco-German Relationship in the European Union* (London & New York: Routledge 1999), p. 177.
6. A full account of the background is given by Valerie Guérin-Sendelbach, *Frankreich und das vereinigte Deutschland. Interessen und Perzeptionen im Spannungsfeld* (Opladen: Leske & Budrich 1999). The present chapter deals only briefly with the Maastrich Treaty's "third pillar," on which see further Jörg Monar & Roger Morgan, eds., *The Third Pillar of the European Union. Cooperation in the Fields of Justice and Home Affairs* (Brussels: European Interuniversity Press 1994) and Patrick Weil, "France, Germany and Immigration Policy" in Webber (1999), pp. 159–166.
7. See Morgan (1993), pp. 102–103, and McCarthy in Webber (1999), pp. 41–42.
8. See Wolfram F. Hanrieder, *Germany, America, Europe. Forty Years of German Foreign Policy* (New Haven, CT: Yale University Press, 1989).

9. On the concepts "monetarist" and "economist" (used in the EMU context in a way distinct from their normal meanings), see Loukas Tsoukalis, *The New European Economy,* 2nd ed., (Oxford University Press 1993), esp. pp. 178–179.

10. See Eric Richard Staal, *European Monetary Union. The German Political-Economic Trilemma* (Bonn: Center for European Integration Studies 1999) and Amy Verdun, *European Responses to Globalization and Financial Market Integration. Perceptions of Economic and Monetary Union in Britain, France and Germany* (Basingstoke & New York: Macmillan 1999).

11. For detailed accounts of the 1990–1991 period, see Colette Mazzucelli, *France and Germany at Maastricht* (New York: Garland 1997) and Kenneth Dyson & Kevin Featherstone, *The Road to Maastricht. Negotiating Economic and Monetary Union* (Oxford University Press 1999).

12. Elizabeth Pond, *The Rebirth of Europe* (Washington, DC: Brookings Institution Press 1999), p. 46. This excellent and solidly documented work has been used extensively in the next section of this chapter.

13. Pond (1999), pp. 47–48.

14. Morgan (1993), esp. pp. 94–95.

15. Pond (1999), p. 50. On French and German attitudes to enlargement, see McCarthy in Webber (1999), pp. 41–57.

16. See Jonathan Story, "Monetary Union: Economic competition and political negotiation" in Webber (1999), pp. 20–40.

17. Quoted by Pond (1999), p. 89.

18. Ibid., p. 90

19. Ibid., p. 98.

20. Story in Webber (1999), p. 34.

21. Pond (1999), p. 100.

22. Ibid., p. 108.

23. See, for instance, the contrasting views of French and German contributors in *Will EMU Lead to a European Economic Government?* (London: Centre for European Reform 1999).

24. Story in Webber (1999), p. 30; his summary, "Conflicts and Partial Accords," ibid., p. 36.

25. Quoted in Morgan (1993), p.108.

26. Pond (1999), p. 94.

27. Ibid., p. 95.

28. Ibid., Chapter 5.

29. On the background, see Weil in Webber (1999), loc. cit.

30. The standard account is by Simon Nuttall, *European Political Cooperation* (Oxford, Clarendon Press 1992).

31. See the present writer's two articles, "How Common Will Foreign and Security Policies Be?" in Renaud Dehousse, ed., *Europe after Maastricht: An Ever Closer Union?* (Munich: Law Books in Europe, 1994), pp. 189–199, and "The Prospects for Europe's Common Foreign and Security Policy," in

Armand Clesse et al., eds., *The International System after the Collapse of the East-West Order* (Dordrecht: Nijhoff 1994), pp. 413–423.

32. For a good assessment of WEU, including French and German views, see Anne Deighton, ed., *Western European Union, 1954–1997. Defence, Security, Integration* (Reading, UK: Interdependence Research Unit of St. Antony's College, Oxford 1997).

33. See Lothar Rühl, *Conditions and Options for an Autonomous "Common European Policy on Security and Defence" in and by the European Union in the post-Amsterdam Perspective Opened at Cologne in June 1999* (Bonn: Center for European Integration Studies 1999).

34. See "Rudolf von Thadden, Marriage-Guidance Counsellor" in *The Economist,* October 2, 1999. For an important Franco-German exchange of views on the budgetary and other aspects of Europe's future, see Jean-Louis Arnaud, *Le Moteur Franco-Allemand a l'Epreuve de l'Agenda 2000* (Paris: Notre Europe 2000).

Chapter 6 ✤

Security Relations:
Mehr Schein als Sein

Anand Menon

S ince the end of the Second World War, security relations have fea-
tured prominently on the agenda of Franco-German bilateral relations. In particular, once the immediate issue, for France, of dealing
with the possible resurgence of a German military threat had receded, bilateral security cooperation became one of the key mechanisms through
which the two states hoped to cement their newfound friendship. Yet, as
this chapter argues, despite the bewildering proliferation of cooperative
ventures and institution-building initiatives undertaken by the two states,
only limited progress has been made in forging a meaningful military partnership between Paris and Bonn. In particular, it is striking to note the degree to which the problems that hampered cooperative endeavors in the
past continue to do so today. Security cooperation has not, in other words,
progressed to the point of altering the basic security preferences and interests of the two countries.

The chapter is divided into three sections. The first explores the various
considerations that led both France and Germany to pursue strategies aimed
at fostering bilateral cooperation in the period since the Second World War.
In particular, it highlights the implicit and explicit tensions between their
motivations and preferences, and suggests that the existence of these did not,
and indeed does not, bode well for the bilateral security relationship. The
second section briefly traces the course of Franco-German security cooperation. The final section critically analyses this cooperation, pointing out its
limited achievements and the continued inability of France and German to

overcome some of the crucial divergences that have continued to limit their ability to cooperate for some decades.

The Bases of Partnership

Looking back at the development of Franco-German relations since the end of the Second World War, it is striking that both sides have, to a significant extent, been keen to give security relations a privileged place among the myriad of cooperative ventures that have been undertaken.

The motivations underpinning security cooperation have been multifarious, complex, and in some cases contradictory. Following the end of the Second World War, France and Germany shared a common desire to overcome their troubled history and prevent further conflict between themselves. Both, moreover, as the Cold War got underway, were confronted with the fact that the greatest threat to their security came not from each other but from the Soviet Union. While seen as useful in its own right, the bilateral security relationship has been, and continues to be, viewed on both sides of the Rhine as a means to a greater end. As one French observer has put it, from "the outset, Franco-German cooperation in security and defense has . . . been linked to the broader logic of European construction and integration."[1] Yet behind such apparently persuasive shared concerns there lurk a number of issues that have divided the French and Germans concerning the reasons for, and the objectives and nature of, their bilateral security cooperation.

The first such factors have to do with the motivations behind the shared objective of promoting such cooperation. Somewhat paradoxically, French interest in cooperation with its eastern neighbor since the Second World War—an interest often expressed in glowing terms of rapprochement and reconciliation—has always rested, if only in part, on a sense of profound distrust. Clearly the postwar French obsession with Germany initially stemmed from fear of the resurgence of a German threat. Thus even as the American administration was pronouncing its Truman doctrine, France and Britain became signatories to a Dunkirk Treaty that underlined their intention to collaborate in measures of mutual assistance in the event of any renewal of German aggression. Overt distrust outlived the Dunkirk Treaty. Indeed, Korea notwithstanding, such distrust was apparent in the European Defense Community proposals tabled by French Defense Minster René Pleven, whose objectives were to "simultaneously deter a Soviet attack in Europe and prevent the resurrection of German power." Those in favor argued that France faced a choice: "the EDC or the Wehrmacht."[2]

Moreover, such considerations persisted beyond the 1950s, and indeed persist to the present day. In the early 1980s, renewed momentum for bilateral security cooperation was provided by French concerns regarding a possible "drift toward neutrality" on the part of the Federal Republic. With German unification, concern about Germany reached levels not experienced since 1945. The reasons for this were twofold. First, the new German state, freed from the constricting embrace of superpower conflict, would not only enjoy more international autonomy than had the Federal Republic, but would also represent a far more powerful state—particularly economically— than the FRG (Federal Republic of Germany) had been. The momentous events of 1989 profoundly altered the balance of power between France and Germany with the "strengthening of Germany's relative power [being] most evident in the defense and security domains."[3]

Second, the very way in which unification was achieved alerted French political leaders to the dangers of a united Germany being far more assertive internationally than its predecessor had been. Unilateral German initiatives around the time of the collapse of the Berlin Wall, such as Chancellor Kohl's ten-point plan for unification, raised the specter of a politically active and militarily unfettered German state over which Paris had no control.[4] Significantly, it was the West German government, working together with the superpowers, that played the crucial role in negotiating German unification. The July 16, 1990, agreement on German membership in NATO was negotiated directly by Kohl and Gorbachev with no direct French involvement. Unsurprisingly, French fears about the implications of unification spawned a burst of enthusiasm in Paris for Franco-German cooperation in the security sphere.

Concerns about German trustworthiness spawned a second area of potential tension, shaping French aspirations concerning the nature of cooperation in such a way as to render them potentially contradictory with their German equivalents. For Germany, cooperation with France, and indeed participation in multilateral institutions in general, represented a means of regaining a degree of influence and autonomy in international affairs. Influence within institutions was the key to this aspiration. High levels of integration, moreover, did not pose a problem for political leaders anxious to downplay the possibility of German unilateralism.

French attitudes, however, were and still are very different; institutions have been seen as a way of tying down Germany while Paris enjoyed greater room for maneuver, as was the case, notably, with NATO. This had two major consequences in terms of the kinds of cooperation envisaged in Paris. First, it implied that Germany remained firmly tied within multilateral organizations. Thus, in the early 1980s, France acted quickly to reinforce German loyalty to NATO in order to ensure that West German leaders did not attempt to emulate the freedom from NATO that Paris had acquired in 1966. Moreover, as the plans for the abortive EDC made clear, French leaders were inclined to prefer institutional mechanisms that placed additional constraint upon their eastern neighbor, rather than aspiring to equality within multilateral institutions.

Second, the desire to enjoy supremacy over Germany imposed limits on the lengths to which France would go in its cooperative ventures. Nonintegration in NATO, or indeed within any institution threatening French autonomy in the security sphere (note the arguments of the opponents to the EDC in the 1950s) as well as the possession of a national nuclear force under national command, were immutable elements of French security policy—not least because they helped to ensure a comparative advantage in terms of freedom of maneuver over the Germans. For Paris there was no contradiction between, on the one hand, France's possessing a defense policy that clearly prioritized national, as opposed to allied (including German) security, and on the other hand, its professions of faith in the Franco-German security relationship—even when France's defense policy included possession of tactical nuclear weapons targeted on Germany.[5] Cooperative ventures threatening either of these central planks of French military policy, therefore, were not to be considered. France wanted independence while Germany would be controlled within multilateral institutions.

A desire to maintain the upper hand in security affairs was, of course, explicable partly in terms of a belief that, given the history of Franco-German relations, military superiority was desirable *en tant que tel*. Such superiority also, moreover, allowed for the reinforcement of bilateral relations more generally through the existence of what Stanley Hoffmann has termed an *équilibre des déséquilibres*. European integration represented a particularly useful means to trade relative French military and political weight—while such ideas still had any meaning—for German concessions in other spheres. Thus Jacques Isnard, the respected defense correspondent of *Le Monde*, stated that if:

> France is ready to make a decisive contribution to the security of Europe, if need be by modifying its own defensive doctrines and organization, its West German ally will have to make a comparable effort in showing itself to be more supportive in the political, economic, and monetary spheres.[6]

Consequently, following German unification, when fears concerning German economic power reached their zenith, French policymakers came increasingly to stress the need to tie Germany more tightly into West European structures: *Plus nous irons vite vers l'union, moins notre voisin pourra faire cavalier seul.*[7] A Socialist Party poster urging the electorate to vote "Yes" in the forthcoming Maastricht referendum provided a vivid illustration of this. The poster showed a picture of a short man with a small moustache in German military uniform alongside the caption *Vive l'Europe pour que vive la paix.* The point this makes is not that fear cannot motivate far-reaching political action. Rather it is simply that one cannot but doubt the potential efficacy of supposedly far-reaching cooperative ventures if one partner in such cooperation is still consumed with deep distrust for the other.

More broadly, Franco-German security cooperation has been routinely portrayed as representing a catalyst for broader collaborative initiatives in Western Europe. Here again, though, a certain contradiction has existed between the objectives of the two sides. For Germany, NATO was, and remains, the bedrock of its defense posture. In his first statement as chancellor of West Germany, Helmut Kohl declared that "the Alliance is at the heart of the raison d'état of the Federal Republic of Germany."[8] For Paris, on the other hand, European defense cooperation, including bilateral initiatives with Germany, was, on occasion at least, seen as a way of launching initiatives to rival NATO. This was very much the case with de Gaulle's Franco-German initiative of the early 1960s, and was again apparent in the early 1990s when France, often acting in tandem with its German partner, launched schemes that, in Paris at least, were intended to challenge the predominance of the transatlantic alliance.

Finally, and more specifically related to the security sphere itself, "German and French strategic conceptions, and defense philosophy, diverge."[9] The German tendency to emphasize, even in the post–Cold War world, the primacy of territorial defense; to question, especially in the post–Cold War World, the legitimacy and utility of nuclear weapons; indeed, to "remain chary about military action" *tout court,* are all in stark contrast to France's more "muscular" approach to military affairs. Thus Defense Minister Rühe, reacting to the French announcement of plans to abolish conscription precisely in order to facilitate French involvement in multilateral out-of-area operations, emphasized the continued primacy for his government of territorial defense. German attitudes to the resumption of French nuclear testing in 1995 was nicely summarized by the Socialist MP Freimut Duve who declared that "Germany has once and for all renounced nuclear weapons and considers itself today as a chief proponent of nonproliferation."[10] Although the July 12, 1994, decision by the German Supreme Court lifted any legal ambiguity surrounding German participation in nonterritorial defense missions, by providing a clear justification for participation of German armed forces in multilateral peacekeeping and peace enforcement actions under the framework of the United Nations, WEU, or NATO, doubts persist about Germany's ability or willingness to participate in such operations.

Security Cooperation

The history of Franco-German security relations since the Second World War has been described in detail elsewhere; hence a brief descriptive summary of developments will suffice here.[11] Whereas the years preceding the so-called Elysée Treaty of 1963 had not been devoid of bilateral discussions of security affairs, perhaps this treaty marked the first development of note in purely bilateral relations. (The Federal Government in Bonn had suggested to their French counterparts that the document take the form of a treaty rather than a simple declaration, with ultimately disastrous results as it was this decision that necessitated ratification in the Bundestag.) The Elysée Treaty, signed in January 1963, stipulated that:

> Heads of State or Government would meet at least twice a year.
> Defense and Foreign Ministers would meet at least once every three months.
> Chiefs of Staff would meet at least once every two months.

Moreover, apart from such provision for regular meetings, and others dealing with the need for exchanges of personnel and for armaments cooperation, the Treaty envisaged far-reaching cooperation on the substance of defense policies:

> As far as strategy [and military] structures are concerned, the competent authorities in the two countries are committed to bringing about a *rapprochement* between their doctrines, with a view to arriving at common concepts.[12]

For all the brave and undoubtedly ambitious intentions of the Treaty, however, its fate was effectively sealed, for the medium term at least, when the Bundestag added a preamble to the text reaffirming Germany's staunch attachment to NATO; this initiative, for many French officials, robbed the document of its major significance.

The next major development was in fact the reactivation of the Treaty, whose security clauses were left in abeyance following the shift in de Gaulle's policy priorities in the mid-1960s toward rapprochement with Moscow. The accession to power of François Mitterrand provided an almost immediate fillip for security relations between the two states. As intimated above, French concerns regarding a possible neutralist slide by the Federal Republic led to Franco-German security discussions, opened in 1982, that represented for France a means of reinforcing the Atlanticist loyalties of the Federal Republic.[13] These discussions led in turn to the reactivation of the security clauses of the 1963 Elysée Treaty and the creation of a Franco-German Commission on Security and Defense. Both developments were motivated by France's desire to tie the Federal Republic more firmly into Western security structures and combat the rising tides of pacifism and neutralism that were in evidence across the Rhine.[14] These initiatives were soon to be built upon; first in 1987, with the creation of a joint brigade,[15] and subsequently the following year with the signing of a protocol that created a new Franco-German Council for Defense and Security at the levels of Heads of State and Government.[16]

Mitterrand's presidency also witnessed the first signs that Paris might be willing to alter some of the more overtly nationalist elements of its defense strategy in order to take into account the sensibilities of its eastern ally. While Chirac hinted at a possible shift in France's staunch insistence that it could not commit itself to the defense of its allies in advance, declarations from the Elysée seemed to indicate that even French nuclear strategy could be revised as a response to German sensitivities. In 1986 Mitterrand tantalizingly raised the possibility both of consultation with the Federal Republic on the use of tactical nuclear weapons,[17] and of not targeting sites in Germany with these weapons.[18] France also consented, from 1987, to engage in secret discussions between French and West German chiefs of staff concerning nuclear questions and in particular the Hadès missile project.[19]

As if all this were not enough, the end of the Cold War, for the reasons outlined in the previous section, led to a renewed burst of activity in bilateral security relations. Franco-German initiatives dominated the Maastricht IGC, with the two states playing the leading role in pressing for the EU to acquire some kind of role in defense policy. The two states also were responsible for the launch of the Eurocorps—a multinational unit that, at least according to statements made at the time, had the potential to develop into an embryonic European Army. A couple of years later, the German Government underlined its continued commitment to the bilateral relationship in its Defense White Paper of April 1994. This stressed the basic security interests of Germany: maintenance of a strong transatlantic link, maintenance of NATO, development of CFSP. However, it was the "advancement of European integration around the Franco-German axis" that held pride of place at the top of this list of German priorities.

More practically, Paris and Bonn continued with their attempts to construct a European satellite reconnaissance system. On December 7, 1995, the Franco-German armaments agency was created. The Franco-German Foreign Ministers' seminar at Freibourg in February 1996 proposed the creation of a European Forecasting and Analysis Unit.[20] In November 1996, the two countries signed a naval agreement whereby the two naval chiefs of staff would supervise joint planning of naval operations and joint exercises, procurement, research, and development, and the use of joint naval forces.[21] Perhaps most strikingly, on December 9, 1996, at Nuremberg, the two states signed the so-called common strategic concept that took military cooperation between them to new levels. This incorporated far-reaching declarations concerning the indissociable nature of the security interests of the two countries, and spoke in ambitious terms of their European ambitions.[22]

This common concept marked an apparently striking development in that it made reference to the "increasingly inseparable" security interests of the two states and the need to assure the integrity of both national territories. The document spoke of Franco-German willingness to search for complementarity between their respective armed forces and to put into place common military means. It also raised the possibility of arriving at a system for the joint planning of military needs. France, moreover, for the first time publicly announced its willingness to discuss nuclear issues with its eastern neighbor.[23] Indeed, a couple of years earlier, statements by Prime Minster Juppé in September 1995 raised the prospect of "concerted deterrence" as a means of overcoming the overwhelmingly national focus of French nuclear strategy.

Limited Achievements

A lot has been done, therefore, to promote Franco-German security relations. And let us not forget, given the nature of Franco-German relations during the decades before 1945, these efforts should not be lightly dismissed. Yet all these various and varied initiatives notwithstanding, it is striking to what extent they failed to have any lasting practical significance. Thus some have dismissed the military worth of the Franco-German brigade,[24] while others have been critical of the Eurocorps, labeling it as nothing but an expensive "language school."[25] As for the hype surrounding Franco-German initiatives in their guise as catalysts for broader European defense ventures, this has been shown to have been overstated. Although Paris and Bonn had worked closely in their efforts to produce meaningful outcomes in the defense sphere, the Maastricht Treaty was something of a damp squib in this respect.[26] More strikingly, in the (unlikely) event that current initiatives in the defense sphere lead to more impressive developments in the EU, these developments will have been a result of intense bilateral discussions between, and multilateral lobbying by, Britain and France. In other words, the practical military significance of many Franco-German initiatives has been doubtful, to say the least. More importantly, the tensions between French and German ambitions and objectives in fostering cooperation, alluded to in the first section—tensions never, to this day, successfully resolved or overcome—have played a crucial role in limiting meaningful accomplishments. The first major constraint on progress stemmed from disagreements concerning the degree of integration to be undertaken in the defense sphere. Whereas integration was, for France, too high a price to pay to achieve closer ties with even its German ally, for Germany—accustomed to and reassured by far-reaching integration—it was a *sine qua non* of meaningful military collaboration. Bilateral cooperation between the two states during the Maastricht IGC faltered because of differences between the strongest protagonists of a European defense organization—France and Germany. Simply put,

> [The] Defense Ministry in Bonn began to think that French reluctance to move beyond declaratory policy to the level of detailed military integration reflected an unwillingness to consider any form of military integration, which for Bonn was *the* most important purpose of any European defense identity.[27]

Consequently, the Franco-German partnership failed effectively to push its partners in the direction of ambitious cooperative defense schemes. The weak defense provisions of the EUT resulted. Increasingly, the Germans came to express their frustration with what they saw as unwarranted French recalcitrance over this issue. The now infamous CDU/CSU paper on the forthcoming Maastricht 2 IGC, with its ambitious schemes for furthering integration, was not at all warmly received in Paris, not least because of its rather pointed assessment of French policy:

> France . . . must rectify the impression that, although it allows no doubt as to its basic will to pursue European integration, it often hesitates in taking concrete steps towards this objective—the notion of the unsurrenderable sovereignty of the "État nation" still carries weight, although this sovereignty has long since become an empty shell.[28]

Similarly, the progress of bilateral cooperation was hampered by tensions stemming from Paris's determination to cling to a nationally centered defense policy and Bonn's desire to see its ally make concessions toward it. French nuclear strategy, its national bias, its refusal to countenance meaningful consultation with partners, and in particular its tactical nuclear weapons, were bones of contention for many years.[29] As one observer put it:

> France's reticence regarding consultations on nuclear employment questions with Germany and other allies lessened the credibility of French professions of interest in building a Western European defense identity and placing French nuclear weapons at the service of this entity.[30]

Indeed, as one prominent observer pointed out, it represented a sad indictment of France's position that:

> When one of our Defense Ministers [Charles Hernu] pronounced the essential truth—not to say truism—that France and the German Federal Republic have security interests in common—this platitude was considered [in France] as an important political event.[31]

Rhetorical French initiatives intended to assuage German fears produced little in the way of practical consequences. Declarations concerning possible consultation over the use of tactical nuclear weapons emphasized that this would take place within "the limits imposed by the rapidity of such decisions," leaving France with an obvious opt-out. Similarly, Mitterrand's remarks about targeting arrangements made little sense if these weapons were based in France. As the defense correspondent of *Le Monde* pointed out, avoiding German targets implied deployment toward the intra-German frontier—with all the attendant dangers in terms of national autonomy that this implied.[32]

A similar pattern has been evident under the presidency of Jacques Chirac. In a keynote broadcast televised in February 1996, Chirac outlined plans for a wholesale reform of the French military machine, a reform predicated on the need for France to be able to participate more effectively in multilateral out-of-area missions. Yet even when reforming its defense posture, nominally at least, in order to facilitate inter-allied cooperation, Paris proved unable to do so without worrying, if not alienating, the Germans. Despite frantic press speculation concerning the possible implications for Franco-German cooperation of professionalization and planned force reductions, Paris did not discuss its plans in advance with Bonn.[33] A senior Bundeswehr officer complained that the decision to professionalize the French forces should have been subject to prior consultation, given its implications for military cooperation between the two countries.[34]

Indeed, many German officials viewed with suspicion the professionalization of French forces, seeing it as part of a broader process by which Paris was distancing itself from its supposedly privileged partner. As one French observer put it, "For many Germans, France's NATO *rapprochement,* together with . . . the abolition of conscription and the emphasis on projection capabilities . . . means that France is more interested in military ventures with [its] Anglo-Saxon allies in 'out-of-area' scenarios than in building, together with Germany, a European defense."[35] These apparent shifts in French priorities in fact led the Germans to express public disquiet about the future of the Eurocorps and about French attempts to steal a march on its eastern neighbor. As a senior German official put it: "We get the trenches in central Europe, you [French] get Africa and the sexiest missions."[36]

Even Chirac's attempted restructuring of the French arms industry—a restructuring again loudly proclaimed to be undertaken in the name of European cooperation—raised fears across the Rhine. French hesitations over restructuring, and particularly its vacillations over the Thomson privatization, led to disquiet especially in Germany, where firms clearly perceived the need to forge alliances and were eager to do so with French partners. They were, however, increasingly impelled to find American allies because of the failure of France to offer a level playing field by releasing its firms from state control. The decision by the Jospin government to halt the privatization of Thomson led to profound disappointment among German industrial circles and especially within DASA.[37] European firms were unwilling to pursue structural links with French state-owned enterprises. Indeed, such was the constraint that their nationalized status implied that Aérospatiale and Thomson complained to the National Assembly Defense Commission that they risked finding themselves isolated unless privatized.[38] More generally, Chirac's intention to create powerful French champions capable of dominating a future European market aroused suspicions that France was merely attempting to gain comparative advantage over its partners while employing the rhetoric of European cooperation. A senior German official described French tactics as "an approach which is sometimes reminiscent of the nineteenth century."[39] So much for overcoming the past.

Disturbingly from the perspective of Franco-German cooperation, repeated disappointment with French actions had the effect of alienating the Germans. Rather than offer their support for French intimations of a possible return to the NATO integrated command structures (as did Great Britain), German officials increasingly expressed irritation at apparent attempts by France to gain a privileged place for itself within NATO. Klaus Naumann, former inspector general of Bundeswehr and president of the NATO military committee, stated that "French participation in the military committee without its forces being put at [NATO's] disposal will not happen."[40] Similarly, both Germany and Italy expressed disquiet at the prospect of the allocation of too large, or too important a command to France, feeling this would be rewarding France for having stayed out of NATO.[41]

Contrasting and indeed contradictory attitudes toward NATO in fact represented a further crucial impediment to effective cooperation. Obviously, this had scuppered de Gaulle's ambitious plans for the Elysée Treaty. More recently, the tension between periodic French irritation with the American-dominated NATO, and German attachment to it, have made it ever more difficult for the two states to reach agreement on European defense initiatives. Certainly, such problems are not necessarily insurmountable. A case in point was (reluctant) French agreement to German insistence that the Eurocorps be linked to NATO to enable its effective participation in the common defense. Consequently, after weeks of negotiations, on December 2, 1992, France and Germany presented plans allowing for the transfer of operational *command* over the Eurocorps to NATO. On January 21, 1993, a formal agreement was signed between French Chief of Staff Admiral Jacques Lanxade; his German counterpart, Klaus Naumann; and the

SACEUR (Supreme Allied Commander of Europe), John Shalikashvili. For all this, however, it seems incontrovertible that contrasting—indeed contradictory—stances toward the role of NATO will continue to represent an enormous hurdle to future cooperative initiatives between France and Germany (as indeed they doubtless eventually limit, if not undermine, Anglo-French cooperation). Finally, the bilateral relationship continues to suffer from the fact that the two countries still possess very different military cultures, policies, and ambitions. The nuclear issue is the best illustration of this. Shortly after his election Chirac announced his decision to resume French nuclear testing, with senior officials going out of their way to claim that this was being done so that Europe as a whole could "benefit" from the French nuclear deterrent. This flew in the face of German thinking about nuclear policy. Only three years earlier, comments by Mitterrand concerning a possible future European deterrent force, made without prior consultation with Bonn, were greeted in France as a courageous initiative heralding a bright future for European defense cooperation, but they were not well received by many in Germany.[42] Reactions to the resumption of testing itself verged on the apoplectic. German Foreign Minister Klaus Kinkel exclaimed angrily that "We don't want to be a nuclear power, and not even through the back door."[43] In short, the test program—seen by Chirac as central to France's defense posture and to the development of meaningful European security structures—distanced France from Germany, and consequently had the effect of undermining attempts to form a coherent European front on defense issues. As one commentator put it:

> If Jacques Chirac . . . were to exclaim, when the final test is concluded . . ."*Hourra pour* l'Europe,"[44] the reactions would likely range from anger to embarrassment, from irritation to hilarity. The prospects of even a ripple of applause are negligible. Paradoxically, it may well prove that the tests, and particularly the arrogant style of their presentation, will ring the deathknell of moves towards a European deterrent.[45]

Conclusions

Increasingly, contradictions between the objectives of each state and between their aspirations for military policy have more and more clearly come to hamper attempts to build a meaningful bilateral security relationship. The limited progress made in the security sphere has also been intimately linked to the fact that both France and Germany have explicitly sought to link bilateral cooperation to broader collaborative ambitions for Western Europe. Apart from the differences between France and Germany concerning what these ambitions might be, the very fact that defense collaboration has frequently been seen as a means to an end rather than an end in itself, has been a debilitating factor.

François Mitterrand, in a speech to journalists in 1994, used the following imagery to describe the Franco-German relationship:

> In the Middle Ages, a stranger saw some workmen placing stones one on top of the other. He stopped and asked them: "What are you doing?" "As you can see," came the reply, "we are placing stones one on top of the other." He then turned to another group, further away and engaged in the same task, and asked them the same question: "What are you doing?" And the workmen replied: "We are building a cathedral."[46]

Typically Mitterrandian. Yet to build a cathedral, one must have plans. And those plans will illustrate the precise position of each stone in order that the finished product be perfect. In the Franco-German case, it would seem as if random stones, placed in random locations, are portrayed as useful first steps on the way to building the cathedral of a meaningful European defense organization. Yet as the joint brigade and the abortive attempts to reach some kind of understanding about nuclear weapons have illustrated, many of these stones are incapable of holding any weight. In contrast, the current far-reaching discussions on defense collaboration between Britain and France are not based on vague visions of the future. Rather, they are based on practical experience, notably in Kosovo, and hence the cooperation process has been far more utilitarian than ideological.

Of course, an essential prerequisite of such utilitarian, and highly effective, collaboration is that a minimum of convergence exist concerning objectives between the participants. It is precisely here that the Franco-German relationship has failed to make significant progress. It is striking to note that the same problems have continued to bedevil the bilateral security relationship virtually from the 1950s to the present day. A desire to preserve national control has continually hampered French attempts to foster closer relations with the Germans, in the 1960s as today—particularly in the nuclear sphere.[47] French refusal to contemplate a decrease in the degree of political autonomy it enjoys in deciding on its own military policy was an important fact limiting progress in Franco-German initiatives in preparing for Maastricht, just as it had been during the EDC debates of the 1950s. Differing conceptions of the role and place of European and Atlantic security structures have dogged recent security discussions between the two states as they undermined de Gaulle's vision of the Elysée Treaty. Indeed the final two issues are interrelated. Those Germans who favor the more intergovernmentalist arrangements proposed by France for defense cooperation favor it within a NATO framework. Conversely, those Germans who support the

French initiative to create effective European structures tend to be in favor of a higher degree of military integration than Paris is willing to accept.[48] To return to Mitterrand's metaphor for the last time, the Franco-German "cathedral" is being built by workmen who have fundamentally different conceptions, not only concerning its ideal location—in the grounds of NATO or some distance from it—but also its ultimate purpose.

Paradoxically, in many ways, the most impressive thing about the Franco-German security relationship is not what it has achieved but rather that it has endured for so long, and that it maintains a high priority for both states despite the limits of its practical achievements to date. As one scholar has put it, the bilateral relationship seems to be characterized by a "partnership prejudice," or, in other words, a "bias toward bilateral cooperation for cooperation's sake and a desire to do everything possible to avoid both the impression and the existence of divergence."[49]

All this raises important and potentially difficult questions for students of political institutions. While it is not appropriate in an empirically focused volume such as this to devote much time to these questions, it is worth at least pointing out that Franco-German security relations are of significant theoretical interest. Why have both sides insisted on the importance of their bilateral relationship despite its limited practical consequences? Why have the security institutions created in 1963 endured? Given the limits of such a process, in this case, under what conditions can we expect interaction within an institutional structure to result in the convergence of preferences between the actors involved?

Notes

1. Amaya Bloch-Lainé, "Franco-German Co-operation in Foreign Affairs, Security and Defence," in D. Webber, ed., *The Franco-German Relationship in the European Union* (London: Routledge 1999), p. 150.
2. N. Gnesotto, "Le Dialogue Franco-Allemand depuis 1954: patience et longueur de temps," in K. Kaiser and P. Lellouche, eds., *Le Couple Franco-Allemand et la Défense de l'Europe* (Paris: IFRI 1986), p. 13.
3. Simon Bulmer and William E. Paterson, "Germany in the European Union: Gentle Giant or Emergent Leader?" *International Affairs* 72, 1, 1996, p. 18.
4. See D. S. Yost, "France in the new Europe," *Foreign Affairs* 69 (Winter 1990–91), p. 112. For the ten-point plan see *Le Monde,* November 30, 1990.
5. See Anand Menon, *France, NATO, and the Limits of Independence 1981–1997: The Politics of Ambivalence* (London: Macmillan 2000), especially Chapters 4 and 5.
6. *Le Monde,* October 20, 1987.

7. "The quicker we move towards Union, the less our neighbour can go it alone." The phrase is that of H. Froment-Meurice, in *L'Express*, February 14, 1992.
8. Helmut Kohl, "Regierungsklärung vom 13.10.82," *Stichworte zur Sicherheitspoilitik* 10, 19, 1998, p. 1.
9. Michael Meimeth, "Germany," in M. Brenner, ed., *NATO and Collective Security* (London: Macmillan 1998), p. 109.
10. *Le Monde*, August 24, 1995.
11. See particularly Georges-Henri Soutou, *L'Alliance Incertaine: Les Rapports politico-stratégiques franco-allemands, 1954–1996* (Paris: Fayard 1996).
12. Ibid., pp. 246–247.
13. On this, see N. Gnesotto, *Le Dialogue Franco-Allemand depuis 1954*, op. cit., pp. 24–28. See also R. Grant, "French Security Policy," in R. Laird, ed., op. cit., p. 21.
14. See, for instance, C. Cheysson's comments in "Diplomatie: l'Empreinte Française," *Politique Internationale* 20, summer 1983, p. 16. The Commission was under the authority of the Ministers of Foreign Affairs and Defense and was comprised of high-level civilian and military officials from each side. For more detailed information on the workings of the Commission from participants in the events of the time, see F. Heisbourg and P. Boniface, op. cit., pp. 241–243.
15. See W. Feld, "Franco-German Military Co-operation and European Unification," *Journal of European Integration* 12:2–3 (Winter 1989), pp. 151–164.
16. For a discussion of the Protocol of January 1988, see E. Guldner, "Le Traité de l'Elysée et la Coopération Franco-Allemande en Matière de Défense," *Stratégique* 1 (1989), pp. 133–150.
17. *Le Monde*, March 2–3,1986.
18. *Le Monde*, October 21, 1987.
19. *Le Monde*, January 30, 1997.
20. Guidelines adopted by the Franco-German seminar of Ministers of Foreign Affairs, Freibourg im Breisgau, February 27, 1996, in *France Statements* (London: French Embassy, March 7, 1996), p. 19.
21. *The Independent*, November 8, 1996.
22. The full text of the Franco-German common concept can be found in *Le Monde*, January 30, 1997.
23. *Le Monde*, January 30, 1997.
24. Lawrence Freedman, for instance, has written that the brigade was of minimal military relevance, and, moreover, failed to bridge any of the key strategic differences dividing France and Germany. See L. Freedman, "Defence Cooperation in Political Context," in W. Taylor Jr., ed., *Beyond Burdensharing* (Brussels: United States Mission to NATO, Atlantic Papers, Proceedings no. 1, April 1989). Also, proceedings of a seminar for Permanent and Military Representatives to NATO sponsored by the U.S. Mission to NATO, December 12, 1988, Brussels, p. 25.

124   *Anand Menon*

25. Interviews, NATO Headquarters, July 1997.
26. See A. Menon, "Defence and integration in Western Europe," *Contemporary Security Policy,* October 1996, pp. 264–283.
27. A. Forster, *Empowerment and Constraint: Britain and the Negotiation of the Treaty on European Union,* D. Phil Thesis, University of Oxford, 1995, p. 170.
28. CDU/CSU Fraktion des Deutschen Bundestages, "Reflections on European Policy," September 1, 1994.
29. *Le Monde,* November 30, 1982. See also Wolfgang Schlör, German Security Policy Adelphi Paper 277 (London: International Institute of Strategic Studies, June 1993), pp. 25–27.
30. D. S. Yost, "Nuclear Weapons Issues in France," op. cit., p. 57.
31. F. de Rose, *Défendre la Défense* (Paris: Juillard 1989), p. 150.
32. *Le Monde,* October 24, 1987.
33. *The Guardian,* February 14, 1996. Interviews, Paris, NATO Headquarters, July 1997.
34. *Le Monde,* February 15, 1996.
35. F. Bozo, "France," op. cit., p. 75.
36. *Le Monde,* March 22, 1996.
37. *Le Figaro,* July 14, 1997. Thompson is a large MWC with a strong military component. The denationalization of all or parts of Thompson, which was nationalized in 1981, has been a burning issue in French business circles.
38. *Defense News,* July 21–27, 1997.
39. *Le Monde,* June 6, 1997.
40. *Le Monde,* March 22, 1996.
41. *Le Monde,* July 21–22, 1996.
42. Ibid. Interviews, Paris, December 1995.
43. *Wall Street Journal,* September 11, 1995.
44. De Gaulle had exclaimed *"Hourra pour la France!"* following the explosion of the first French nuclear weapon.
45. J. Howorth, "'HiroChirac' and the French Nuclear Conundrum: A Testing Time for the Pursuit of Grandeur," *French Politics and Society* 13:3 (Summer 1995), p. 14.
46. François Mitterrand, *De l'Allemagne, de la France* (Paris: Editions Odile Jacob 1996), pp. 239–240.
47. Compare, for instance, the comments of former defense minister Franz Josef Strauss: "Germany does not want atom patronage, but atom partnership" in *The Grand Design* (London: Wiedenfeld and Nicolson 1965), pp. 63–64, with those of German MP Freimut Duv in response to Juppés speech about concerted deterrence: "Will we have a right to be consulted or of co-decision over [the use of French nuclear weapons]?" *Le Monde,* August 24, 1995.
48. G-H Soutou, op. cit., p. 436.
49. Philip H. Gordon, *France, Germany and the Western Alliance* (Boulder: Westview 1995), p. 102.

Chapter 7 ✥

A New European Role for Italy?

Anja Dalgaard-Nielsen

Abstract

I taly undertook efforts to modernize during the 1990s and has been seeking a more central position in European cooperation. This chapter will
discuss what resources Italy can muster in order to support this ambition, and will seek to identify the major problems that might compromise
it. The chapter will discuss how ideological commitment and material interests interact and shape the European engagement of Italy. It will show
how "Europe," "modernization," and "a stronger Italian state" are seen as in-
terconnected and how this "myth of Europe" provides for a strong Europeanism within the elite and within the general population. The
Europeanism has proven critical in the reforming attempts of the 1990s; it
is argued that it lends plausibility to Italy's quest for a more central position
in the European cooperation of the future. The chapter will conclude with
a discussion of how the internal cleavages of Italian society might jeopardize
Italy's European ambitions, and argues that Italy will have to balance its own
internal contradictions through a balanced cooperation with both France
and Germany.

Introduction

In 1995 Lucio Caracciolo, editor of an Italian journal of international relations, launched a proposal to merge France, Germany, and Italy in a
super-hard core to secure the pace and efficiency of European integration
in a future enlarged union.[1] Such a bold proposal would probably surprise and maybe amuse those who have gotten used to thinking of Italy

as one of Europe's lightweights on the diplomatic front. It is true that Italy, burdened by internal problems and constrained by geopolitical realities of the Cold War, has pursued a low-profile foreign policy in the second half of the twentieth century. But, as displayed in the vision of Caracciolo, today Italy is moving. It is seeking a more central position in the European cooperation, and would like to see itself as part of the Franco-German engine.

The chapter will first explore the background of Italy's European engagement and illustrate how ideological commitment has interacted with tangible material benefits to establish a strong "myth of Europe" in the Italian political universe. This myth has been a central driving force in Italy's commitment to Europe and played a pivotal role in the modernization efforts of the 1990s, a modernization that now enables Italy to claim a more central position in the cooperation. This chapter will argue that the most imminent challenge for Italy, and at the same time the greatest opportunity for enhanced influence, is to give body to the myth of Europe—that is, to move beyond the negative definition of Europe as different from Italy to a positive definition of what Europe Italy wants. The chapter concludes that if Italy succeeds in doing this without widening the internal cleavages of her own society, she will find herself in a strong position to influence the future design of Europe.

Driving Forces

When one looks at the political debate about Europe in the major Western European states, Italy stands out. Nowhere else are the concepts of Europe, modernization, prosperity, and efficiency so closely linked as in Italy. And nowhere else are these concepts so clearly juxtaposed to the notion of the individual nation-state.[2] This constellation of ideas, which I shall term "the myth of Europe," is critical in understanding Italy's European engagement. The following section traces the background and development of the myth.

The Italian Inferiority Complex

The myth of Europe must be understood against a persistent Italian self-perception of being a weak nation-state. The roots of what may be called "the Italian inferiority complex" go back to the country's unification. Italy was a latecomer among the established great powers of Europe and clearly the weakest among their number in all dimensions of statehood: material and economic strength, institutional efficiency, and national ideology. The newly unified state had to struggle with the economic underdevelopment of the South, inefficient political institutions, and lack of a unifying national culture.[3] But instead of concentrating on her own internal consolidation, Italy, in tune with the mood of the time, embarked on seeking affirmation of her nationhood in international grandeur. This was an ill-fated attempt. It resulted in a legacy of colonial adventures culminating in the crushing defeat at Adua in 1896. This defeat inflicted a serious wound on a nation whose leaders had presented war as a test of nationhood.[4] Ultimately the humiliating defeat in the Second World War put an end to Italy's assertive foreign policy and left the country materially and economically devastated. Nationalism was tainted by the fascist experience, and so were the state institutions by dint of having succumbed to the Fascist party.

The postwar era did little to restore Italian self-confidence. External constraints interacted with internal cleavages to consolidate the Italian experience of being a weak nation-state. With the decision to join NATO in 1949, Italy placed herself in the Western camp and followed American directives so loyally as to become known as "America's most faithful ally."[5] Simultaneously the country had the biggest Western European communist party, representing anti-American and NATO-skeptical sentiments. This internal cleavage resulted in a foreign policy in which dependence on the United States in military and security matters coexisted with a discrete, independent policy toward the East that made Italy one of the most important trade partners of the Soviet Union. One might view this situation as an example of how Italy skillfully pursued her own interests under the given international constraints.[6] The other side of the story, however, is that this inconsistent foreign policy prevented Italy from exerting leadership in international affairs. Forced to pursue a low-profile foreign policy in order not to fuel the internal antagonisms of her society, Italy reverted to a policy of *presenza*—of being present in international institutions without seeking to take on an active role.

The domestic repercussions of Italy's international situation was a political system in which no real alternation of power was possible. For geopolitical reasons neither the big Italian communist party, nor the neofascist party, could be included in government at the national level. This resulted in the notorious Italian ills of clientilism and *lottizzazione*.[7] Although ideologically fully committed to supranationalism and integration, the dynamics of the Italian political system prevented Italy from delivering much positive input to European integration. Developments at the international level were often exploited for internal purposes, which meant that in critical situations in which constitutive issues about the European cooperation were at stake, the energies of the Italian political system were consumed by governmental crisis and political maneuvering within and among parties.

Just as the internal East-West conflict excluded Italy from promoting the European cause with more than just words, so it precluded a coherent policy toward the second internal cleavage: the Italian North-South gap.

Serious social and economic problems were subordinated to anticommunism as issues likely to provoke real conflict of interest within the governing coalition were excluded from the policy agenda. When political decisions aimed at promoting economic development of the South were actually taken, their effects were modest due to corruption and inefficient implementation. These practices of nongovernance did nothing to eradicate the enormous socioeconomic and cultural differences between North and South. It also discredited the state by creating widespread disillusionment or outright hostility toward it.[8]

Via its replication inside Italy, the international East-West conflict thus reinforced the existing Italian North-South cleavage and contributed to the Italian self-perception of weakness and marginalization. Engrossed in internal strife and problems, neither the elite nor the broader public took much interest in international affairs. But those who did tended to perceive their state as an object rather than a subject in international affairs.[9] A foreign observer may disagree with this Italian perception. But whatever its objective validity, the perception is real enough in the sense that it has had a decisive influence on Italy's European policy, as shall be argued below.

The Myth of Europe

The myth of Europe developed as a counterpart to the Italian inferiority complex. In Italy, "Europe" is a highly positive symbol that stands for modernity and prosperity, and the myth contrasts inefficient Italy to efficient and prosperous Europe. The key to the development of Italy's strong commitment to Europe lies at the intersection of ideological appeal and material interest.

The ideological commitment goes back to Guiseppe Mazzini and Guiseppe Garibaldi—heroes of the Italian unification. Mazzini favored a European federation in which the existing nation-states would give up their sovereignty. By unifying, Italy could become a stronger promoter of this cause.[10] The concept of internationalist patriotism was contradicted by the foreign policy of Francesco Crispi and Giovanni Giolitti, and ultimately by Mussolini. The fascist experience and the defeat in World War II discredited the notion of a strong independent nation-state, and the resistance movement brought Mazzinian ideals back to the fore. Luigi Einaudi, Italian president from 1948 to 1955, formulated the prevalent mood of the time when in 1947 he claimed that "The myth of the absolute sovereignty of states is the enemy, not only of economic prosperity, but of civilization itself."[11]

Already in the 1950s Europeanism had become a firmly established "postnational" ideology in large segments of Italian society. Besides being an obvious answer to fascism, it had the advantage of resonating well with the strong Catholic subculture of postwar Italy.[12] The idea of a united Europe in which sovereignty is transferred to supranational structures fits the Church's notions of solidarity and subsidiarity well.

On the political left wing, a combination of Mazzinian ideals and classical socialist internationalism made the Italian socialist party embrace the idea of a united Europe. Integration was conceived as a means to expand socialist efforts to a wider field. Initially the Italian Communist Party (PCI) was opposed to European integration on the grounds that it was limited to Western Europe and oriented toward NATO. Already by 1960, however, the PCI stopped advocating that the EEC be abolished, and argued instead that it should be transformed into an integrative structure open to both East and West.[13] Finally in 1973 the party distanced itself from Soviet Communism and declared its support for the EEC, leaving the small neofascist party as the only one not to support the cause of European unity.

Ideological commitment has interacted with material interest. Alcide De Gasperi saw a united Europe as a means to secure peace, but also as a remedy against the structural problems of the Italian economy and the underdevelopment of the South.[14] Though the initial period of federalist enthusiasm ended with De Gasperi's premiership, Italy remained, at least in words, a committed pro-integrationist member of the European cooperation. She had no part in conceiving the two main European initiatives of the 1950s, the Schuman Plan and the Pleven Plan, but the political class embraced the ECSC without hesitation. The first decade of participation in the economic cooperation in Europe was the greatest period of economic growth in Italian history. Unemployment went down, GNP increased, and industrial production went up, as did exports to the EEC partners.[15] For the first time, large-scale concerted efforts could be taken against the underdevelopment of the South.

Though economic prosperity was reinforced rather than caused by the EEC membership, and though the major contribution to development of the South came from Italy's own economic miracle,[16] it is obvious why Europe and prosperity came to be linked in the Italian political universe. The experience of unprecedented economic growth coincided with the strongly pro-European rhetoric of the political and economic elite.[17] The Social Funds agreed upon in the Treaty of Rome, for example, were presented by the government as proof that Italy's European partners were willing to assume responsibility for the Italian problems of unemployment and underdevelopment of the South.[18] Disillusionment with the institutions and politicians of Italy made it easy to persuade the citizens to project hopes of legitimate rule and economic prosperity onto Europe. The ideological Europeanism of the political class thus spread to larger segments of Italian society. Against the backdrop of the Italian inferiority complex, the positive experience of participation in European cooperation consolidated a strong myth of Europe in the Italian political universe.

The end of the Cold War has enhanced Italy's room for maneuver internationally. Internally it freed Italy from a political class that had seemed eternal, and this paved the way for the modernization attempts of the 1990s. But the Italian inferiority complex lingers. The Italians still tend to be pessimistic about the power of their state, and much political debate clusters around the question of how to be taken more seriously by the European partners.[19] The European myth figures prominently in this debate. Common to all the different groups is the fact that modernization is linked to Europe. Europe is seen as Italy's chance of clinging to the Alps instead of drifting into the Mediterranean. Europe promises modernization and prosperity and the possibility that if Italy moves closer to Europe she could overcome her own deficiencies. The myth states that if she can do this Italy will prosper, but if not she will be left to "soak in the Mediterranean."[20] The myth also combines a fear of marginalization with a hope for inclusion in the core of a politically and economically united Europe.

The trauma of the events of September 1992, and the way the political class responded to them, must be seen in the light of the myth: The excesses of the state and the oil crisis pushed the lira out of the European Monetary System (EMS) in September 1992. With this expulsion the Italian feeling of marginalization took on a very concrete form. Giulio Andreotti stressed continued Italian allegiance to Europe, and the Amato and Ciampi governments pursued austerity budgets to allow Italy to reenter the EMS. These efforts were crowned by Romano Prodi's term in office and the entrance of Italy among the founding members of EMU. The Prodi government embarked on a program of structural spending cuts. It also introduced an extraordinary income tax surcharge—the euro-tassa—to reduce the public budget deficit below the 3 percent of GDP as required by the EMU entrance criteria. The impressive effort of bringing down the deficit from almost 7 percent of GDP in 1996 to less than 3 percent in 1997 not only allowed Italy to enter among the founding members of EMU, but set an example of austerity for many other countries. The strategy and achievements of the Prodi government illustrates the positive dialectic between the myth of Europe and internal Italian modernization. By invoking the powerful constellation of ideas that link Europe to prosperity in the Italian political universe and by playing on Italian fears of marginalization, the government could induce the population to accept spending cuts and austerity measures—even new taxes. In Prodi's own words: "Maybe people are not conscious of the fact that without Europe we would have ended up in Latin America two or three times in this postwar period."[21]

Prodi emphasizes how the myth of Europe helped a weak state to reform, as the Italian political class—by invoking Europe—could discipline its own fragmenting tendencies and coax its domestic population. Patrick McCarthy has pointed out that besides coaxing its domestic population by invoking Europe, the Italian political class has also been able to coax its European partners by invoking Italy. Various political leaders have skillfully exploited the weakness of the Italian state to obtain concessions from its partners that would not have been granted to "stronger" states.[22] The extent to which Italy can play this game, however, is likely to decrease as Italian modernization proceeds, and as a general European consensus on the necessity of cutting structural spending and reforming welfare states seems to develop. Spanish Prime Minister Jose Maria Aznar's rejection of Prodi's suggestion to form a block pressing for more lenient EMU entrance criteria for the Southern European countries is an example.

It may appear that Silvio Berlusconi's government (1994) represented a break with the pro-integrationist Italian tradition. Berlusconi and his minister of foreign affairs, Antonio Martino, flaunted their commitment to a "stronger" Italian foreign policy and to a Europe of nation-states in which EU bureaucracy and Brussels technocrats would be placed under firmer national control. In spite of this rhetoric the Italian policy remained fully pro-European, and Berlusconi's brief term in office saw only one spasm of more assertive Italian foreign policy as the government blocked Slovenian efforts to negotiate an association (which would not give Slovenia membership in the EU, but special status with it).[23] It bears witness to the strength of Italian desire to Europeanize that Berlusconi, in spite of the more assertive rhetoric of his government, campaigned on the issue that only the Polo, Berlusconi's center-right coalition, and not a center-left coalition would be able to bring Italy into the EMU.

For many foreigners, Prodi—even more so after his appointment as head of the European Commission—has come to incarnate Italian determination to move closer to Europe. His downfall, however, by no means represents a backlash for the pro-integrationist forces of Italy. Though Massimo D'Alema, who headed the government that took over after Prodi, represents a political tradition with strong interventionist and Keynesian sympathies, his government continued the attempts to cut structural spending and reduce the role of the state in the economy. Labor union resistance seems to have stalled reform of Italy's generous pension system for the moment, but there is a common understanding among unions as well as employers' organizations that the commitment to Europe is fixed and that this requires reform. The government has continued the process of privatization, expressing its commitment to reducing the role of the state in the economy. On the ideological level, the D'Alema government represents a continuation of the strand of thought that wishes to Europeanize Italy—to adapt "abnormal" Italy to efficient Europe. D'Alema even dedicated a book to the theme: *Un paese normale.*[24]

The thread running through the postwar policy of Italy, from De Gasperi to Prodi and beyond, is the attempt to become more European. The myth of Europe has been a critical driving force in Italy's commitment to integration and it has functioned as a lever in her internal development. Throughout the postwar era, most evidently during Prodi's term in office, Italy's European engagement has been a positive impulse to reform her political system and public economy. The next section will address the question of whether this modernization will now finally allow Italy to realize her ambition of "counting more in Europe."

Resources and Challenges

Italy's strong preoccupation with inclusion in the core of the European co-operation must be understood against the background of a lingering inferiority complex and the experience of tangible material gains as a result of participation in Europe. Traditionally, Italy has seen federalism as a means to obtain parity with France and Germany, and today the ambition of becoming part of the Franco-German engine figures prominently in the Italian debate. This section highlights the problems that still compromise Italy's ambition to gain a more central position and discusses what resources Italy can muster to support it.

Italian Modernization Problems

Even though Italy has come a long way in her efforts to modernize, it still has to cope with problems like a big public debt, political instability, and the unsettled debate about constitutional reform.

Italy's public debt is the largest in value terms in the Eurozone. Structural spending cuts, which meet with resistance from labor unions and from factions inside the government, are necessary to reduce the debt servicing costs. At the same time Italy has experienced a period of weak growth due to the fiscal squeeze necessary to qualify for the EMU-entry. Since 1996 Italy's GDP has grown less than France's and Germany's.[25] This has placed the government in a dilemma, as tight financial policies are likely to further hamper recovery. These issues compromise Italy's ambition to move closer to the core of Europe as demonstrated at the Ecofin meeting of Europe's economic and finance ministers in May 1999. Having requested that its budget deficit for next year would be allowed to slip from 2 percent to 2.4 percent of GDP, Italy once again found itself under examination by European partners doubting its capacity to manage its public finances.

Problems of political culture also linger. Cossutta's threat to withdraw from D'Alema's government coalition because of its policy toward the

Kosovo conflict illustrates how factionalism still compromises Italy's ability to pursue a coherent foreign policy: As NATO attacks on Serbia were launched from Italian bases, the Italian government, under pressure from Cossutta's communist party, embarked on several attempts to mediate and reopen the diplomatic process.[26]

Connected to the question of political stability is the issue of constitutional reform. The Italian political system has produced 56 governments since World War II, and political pressure for reform has been building since the 1980s. There was a large but useless "yes" vote in the 1998 referendum, which would have introduced a less proportional electoral system. But the referendum failed to achieve the 51 percent quorum of eligible votes required. This means the continuance of an electoral system that tends to produce a fragmented party system. The failed referendum indirectly influences Italian prospects for enhanced influence in Europe as it affects the perception of Italy among its partners. The Germans, especially with their emphasis on stability and accountability in political life, may be reluctant to rely on an Italy with an unreformed electoral system.[27]

A combination of political and economic factors thus compromises Italy's ambition to become part of the Franco-German engine. But these problems are recognized and Italy has displayed a willingness to address them in her effort to trim public spending and reform politically. Though political culture and public finances still bear witness to a tradition of factionalism and *lottizzazione,* the underlying structure of Italian party politics is transformed. The end of the Cold War has broken the Christian Democratic Party's power monopoly and, though the internal coherence of the two "poles" should not be exaggerated, the Italian political system now has, at least theoretically, two governmental alternatives: a center-left versus a center-right coalition. This changes the incentives of the political actors: Had Cossutta brought down the D'Alema government over the Kosovo conflict, he might have paved the way for a center-right government under Berlusconi—hardly the most attractive prospect for Cossutta's electorate. The existence of two governmental alternatives is likely to prompt more responsible coalition behavior. It holds out the prospect of more stable Italian governments with greater capacity to pursue coherent strategies against Italy's remaining internal problems. Also, in the field of foreign affairs, the stereotype of a confused and meddlesome Italy is challenged. The noise made by Cossutta over the Kosovo intervention should not obscure the fact that the intervention was supported by all political parties except the Communists and the Greens. This historically significant cross-partisan consensus has also influenced the major foreign policy decisions of recent years—support for NATO enlargement and intervention in Albania—as have the Berlusconi government's nomination of Renato Ruggiero as general secretary of WTO and D'Alema's nomination of Prodi as head of the European Commission. These developments are likely to enhance Italy's credibility as a foreign policy actor.

Though political culture does not change overnight, there is little reason to believe that Italy will suffer serious setbacks in the efforts to reform its economy and political system or in gaining increased credibility as a foreign policy actor in the eyes of her European partners.

Which Europe?—The Underdefined Italian Myth

I would contend that the real challenge to Italy's capacity to take on an active and constructive role in the European cooperation lies elsewhere and has a more subtle character.

It has been argued above that the myth of Europe is a motive force in Italy's European engagement and that it has been a critical stimulus for internal reforms. There is a strong desire to move closer to Europe, so strong that it sometimes appears as if the Italians wanted to substitute their own inefficient state for a stronger European entity. The problem is that there does not seem to be much agreement on *what kind of Europe* Italy wants to substitute for the Italian state. Italy's Europeanism might prove to rest on a minimalist consensus of aversion—"rather Brussels than Rome"—but to have little positive content beyond that. The real challenge today is to move beyond that minimalist consensus and give a positive content to the myth of Europe. What kind of Europe is it Italy wants to move closer to?

The problem in this exercise is that the Europeanism of the Italian population rests on potentially conflicting ideas. Europe is a positive symbol to almost everybody. But beneath this surface of unity, a variety of different concepts of Europe exist. Whereas, in the South, Europe is seen as a substitute for an inefficient state power, it is seen in the North as a means to get rid of what is perceived as excessive and inefficient state intervention. The South wants a social Europe, the North wants a free market, to put it sharply. The richer North Italian constituency, whose views are represented by politicians like Antonio Martino[28] and Giuliano Urbani, is in favor of an Anglo-American style of liberalism.[29] The financial establishment, Banca Italia, and groups around the employers' organization "Confindustria" see Europe primarily as a remedy to curb the Italian welfare state and discipline its monetary policy through a "germanization" of the Italian economy.[30]

In the Italian context, "Europe" is a symbol of modernity, but its more specific meaning remains weak. The unifying power of symbols lies in their capacity to gloss over differences. But this is possible only to the extent that they remain underspecified and thus permit different groups to read different meanings into them. This is exactly what has happened in Italy as in many other European states. But what sets Italy apart from the other major players in Europe is that the competing concepts mirror a geographical, economic, and cultural cleavage of such importance that it potentially threatens the unity of the country. The real challenge thus lies in giving a positive content to the myth of Europe without fueling Italy's internal contradictions.

In a sense Italy is in a race against time. Its internal modernization efforts have the potential to blunt the sharpness of the North-South cleavage. These efforts depend on a European integration process that moves ahead and thus places pressure on Italy to keep abreast. But if Europe eventually takes on a direction that clearly favors one of the competing Italian concepts of Europe over the other, the Europeanism that for the moment unifies the country in its dual push for modernization and integration may prove superficial, and thus disappear. Certain external events are likely to add to Italy's problems. An enlargement of the European Union, followed by a shift of resources and attention away from the existing EU's poorer areas to the (new members in the) East, may activate Italy's internal contradictions. Furthermore, enlargement is likely to be accompanied by the creation of a hard core of member-states, or some sort of variable geometry. It would disappoint Italy's ambitions and lead to a credibility loss for the pro-European internationalist discourse if she does not succeed in becoming part of the core. Both developments may give renewed momentum to Umberto Bossi's separatist movement. Though the immediate threat of Bossi's fantasy republic "Padania" breaking away from the central government in Italy seems less imminent now than in the early 1990s, the underlying differences between North and South remain real, and in the economic field they are growing. Prosperity is increasing in the South, but not at the same rate as in the North.[31] In the extreme scenario, the affluent Northern provinces might seek to join the core of an enlarged Union and finally let the Southern provinces "slip into the Mediterranean."

Italy's different Europeanisms thus constitute a challenge but at the same time an opportunity. Measured by conventional criteria,[32] Italy would still be judged a weak state relative to Germany and France. But the strong Europeanist current in Italy's political culture represents a potential source of strength. Though the Italians do not agree on what Europe they want, they do know that they want the European integration to move forward.[33] This ensures a permissive domestic consensus, which gives the Italian political class much room to maneuver in the field of foreign policy as long as it presents its initiatives as attempts to further the European cause. This is an advantageous position from which Italy can pursue proactive strategies, set agendas, and launch visions for the future design of Europe, as she does not have to fight a two-front-war with, on the one hand, her European partners and, on the other hand, her domestic society. The idea of Framanitalia

(France-Germany-Italia) is obviously too wild. European federalism is anathema to French political thinking, and the idea of a "Europa-Staat" is contrary to the German inclination to divide rather than concentrate power. But the proposal illustrates how Italy could become a constructive agenda-setting force, and in this game the Europeanism of the Italian population lends plausibility to her push for further integration.

Following this line of argument, the important challenge for Italy is not simply to undertake structural spending cuts and reduce the public debt. The most important challenge, and the biggest opportunity to exert greater influence in European cooperation, lie in developing a positive, unifying vision of what kind of Europe Italy wants. If she can do this without jeopardizing her internal stability she could take full advantage of a strong Italian Europeanism as a lever, not only in moving closer to an underdefined Europe but in pursuing proactive strategies to shape the Europe of the future.

France, Germany, and the Recession of Political Imagination

One current of thought in Italy tends to see the recent cracks in the French-German axis as something that may provide openings for enhanced Italian influence.[34] This section first discusses the background for the French-German problems, then argues that Italian attempts to build stronger bridges to either of the two traditional core countries must be squared with her need to bridge her own internal cleavages. This means that Italy should not fall for the temptation to exploit the problems in the French-German partnership in order to seek more influence through bilateral alliances, but should instead strive for a balanced cooperation with both in a push to further both European integration and internal modernization.

Problems in the French-German Partnership

France and Germany have always harbored different visions of Europe. The German idea of Europe places emphasis on the necessity of making borders less important, curbing the sovereignty of nation-states, and rendering irreversible the integration process. The Germans tend to view Europe as a process, a configuration of cooperating states, while underlining the economic aspects of the cooperation. The French idea of Europe is focused on the building of a coherent entity, capable of playing a role on the international scene. Hence, the French place more emphasis on the political and military aspects of the cooperation. Whereas it sometimes appears that the Germans want to dilute their own state in Europe, the French, far from seeking a dilution of France, attempt to strengthen their nation-state by recreating France at a European level.

Paradoxically, instead of rendering cooperation difficult, the fact that France and Germany harbored different visions of Europe made cooperation easier as the two countries complemented each other. France could stress her historical tradition and act as the political leader of the group, while Germany downplayed her own political heritage and focused instead on economic performance.[35] Today this "balance of imbalances" has broken down. Germany is reunited and has apparently started claiming a more central political role in the cooperation. The last years of the integration process have been marked by difficulties, which could be seen as stemming from the overwhelming concentration on pushing forward monetary integration. One could argue that the kind of Europe taking shape with the Maastricht Treaty is very much a German, and not so much a French Europe. Though France has gained a measure of control over German monetary policy through the EMU, the European Central Bank is shaped in the image of the Bundesbank and thus functions in line with a German economic paradigm. Political integration did not take a leap forward with the Maastricht Treaty, and Europe today remains a far cry from being a coherent international actor that can promote European values and interests in the world.

Though it can be argued that Europe is moving Germany's way, Germany hardly projects a positive unifying vision to keep up the pace of the integration process. In Germany, Europe is about aversions. It is about avoiding the excesses of unbounded nation-states and the danger of economic decline in a globalized[36] world. The Germans have tended to focus on the *process* of integration instead of final constructions. For Germany, the European choice represented a fundamental break with the "Machtstaat tradition" of the past. The Germans believed that, through cooperation, states would eventually be transformed into more peaceful entities; therefore, keeping the process moving became the main German goal. Pondering the final institutional or political shape of Europe was considered unnecessary academic exegesis. This discourse certainly has proven to be a powerful unifying force in postwar Germany, but it is questionable whether it will remain convincing as a new generation of politicians take over in Europe.

Tony Blair and Gerhard Schröder's "third way," with its ideas of how to adapt the European welfare states to a globalized world economy, may appear a candidate for a new unifying vision in a Europe dominated by center-left governments.[37] But though it arouses enthusiasm in Britain, and eventually could provide the discourse that will make Britain enter the EMU, I contend that it has scant unifying potential on the European level. As the reception of the Blair/Schröder paper in France demonstrates, the third way is not the French cup of tea. In the French tradition of political thinking, the state embodies the universal values of the French revolution and therefore the state should be active, not just domestically but also on the international scene, in promoting these values. The French do not project themselves as participants in a Europe that does not strive to play a great role in the world, and in which the states increasingly abdicate power to the market.[38] Not even internally in Germany does the third way or *Neue Mitte* seem to provide for a common vision. It is resisted by strong forces within the government, and viewed with skepticism in the new Bundesländer that are most in need of an active German state for their development.[39]

The major European players apparently have difficulty agreeing on a positive unifying vision of where the continent should be heading. The minimalist consensus of today seems to center on attempts to rally support for the European cause by invoking the necessity to adapt to globalization—to avoid economic decline in a competitive world economy. This discourse is probably much too sterile and nakedly rational to arouse much enthusiasm. It invokes an external menace as an incitement, an excuse for deregulation and welfare cuts, but it does not create a positive vision of where to go. It is more likely to produce apprehension and apathy than enthusiasm for the European cause, as the low turnout at the European elections of June 1999 indicates.

Europe seems to be suffering from what Patrick McCarthy has called "a recession of political imagination."[40] The postwar quid pro quo is threatened, and the traditional French-German motor seems to have difficulty coming up with a common project for where the continent should be heading.

Bilateral Temptations

This state of affairs may tempt Italy to seek enhanced influence through bilateral alliances. The constellation of Italy, France, and Germany suggests different possible roads to influence.

There is a clear convergence of worldviews between the political and intellectual elite of Italy and that of Germany. Because of their historical experiences, the elite of both countries have an uneasy relationship with unbounded nation-states. Originally the European choice for both Italy and Germany hinged on overcoming their own recent past and gaining rehabilitation in the international community; today both countries perceive their economic prosperity as inseparable from a forward-moving integration process. In the national debates of both Italy and Germany, national interests are seldom distinguished from European interests, and nation-states are depicted as increasingly anachronistic in the interdependent world of today. These ideological backdrops make both Germany and Italy keen on keeping the integration process on track, and one could speculate about the possibility of Italy taking over the role of France as the primary German partner in keeping the process moving. But even though Italy has improved her credibility and foreign policy profile, the German view on Italy remains one of polite reservation. Furthermore, a strategy of entering the European core by becoming a German junior partner may run counter to Italy's geopolitical interests. As argued above, she stands to lose if the EU center of gravity drifts too far to the north and the east, as this development may widen her own internal North-South cleavage. This points to France as a more likely and suitable ally. Italy and France share an interest in the Mediterranean area and this convergence of geopolitical perspectives is likely to become activated with the enlargement of the EU. An alliance with France in order to halt a refocusing of both attention and aid to the countries of Eastern Europe might appear the obvious solution for Italy. But I contend that this would not further Italian stability and prospects for influence. The "logic of balance" that underlies such a strategy would run counter to the broader Italian political culture, with its strong currents of internationalism and Catholicism. Such a European policy would not unify Italy and it would divide Europe. Attempts to counterbalance Germany may deadlock the European integration and tempt Germany to go it alone in "Mittel Europa."

There are no bilateral shortcuts to "counting more in Europe." As argued above: It is urgent for Italy to move closer to the core of Europe; but it is equally urgent, with respect to Italy's attempts to modernize internally, that Europe keep moving. If Italy tries to realize its European ambitions through bilateral alliances, she will end up threatening her own stability and prosperity. While Italy is striving to bridge her internal cleavages she must be careful to balance her own contradictions through a balanced cooperation with both France and Germany.

The challenge lies in not reverting to the traditional role of Italy as mediator between France, Germany, and Britain—a role that often covered over the fact that Italy, due to her internal lack of cohesiveness, did not have the capacity to develop and pursue a substantive policy of her own.[41] This brings us back to Italian Europeanism—simultaneously the biggest challenge and the biggest asset. In the worst case, Italy's contradicting concepts of Europe force her to stick to ad hoc activism and reactionary policies vis-à-vis the overall shape of a future enlarged Union. In the best case, Italy would take advantage of having developed a sensitivity, through its own internal problems, toward the potential contradictions between North and South, East and West in an enlarged Europe. If Italy can exploit this sensitivity in a positive way, she may be capable of formulating a convincing unifying vision for Europe, and use the Europeanism of its population to back it up. Gianni de Michelis's 1990 scheme of a "neo-mitteleuropean" group, consisting of Italy and Austria providing a bridge between the Eastern European states and Western Europe, foundered on Italy's lack of the vast financial resources needed to establish a common infrastructural network with these states. Italian economic aid and investments were soon outdistanced by German, Japanese, and American investments in the area.[42] But today, as the initial burst of post–Cold War capitalist enthusiasm seems to have waned, the nonmaterialist and Catholic strands of Italian culture may prove attractive to the Eastern European states. Economically, the small-sized Italian companies have been effective in penetrating the Eastern European markets in the wake of the German giants that established themselves in these countries.[43] So the Italian ambition of becoming a political, economic, and cultural bridge between the former Soviet satellites and Western Europe may not be that unrealistic after all, especially now that Italy, respective to the situation in 1990, is more firmly placed at the core of European integration.

Much the same argument could be made regarding her opportunity to bridge the difference between Northern and Southern members of the EU. A more efficient state that does not waste resources, and does not let transfer payments disappear in corruption networks, is in a better position to defend the vision of a social Europe without appearing hypocritical to its Northern partners and illegitimate to its own Northern regions.

In a Europe apparently at a loss of strong visions about where to go, Italy, because of the generally pro-European sentiments of her society, is in a favorable position to push forward integration by launching visions and ideas for the future shape of the continent—by becoming a provider of political imagination. But if Italy is to take full advantage of the Italian people's pro-European sentiments, she will have to move beyond the minimalist consensus of "rather Brussels than Rome" and develop a substantive consensus on what Europe it wants. If Italy can do that, she will find itself in a very strong position to shape the future design of Europe.

Ideas constitute a source of influence in their own right. Politics is an act of unification, and the country that can deliver a vision around which expectations and actions can cluster exerts a strong influence. But the moment Italy can back up its visions by enhanced political credibility and economic weight, the likelihood of actually realizing those visions obviously increases. This credibility can be attained only if Italy sustains her modernization efforts and takes real measures to bridge the internal development gap, and, as has been argued above, if she moves faster than external developments at the European level that would threaten both her internal stability and Europeanist consensus. With the fundamental changes in Italian party politics accelerated by the end of the Cold War, Italy seems capable of sustaining these efforts. As Mario Monti put it: "What Italy lacks now is not the strategy or the willingness to change, but the sense of urgency."[44]

Notes

1. Lucio Caracciolo, "L'esperimento Framania," in *Limes*, 2/1995, pp. 7–13.
2. See for example Francesco Cossiga, "Perché contiamo poco," in *Limes*, 3/1995, pp. 13–21; Romano Prodi, "Non faremo i satelliti di nessuno," in *Limes*, 3/1996, pp. 23–28; Lucio Caracciolo, "Ci conviene Framania?" in *Limes*, 2/1995, pp. 7–34.
3. Patrick McCarthy, *The Crisis of the Italian State: From the Origins of the Cold War to the Fall of Berlusconi* (New York: St. Martin's Press 1995), p. 14.
4. Denis Mack Smith, *Italy: A Modern History* (Ann Arbor: The University of Michigan Press 1959), p. 186.
5. Paul Ginsborg, *A History of Contemporary Italy* (London: Penguin Books 1990), p. 158.
6. See McCarthy, *The Crisis of the Italian State*, p. 46.
7. *Lottizzazione* refers to the stalled political process in which the centrist forces of Italian politics grouped around the Christian Democratic Party laid aside internal quarrels and joined in parceling out power and jobs between themselves, thereby securing a permanent exclusion of the communist party, PCI, from power.
8. Paul Ginsborg, *A History of Contemporary Italy*, p. 185.
9. See, for example, Cossiga, "Perché contiamo poco;" also Luciano Bozzo, *Italian Foreign Policy and the European Integration Process After the Cold War*, Manchester University Paper No. 1/1998.
10. Gordon A. Craig, *Europe, 1815–1914* (New York: HBJ 1971), pp. 188–190; Thomas Haarder, *Italien* (Copenhagen: Samleren 1997), p. 37.
11. Quoted in Giuseppe Sacco, "Europeisme in salsa italiana," in *Limes*, 4/1993.
12. According to a survey from 1996, more Italians feel represented by the Church (17.1%) than by shifting governments (4.5%) or by parliament (6.7%). Actually, the number of Italians who claim that they feel represented by the Catholic Church is exceeded only by the number who claim that they do not feel represented by anybody (19%). *Weekendavisen*, December 19–26, 1996, p. 5.
13. Primo Vanicelli, *Italy, NATO, and the European Community*, (Cambridge: Center for International Affairs, Harvard University 1974), p. 35
14. Alcide de Gasperi, *Per l'Europa* (Rome: Cinque Lune 1952).
15. Primo Vanicelli, *Italy, NATO, and the European Community*, p. 44; Frank Roy Willis, *Italy Chooses Europe* (New York: Oxford University Press 1971), p. 72.
16. As pointed out by McCarthy, *The Crisis of the Italian State*, pp. 50–54; and Willis, *Italy Chooses Europe*, pp. 66 and 91.
17. Initially the big industrialists were skeptical toward ECSC but Italian membership was pushed forward by the political elite. During the first decade of participation the economic elite became converted and were strong supporters of further integration. Willis, *Italy Chooses Europe*, p. 77.
18. Willis, *Italy Chooses Europe*, p. 89.

19. See for example Cossiga, "Perché contiamo poco"; Romani Prodi, "Non faremo i satelliti di nessuno," *Limes,* 3/1996. For surveys of mass public opinion see figures in Federico Rampini, "America o Germania? L'Italia si dilania," *Limes,* 3/1994.

20. In Caracciolo's terms, Italy would "suffocate" in the "Mediterraneo *arabo-balcanico.*" In Caracciolo, "L'esperimento Framania."

21. "Forse non ci rendiamo conto che senza l'Europa in questo dopoguerra saremmo finiti già due o tre volte in America Latina . . ." Romano Prodi, panel discussion in *Limes,* 2/1995, p. 19.

22. As argued by McCarthy in *The Crisis of the Italian State.*

23. Italy demanded that Slovenia compensate Italians expelled in 1945 for lost property, and that it change its constitution in order to permit foreigners to purchase property in Slovenia.

24. Massimo D'Alema, *Un paese Normale* (Milan: Mondadori 1995).

25. *Financial Times* country survey, June 29, 1999.

26. Cossutta's party represents pacifist sentiments skeptical to the use of violence in international affairs. But Cossutta also played the age-old Italian game of exploiting international events for internal purposes: Ten years ago D'Alema was on the streets protesting against the Gulf War. During the Kosova crisis he had to defend the same NATO's attacks on Serbia. Cossutta may have hoped to enhance his own influence in the government coalition by placing D'Alema and his party in a critical light right before the European elections in June 1999.

27. The Germans perceive the plurality of parties and the proportionality of the electoral system as a major reason for Italian political instability and they attribute the collapse of Prodi's government to these factors. For an example of this view, see *Die Zeit,* November 8, 1998.

28. Paradoxically elected in Sicily where his family comes from, though hardly because of his economic views.

29. For an example of this Northern perspective see Antonio Martino, "Nella libertà la chiave della costruzione Europea," in *Affari Esteri* No.104 1994, pp. 637–50.

30. Rampini, "America o Germania? L'Italia si dilania," p. 78.

31. Corriere della Sera, (July 22, 1999) "Milano tre volte più ricca di Agrigento."

32. For example, Barry Buzan's three dimensions of statehood: institutional efficiency, material strength, unifying national ideology. Barry Buzan, *People, States and Fear* (New York: Harvester Wheatsheaf 1991).

33. The Italian population is the most federalist of the major European countries, according to a survey conducted by *Limes.* See *Limes,* 3/1996, pp. 9–13.

34. See for example Sergio Romano, "Per noi è una grande occasione," *Limes,* 2/1995, pp. 138–140.

35. See for example Ole Waever, "Three competing Europes: German, French, Russian," in *International Affairs,* Vol. 66, No. 3, 1991, pp. 153–170.

36. Globalization refers to a development starting with the breakdown of the Bretton Woods system, which allowed capital streams to cross national borders unhindered. Later the term has also come to name the process in which big multinational companies allegedly loosen national affiliations and "shop around" for the lowest social and environmental requirements as they choose their locations.

37. See the Blair/Schröder paper on Europe's third way, published June 1999.

38. For the reception of the Blair/Schröder paper in France, see "Europas dritter Dritter Weg," *Die Zeit*, 39/1999.

39. For an example of the Eastern view, see interview with Reinhard Höppner, prime minister of Sachsen-Anhalt, *Die Zeit*, 31/1999.

40. Patrick McCarthy, "The 1993 French Elections: Politics Transformed and Policies Continued" (FPI Policy Briefs, SAIS, Washington DC).

41. Vannicelli argues that, for example, the apparently purposeful Italian mediation efforts in the negotiations of 1958 between EEC and Britain for the formation of a free-trade zone in reality resulted from lack of agreement on a coherent policy within the Italian government coalition. *Italy, NATO, and the European Community*, p. 42. Further examples are provided in Marco Rimanelli, *Italy Between Europe and the Mediterranean* (New York: Peter Lang 1997). See, for example, p. 739.

42. Marco Rimanelli, *Italy Between Europe and the Mediterranean*, p. 792.

43. Rampini, "America o Germania? L'Italia si dilania," p. 78.

44. Quoted in *Financial Times*, October 12, 1999.

Chapter 8 ✤

Mixed Signals: Britain and the Franco-German Relationship

James I. Walsh

Introduction

John Major's elevation to Prime Minister in 1990, and the surprise victory of his Conservative Party in the 1992 general election, promised to put Britain's relationship with the Franco-German partnership on a much more solid footing. The final months of Margaret Thatcher's government were dominated by division over the question of Europe, in particular the Franco-German plan to move toward monetary union. Major came to office promising a new relationship with Europe. His gave his first overseas speech as prime minister at the Konrad Adenauer Stiftung in Bonn, where he concluded: "My aims for Britain in the [European] Community can be simply stated. I want us to be where we belong at the very heart of Europe. Working with our partners in building the future."[1] Things did not work out this way; Major spent most of his time in office fending off challenges from members of his own party who wanted to pull Britain farther away from Europe.

Six years later another newly installed prime minister, Tony Blair, would echo these comments. The "New Labour" government's foreign secretary, Robin Cook, declared shortly after the 1997 election that "Britain wants to be one of the three major players in Europe" and that "I want today to be the start of a new era between Britain and the leading states of Europe. It is our intention that Britain should now be one of those leading members, not a country on the sidelines seeking to be obstructive."[2]

French and German governments eagerly awaited Blair's election in 1997 in the expectation that New Labour would take a much more conciliatory position on their priorities; few could imagine a government as unwilling to compromise as the Major administration had been. New Labour's election manifesto called for Britain to play a "leading role" in Europe and pledged to sign the European Union's Social Chapter that Major had rejected; to consider extending qualified majority voting in the Council of Ministers; to press forward with enlargement and the completion of the single market; and to take a more positive attitude toward the Franco-German project of monetary union.

In fact Britain's relationship with the Franco-German partnership has been marked by continuity. Britain under Blair has remained outside the consensus between France and Germany on the importance of monetary union, and in developing responses to the problems posed by globalization, social policy reform, and high levels of unemployment. It is only in the area of foreign and security policy that the Blair government's position has shifted toward the continental center of gravity. Whereas policy did not change much after the 1997 election, the government's rhetoric has been new. Blair has been careful not to allow New Labour to be torn apart by the question of relations with Europe. But as I discuss in the conclusion to this chapter, this shift in rhetoric will likely be an insufficient basis for Britain to play the leading role in Europe that New Labour espouses.

Major's Troubles on Europe

Domestic politics created most of the Major government's difficulty in living up to its promise to be at the very heart of Europe. Major began his term as an elected prime minister in 1992 with a House of Commons majority of only twenty-one seats. This narrow majority made Major captive to two threats. The first was the relatively small number of committed "euroskeptics" among Tory members of Parliament (M.P.s) who threatened to bring down the government at various points during the 1990s. The second threat was the much larger number of M.P.s whose positions on Europe were less important than was their interest in having a party leader capable of reelection. At difficult moments there was always the possibility that the latter group might join the former, and topple Major.

Britain's withdrawal from the exchange-rate mechanism (ERM) of the European Monetary System in September 1992 was the event that mobilized and legitimized the euroskeptics in the Conservative Party. Reversing its long-standing policy of allowing sterling to float, the Thatcher government had tied sterling's value to other European currencies by joining the ERM in October 1990. Many interpreted this as evidence of a newfound willingness to take seriously the Franco-German project of monetary union. But Thatcher and her chancellor (and successor as prime minister), John Major, remained opposed to monetary union and joined the ERM principally as a mechanism to reduce domestic inflation. ERM entry stabilized sterling's nominal exchange rate; and this, with inflation at 10 percent, led the currency to appreciate in real terms. This reduced import prices and placed downward pressure on the high inflation rate. The ERM also provided a more credible framework in the eyes of international investors, attracting short-term financial investment in sterling. Currency appreciation and greater credibility allowed Thatcher and Major to reduce interest rates before the next general election; between Britain's joining the ERM in October 1990 and the election of May 1992, the Bank of England cut interest rates nine times from 15 percent to 10 percent, and inflation fell from 10 percent to 4 percent.[3]

Although inflation had been conquered by mid-1992, economic growth remained sluggish and this created political pressure for interest rates to go even lower. But further interest rate reductions were inconsistent with maintaining sterling's ERM parity, especially after the German central bank, the Bundesbank, raised its interest rates in mid-July. Recognizing the dilemma facing the British government, in the summer of 1992 investors began betting on the possibility of a sterling devaluation and drove the exchange rate toward its floor in the ERM. The Major government's first response was to reaffirm—indeed, to strengthen—its rhetorical commitment to the ERM. Chancellor Norman Lamont made a widely publicized speech in early July rejecting both devaluation and withdrawal from the ERM on the grounds that either move would reduce the credibility of the authorities and require higher interest rates. Prime Minister Major reiterated the government's commitment to its ERM parity, arguing just days before sterling's exit from the mechanism that a devaluation would be a betrayal of our future. In early September the Treasury arranged a ten billion ECU loan from international banks to augment the Bank of England's reserves and to demonstrate the government's commitment to sterling's current exchange rate in the ERM.

Continued speculation against sterling led Lamont unsuccessfully to press the Germans to reduce interest rates. At a meeting of the European Community's finance ministers and central bankers in Bath in early September, Lamont exploited his position as chair to prevent formal discussion of a devaluation, and to harangue Bundesbank president Helmut Schlesinger to lower German interest rates. Schlesinger refused and almost walked out of the meeting rather than face Lamont's badgering. Given the very different priorities of the British and the Germans, the meeting broke up without a plan of action to address the problem of currency speculation. The development that precipitated sterling's exit from the ERM was a wire service report on September 15, in which Schlesinger was said to have implied that sterling and other ERM currencies needed to devalue in order to end the ERM crisis. When the foreign exchange markets in Europe opened the next day, the Bank of England had to intervene on the markets with about 15 billion pounds, or roughly half its reserves. (In accordance with the rules of the ERM, the Banque de France and Bundesbank also intervened heavily by buying sterling.) The Bank of England raised interest rates to 12 percent at 11 A.M. with little effect; a further increase to 15 percent that afternoon also did not stop sales of sterling. Unwilling to raise interest rates further or to devalue, the government indefinitely "suspended" sterling's participation in the ERM and allowed the currency to float.

At an emergency meeting of the European Community's Monetary Committee that evening (September 16), the British tried to persuade other governments to suspend the entire ERM until after the French referendum the following Sunday, but the latter refused and in the communiqué simply "took note" of the British decision. Major and Lamont laid the blame for sterling's exit squarely on the Bundesbank, especially Schlesinger's interview as well as comments made—often off the record—by officials of the German government and Bundesbank, suggesting a sterling devaluation. Major even went so far as to have the Foreign Office call in the German ambassador to London for a formal dressing-down.

In retrospect it is clear that Major and Lamont must share much of the blame for the events leading up to "Black Wednesday," since they placed all of their credibility on membership in the ERM at an unsustainable exchange rate and refused to compromise with France and Germany on a solution to the crisis that would have preserved the mechanism. Black Wednesday also greatly weakened Major's recently won mandate to lead his party. Major had staked his reputation on his ability to pilot the British economy away from high inflation and unemployment upon taking office, and the ERM was the centerpiece of his economic policy. After Black Wednesday, Major's premiership was dominated by struggles to maintain support in the parliamentary party and the Cabinet. This robbed him of any authority to negotiate seriously with France and Germany regarding such pressing issues as institutional reform of the European Union, the development of a European security identity, and joint responses to the challenges of globalization. A few examples bear this out.

The first sign of difficulty came with the ratification of the Maastricht Treaty. Major won a very narrow victory early in the ratification process when euroskeptic Conservative M.P.s joined with the opposition Labour Party to vote against the treaty on November 4, 1993. Fearing that his thin majority might temporarily collapse and halt the treaty's progress through the legislature, Major delayed its consideration by Parliament until after the Danish referendum scheduled for May 1993. Labour exploited Major's weak position by threatening to vote against the treaty unless the government signed on to the social charter agreed to in Maastricht, while perhaps two dozen euroskeptic Conservative M.P.s seemed likely to vote against the treaty as well. Labour and the euroskeptics used every trick in the parliamentary rulebook to embarrass Major, who managed to have the Commons ratify the treaty in August 1993 only after a vote of confidence in his government.

Euroskeptic criticism of Major led him to adopt unreasonable positions on other issues during the 1990s. The first was the planned enlargement of the European Union to Austria, Finland, Sweden, and Norway. The Major government had long supported this step toward "widening" the European Union with an eye toward restricting its future supranational development. Prior to this enlargement, a group of member-states needed to assemble 23 weighted votes to block the adoption of new legislation under the system of qualified majority voting (QMV) used in the European Union's Council of Ministers. Enlargement meant granting additional votes to the new member-states and, logically, raising the "blocking minority" needed to stop the passage of legislation. All of the member-states except Britain and Spain agreed to accommodate enlargement by increasing the blocking minority to 27 votes without changing the allocation of weighted votes among current member-states. Major chose this somewhat obscure issue to cast himself as the defender of British "sovereignty," threatening to veto enlargement unless the existing minority of 23 votes was retained. He was under pressure from both ends of his party. The euroskeptics were adamant that enlargement not reduce Britain's weight in the European Union, and had Michael Portillo hovering in the wings as a potential challenger in case Major failed to win agreement from other governments. At the same time, prominent pro-European Tories agitated for a more conciliatory position and circulated rumors that Chancellor Kenneth Clarke and Minister of Trade and Industry Michael Heseltine might challenge Major's position as prime minister. Major sent Foreign Secretary Douglas Hurd—himself a committed European—to negotiate a fudge in which the Council of Ministers would do "all in its power" to reach a compromise when faced with a minority of between 23 and 26 votes. The nomination of the successor to Jacques Delors as president of the European Commission also became mired in domestic British politics. Before Delors' term expired at the end of 1994, the French and German governments selected Belgian Prime Minister Jean-Luc Dehaene as their candidate for the job. Every member-state except Britain accepted the Franco-German candidate, albeit reluctantly in some cases. Major vetoed the deal in an attempt to "score political points by caricaturing Dehaene as a rabid Eurofederalist." Two weeks later Major agreed to select Jacques Santer as the Commission's new president despite the fact that that his political views differed very little from those of Dehaene.

British beef proved to be another distraction from the business of being at the very heart of Europe. The European Union imposed a worldwide ban on British beef exports shortly after a government scientific panel announced in March 1996 that there might be a link between a disease common among British cattle, Bovine Spongiform Encephalopathy, and Creutzfeldt-Jacob disease in humans. Major objected to the ban and implemented a policy of "noncooperation" in which Britain would veto all measures in the Council of Ministers that required unanimous support (including many proposals that the British government had long favored). When other member-states objected to these tactics and refused to drop the export ban, Major was forced to relent and the others agreed to gradually lift the ban as part of a large-scale cattle slaughter program.

What Revolution? Blair and the Franco-German Partnership

By the time the British government began preparing for the general election that would be held in 1997, the Conservative Party was at war with itself over Europe. Sir James Goldsmith organized the anti-Europe Referendum Party that threatened to steal votes from the Conservatives; and there were rumors that, to the delight of Labour's election organizers, up to two hundred Conservative candidates would contradict the Major government's "wait and see" attitude and openly oppose British entry into economic and monetary union. Combined with the recent history of British obstinacy, these divisions made Chirac in France and Kohl in Germany reluctant to engage Major on important issues, and they ensured that the intergovernmental conference aimed at reforming the European Union's institutions would not be completed until after the 1997 general election. Both leaders expected that the Labour Party would win this election and take a much more conciliatory view of their priorities. The reality has been quite different. Whereas one of the architects of Labour's electoral revival promised that the Blair government would begin a "revolution" in British politics and policy, in practice its positions on many European questions have been quite similar to those of Major. This is particularly clear for two of France and Germany's top priorities in the 1990s: the successful move to full monetary union, and coordinated efforts to combat unemployment. The Blair government's relationship with the Franco-German partnership has been changed only in the area of foreign and security policy.

Monetary Union

"Black Wednesday" had a powerful influence on subsequent economic policy and the attitudes of the Conservative and Labour Parties toward the pro-

ject of monetary union. Sterling's ejection from the ERM led Major and Lamont to abandon any effort at monetary policy coordination in Europe, and
instead to reduce interest rates aggressively to promote economic growth
(and the government's popularity).[4] By January 1993, interest rates had been
cut from 10 percent to 6 percent. Despite comments from Major that there
were "fault lines" in the ERM that needed to be corrected, the British did
not present any detailed plans to reform the mechanism and evinced little
enthusiasm for rejoining.[5]

Other European countries maintained their commitment to monetary
union by reducing fiscal deficits and establishing the predecessor of the European Central Bank during the mid-1990s. The Major government ob-
served these steps from the sidelines in the conviction that monetary union
would not start on time or that it would collapse quickly. The British developed a new paradigm for monetary policy that gave little attention to the relationship between sterling and Europe's other important currencies, the
franc and the mark. The government announced that it would target the inflation rate with the intention of keeping the rate of increases in consumer
prices (excluding mortgage interest rates) below 2.5 percent by the end of
the sitting Parliament in 1997. The Blair government immediately strengthened this orientation toward domestic stabilization; one of the first actions
of Prime Minister Tony Blair and Chancellor Gordon Brown was to grant
full independence to the Bank of England. On May 6, Brown announced
the creation of a Monetary Policy Committee made up of Bank of England
officials and outside experts that would have authority to control interest
rate policy in order to achieve the new government's inflation target of 2.5
percent. This shift had little to do with the development of monetary union,
although it occurred less than a year before most other EU member-states
agreed to create an independent but supranational European Central Bank
to manage the single currency. Although the Labour government was now
convinced of the merits of central bank independence, it was unwilling to
achieve this goal through international cooperation. Instead, its ministers
preferred to give up control over interest rate policy to the domestic central
bank, which would be responsible for meeting a domestic inflation target
rather than pursuing exchange-rate stability.[6]

From Maastricht onward, Major made it clear that his government would
likely exercise the opt-out clause in the treaty that allowed Britain not to participate in monetary union even if the country met the convergence criteria.
Yet Major was reluctant to commit himself to never joining the euro at any
time in the future. Instead he argued for a "wait and see" policy that involved
tracking the development of the single currency and its influence upon
Britain's place in Europe. This was insufficient for the euroskeptics, who first
called upon Major to declare in mid-1996 that, if reelected in 1997, he

would organize a referendum before joining. Major duly acquiesced. The next year the euroskeptics escalated their demands and called for a commitment from Major *not* to join monetary union; as Hugo Young puts it, during this period, "There was no week when this question failed to intrude upon the life, and dominate the manoeuvres, of the grimly tormented figure in 10 Downing Street."[7]

The Labour government elected in May 1997 portrayed itself as more pragmatic on the issue of participation in monetary union, holding that it would base a decision on a "hard-headed assessment of Britain's economic interests" rather than ideological opposition to further European integration. But recognizing that the issue was not popular among the public and some rank-and-file and senior members of the Labour Party, the Blair government moved very cautiously on the issue and never made a straightforward argument for British participation in the single currency. Instead it laid out a series of challenging political and economic hurdles that would have to be cleared first. Labour would consider joining monetary union only after it passed five economic tests: the British and European business cycles would have to be synchronized; monetary union would need to have a positive influence on employment, international investment, and British financial firms; and there would have to be sufficient labor market flexibility for member-states to respond to unforeseen economic shocks. In addition to these economic tests, a decision to move to monetary union would have to receive political approval from the Cabinet, Parliament, and the electorate in a referendum. After taking office the Blair government stated that it favored joining the single currency "in principle," but probably would not seek to do so until after the next general election in 2002.

By late 1999 the Labour Party had united around the idea of holding a referendum on monetary union early in the next Parliament if the government's five economic tests were met. Blair also agreed to sponsor, along with pro-European Conservative politicians Michael Heseltine and Kenneth Clarke and the leader of the Liberal Democrats, Charles Kennedy, the launch of the business-lobbying group Britain in Europe, although only after it promised not to campaign openly for participation in monetary union and instead to stress the benefits to Britain of membership in the European Union.[8] This formula has created a number of ways for Labour to avoid serious consideration of monetary union well into the future. None of the five economic "tests" is stated very precisely; it is not clear, for example, how one would know that monetary union would have a "positive" effect on employment or investment, or how to measure labor market flexibility and short-term economic cycles with any degree of precision. Requiring the electorate to approve monetary union in a referendum also makes it possible for the government to delay a decision on the grounds that it did not want to risk an electoral failure.

Some of the potential political effects to Britain of staying out of monetary union were evident even before the euro was introduced in January 1999. In the mid-1990s French politicians began calling for the creation of a Euro Council consisting of finance ministers only from member-states adopting the single currency. The Euro Council would oversee implementation of the Stability Pact governing fiscal policy and be responsible for formulating external exchange-rate policy, coordinating fiscal policy, and serving as a political counterweight to the European Central Bank by advising it on monetary policy. To the Germans this request looked like a revival of French demands during the negotiation of the Maastricht Treaty for an "economic government" that might threaten price stability and central bank independence. Bundesbank and German government officials refused to endorse the French ideas until March 1997, when they won a series of important concessions, including these: the Euro Council would be an informal, consultative body not subject to the European Union's regular decision-making procedures; it would not discuss monetary policy or impinge on the independence of the European Central Bank; and political responsibility for exchange-rate policy would remain with the full Ecofin Council.

But after reaching agreement among themselves, the French and Germans had difficulty securing formal European Union approval for the informal Euro Council. The four member-states unlikely to participate in full monetary union from the beginning—Britain, Denmark, Greece, and Sweden—opposed creating a Euro Council limited only to countries adopting the single currency, fearing that it might in effect take over from the full Ecofin group. The compromise reached at the Luxembourg Summit in late 1997 held that Ecofin would remain the sole formal decision-making body, but that the Euro Council could invite other member-states to its discussions that concerned "matters of common interest." Although German demands have made the Euro Council much weaker and more informal than the French would have liked, it is still possible that the body could become the nucleus of closer economic policy coordination and, by facilitating negotiations among members of the euro zone, allow them to present a united front when meeting with Britain and the other three monetary union "outs" in the full Ecofin council.

Fearing that these "outs" might unilaterally devalue their currencies and undercut the competitiveness of firms in the euro zone, the French and German governments began negotiations in 1996 over a new exchange rate mechanism intended to link these currencies to the euro.[9] The British objected to this presumption that the monetary union "outs" would be expected to synchronize their economic policies with those of the euro zone. They also feared that the creation of a new ERM would require them to abide by the Maastricht Treaty's convergence criterion that member-states participate in the ERM for two years before adopting the single currency. The first concern was met when the other member-states agreed that participation in the new ERM would be voluntary, but the second remains unresolved. The British argue that the widening of the ERM fluctuation bands in August 1993 from 2.25 to 15 percent essentially did away with the ERM, and that the criterion therefore would not be applicable should Britain apply to join monetary union. Most other member-states, as well as the European Commission, hold that the treaty provision applies to the new ERM, therefore requiring British participation for two years before joining monetary union.

European Security

The Major government's perspective on questions of European security differed in important ways from those of French and German governments. The Germans and especially the French felt that the threats to European security after the Cold War required stronger European security institutions and the transfer of some authority from the North Atlantic Treaty Organization (NATO) to the European Union. France favored a greater role for strictly European security institutions, to forestall unilateral foreign policy choices in Bonn and to enhance French influence by excluding the Americans.[10] The Kohl government in Germany had a different set of interests that complemented the French program for European security. Germany's principal security concerns lay in Eastern Europe, where ethnic conflict and economic difficulties threatened Germany with economic migrants, refugees, and demands for political and military intervention in local conflicts. A European security identity would provide a multilateral forum through which Germany and other states could intervene to prevent or manage such conflicts. Stronger European security institutions consistent with continued membership in NATO also would reassure other states that Germany would not pursue a unilateral foreign policy.

Although British officials initially reacted with concern to the prospect of German reunification in 1990, they soon concluded that the end of the Cold War greatly reduced the threats to British security. This made them reluctant to cede freedom of maneuver over security, and especially military policy, to European institutions. Instead, the Major government stressed the importance of maintaining and revitalizing the NATO alliance. A stronger NATO with a new, post–Cold War mission would help keep the United States involved in European security and could prevent an erosion of Britain's "special relationship" with America.[11]

Major did acknowledge that limited and carefully constructed European institutions could supplement the Atlantic alliance. The unwillingness of the

Clinton administration to resolve the war in Bosnia until 1995, and the willingness of American congressional leaders to contemplate lifting the arms embargo on states in the former Yugoslavia and thereby endanger British peacekeeping troops, led the British to conclude that the United States might be unwilling or unable to involve itself in future European conflicts. The British view was that, in such circumstances, European countries should be prepared to cooperate among themselves through a strengthened Western European Union (WEU). Nonetheless Major (supported by the Danish and neutral member-states) opposed the French desire to incorporate the WEU into the European Union, preferring to preserve the former institution's strictly intergovernmental character. The Amsterdam Treaty signed in mid-1997 did not decide this issue and spoke only of "the possibility of the integration of the WEU into the EU."

Their general unwillingness to strengthen European security institutions also made the British reluctant to adopt the French and German preferences for making the European Union's common foreign and security policy (CFSP) more effective. During the intergovernmental conference of 1996–1997, the British argued for retaining unanimity when making major CFSP decisions. Kohl held that qualified majority voting should become the norm for decisions on implementing CFSP decisions, while consensus should be the normal decision-making rule when the European Council dealt with more important issues. The Germans felt that unanimity would render CFSP useless since there likely would always be one state that opposed a particular action, and that this problem would become more pressing with the enlargement of the EU in 1995 to include the neutral countries of Sweden, Finland, and Austria. The Major government held that further modifications to the CFSP decision-making procedures agreed on in the Maastricht Treaty were unnecessary, since existing procedures urged (but did not require) states not to block a policy that had support from a majority of member-states. The British instead advocated that member-states decide on participation in military tasks other than collective defense (handled, of course, through NATO) on a "case-by-case basis."[12] The final compromise struck at Amsterdam institutionalized the principle of "constructive abstention," according to which a member-state unwilling to support a CFSP action would allow others to do so.

The Blair government abandoned this caution, at least at the level of principle. Initially the new government's attitude was similar to that of the Conservatives; the party's 1997 election manifesto promised that "[o]ur security will continue to be based on NATO." New Labour was interested in greater European security cooperation with France and Germany for at least three reasons. First, the government realized that the United States might not be willing to use force to counter security threats that the European states considered dangerous. Second, Europe was too reliant on American aircraft and sophisticated weaponry, military transport, and intelligence capabilities to be able to respond to even minor crises effectively. This became clear as early as the fall of 1998, when NATO threatened to bomb Yugoslavia for its crackdown on Kosovo Albanians. British officials estimated that the United States would have provided two-thirds of the aircraft even though the European members of NATO collectively accounted for sixty percent of the alliance's population and uniformed personnel.[13] These predictions were borne out in the NATO-led bombing campaign that began in early 1999. Third, security and defense policy was an area in which the British could take the lead, given their relatively large and mobile forces. This allowed the Blair government to successfully maintain Major's policy that the development of a European security and defense capability would not come at the expense of participation in NATO.

All of these developments led the government to play a leading role in the debate over Europe's defense capability. The first step was an agreement with France at the bilateral summit meeting in Saint-Malo in December 1998. The two governments agreed that "the European Union needs to be in a position to play its full role on the international stage . . . [and] decide on the progressive framing of a common defense policy . . . the Union must have the capacity for autonomous action, backed up by credible military forces . . . in order to respond to international crises." This forthright statement in favor of a European defense identity was hedged with qualifications about the relationship to NATO, however. At the insistence of the British, future institutional developments would have to be "in conformity with our respective obligations in NATO," while the French demanded that "the different situations of countries in relation to NATO must be respected."[14]

The resolution also left a number of questions unanswered. For example, as of early 2000, Chirac continued to advocate incorporating the WEU into the European Union while Blair was only willing to discuss this step and emphasized that any future developments must not weaken NATO.[15] No doubt these and other topics will be widely debated and subject to bargaining in the near future. Nonetheless the Saint-Malo declaration will likely form the basis of such discussions, particularly because Chirac and Blair stressed the importance of incorporating other states, especially Germany, into the arrangements. And by mid-1999 there did seem to be some progress on the question of European security cooperation. The Cologne Summit of the European Council in June affirmed many of the goals laid out at Saint-Malo, and stressed the need to develop new consultative bodies within the European Union to handle defense questions and to work to strengthen the member-states' ability to coordinate the development of forces that could be deployed quickly to respond to crises.[16]

Globalization, Unemployment, and Social Policy

New Labour's approach to social and economic policies differs quite dramatically from that of earlier Labour governments. As Colin Hay and Matthew Watson demonstrate, New Labour justifies these differences in the language of globalization. The globalization of economic activity is said to place strong constraints on the success of "Old Labour" priorities of active macroeconomic policies, state intervention and ownership, and supporting trade union demands. New Labour holds that a reputation for keeping inflation low is a prerequisite for economic stability and attracting investment to Britain, and it therefore granted the Bank of England operational independence when implementing monetary policy. The government sees its role as ensuring that markets function efficiently, rather than as intervening in the decision-making processes of firms. This means that public policy needs to focus on promoting competition and upgrading the country's physical and human resources through spending on education, training, and public investment. New Labour also emphasizes its conception of the role of the government in the labor market. Here the key is "flexibility"—which in practice involves forging a much closer relationship with business, keeping the trade unions at a distance by reducing their influence within the party, and retaining most of the anti-union labor market laws passed during the Thatcher and Major governments.[17]

The Blair government emphasizes not only its break with past Labour priorities in Britain but also stresses to its European partners the superiority of such "third way" thinking. Germany has been the focus of this proselytizing; the French Socialist government has been seen as hopelessly interventionist. Shortly after the 1997 general election, Blair criticized Prime Minister Lionel Jospin's plea for centralized European policies on unemployment as hopelessly out of date with the realities of the new, globalized economy. Blair then went on to declare after the Amsterdam Summit of June 1997 that his Third Way program was a viable solution to the continent's problems of persistently high unemployment: "We have shown that alongside low inflation and sound public finances, Europe needs a new approach to employment and growth, based on British ideas for competitiveness, including more flexible labor markets."

Particularly since the election of Chancellor Gerhard Schröder, Germany has seemed to the British a much more promising partner than France for developing a pan-European solution to the problems of globalization. Before his election in 1998, Schröder created a public image and platform for the Social Democratic Party similar to that of Blair and New Labour, emphasizing the importance of "die neue Mitte" and policies that included cuts to corporate tax rates and welfare state reform. A close aide to Schröder, Bodo Hombach, published a book shortly after the 1998 election that called for tax cuts, reducing the role of the state in the economy, and substantial changes to Germany's system of extensive social welfare payments.[18]

The rhetorical similarity between Schröder and Blair culminated in a joint manifesto, "Europe: The Third Way/Die Neue Mitte," issued in June 1999. The manifesto closely followed the New Labour program in stressing the constraints that globalization imposed on national economic and social policies, and the importance of promoting labor market flexibility and of encouraging enterprise. Schröder and Blair emphasized that European economies would be able to address the problems of unemployment and expensive welfare states only by reducing the tax burden, redirecting public spending toward training and education, introducing structural reforms to social security systems, and lifting costly regulations that inhibit innovation, growth, and trade.

Two things are interesting to note about the consensus captured in this manifesto. First, New Labour's policy actions bear a remarkable similarity to those of its Conservative predecessors; it was the Thatcher and Major governments that started focusing on low inflation, reducing subsidies, deregulation, privatizing state-owned firms, and granting some independence to the Bank of England. The Major government stressed the importance of labor market flexibility as far back as 1990, and successfully insisted that the Maastricht Treaty at least mention its importance for a successful monetary union. Second, as Hay and Watson have described, the influence of globalization on the British economy is more rhetoric than reality.[19] This skepticism about the impact of globalization is reinforced by a number of recent academic studies that conclude that national patterns of production are quite resistant to pressures for change from globalization.[20]

Both of these factors make it difficult for the Blair government to forge a consensus with its European partners over how to manage their economic and social policies. Despite rhetoric about the importance of social inclusion, the economic policies that New Labour has implemented to date remain almost as far from the center of continental practices and concerns as were those of Thatcher and Major. For example, while Schröder stresses that his government marks a break with past Social Democratic policies, even before his election in 1998 some major policy pronouncements were diametrically opposed to New Labour's ideas. Schröder stressed the creation of an "alliance of jobs" between the government, labor unions, and employers, which sounds to British ears suspiciously like tripartism and corporatism. This language also found its way into the joint manifesto, where it sits uncomfortably alongside calls for greater flexibility and social security reform. Assuming that he is committed to the ideas expressed in the manifesto, Schröder will have a much more difficult time than Blair in turning them into reality. Tony Blair commands an overwhelming majority in the House of Commons and has proven quite ruthless in stifling dissent within the Labour Party. Schröder, in contrast, must share power in coalition with the Greens and depends on the Länder governments—some controlled by the Christian Democrats—to approve and implement many policies. His principles also have attracted strong opposition from within the Social Democratic Party and its allies. Schröder's first finance minister, Oskar Lafontaine, resigned in part to protest the chancellor's conversion to neoliberal orthodoxy. More problematic is the fact that the labor movement treats the call for "die neue Mitte" with suspicion. Dieter Schulte, head of the DGB (the German umbrella trade union), was quick to point out that the British and German economies differed in important ways and that one economic ideology might not work in both countries. Unlike Britain, Germany has a productive and export-oriented manufacturing sector that could afford higher wages and social charges as long as government and employers promote productivity and investment. Poor showings in the European parliamentary elections and a string of state contests in 1999 did nothing to increase confidence in Schröder's ability to engineer dramatic policy changes. By October, Schröder admitted that his failure to debate these issues within the Social Democratic Party before issuing the joint manifesto was a mistake; and Franz Muntefering, recently appointed as general secretary of the party, announced that the paper had no "direct concrete consequences" for government policy.[21]

Conclusions and Prospects

Britain has not shared many of the concerns of France and Germany despite its change of government in 1997. Both the Major and Blair governments remained on the sidelines as France, Germany, and nine other European Union member-states adopted the single currency and European Central Bank in 1999. The Blair government has pledged not to consider joining monetary union until after the next election, and even then may fail to do so if the move is opposed by British voters. Failure to join soon may have a damaging effect on Britain's influence and reputation in Europe in a number of ways. First, it is possible that the monetary union "ins"—France and Germany in particular—will see each other as natural partners for further integrative steps in related areas, such as fiscal policy. Of course it has always been the case that France and Germany have turned first to each other and then to Britain, and the possibility of Britain's opting out of monetary union has been a possibility since the finalization of the Maastricht Treaty in 1991. But now that the possibility of self-exclusion from monetary union has become a reality, British leaders may have an even harder time trying to convince their French and German counterparts that their desire to play a leading role in Europe is more than rhetoric.

Britain has also remained out of step with its European partners regarding the appropriate responses to unemployment and globalization. British governments of left and right have emphasized eliminating budget deficits, keeping inflation low, and promoting flexible labor markets. German and especially French governments adhere more closely to the traditional social-policy priorities of the Socialist and Christian Democratic parties. To date these differences have not had much practical effect on the European Union since most social policies remain the responsibility of national governments, and European pronouncements in this policy area have often remained earnest but unfulfilled avowals to take action. Differences in national welfare states will not disappear anytime soon, but if the French and Germans were to agree on a common continental model for tackling unemployment they likely would provoke a hostile reaction from Britain regardless of which party is in power.

The one important exception concerns security policy coordination in Europe. Here New Labour has taken a much more positive attitude than its predecessor by showing a willingness to discuss creating a genuine European component of the NATO alliance that could operate independently of the United States. This has created a great deal of excitement on the European continent, where it is recognized that Britain's military posture, along with that of France, could play a leading role in giving substance to a European security and defense identity.

Yet even here the Blair government moves cautiously and is not willing to commit itself to discussing a wholesale revamping of Europe's security institutions. The common factor that ties together Blair's attitude toward the single currency, social policy, and security cooperation is the hysterical attitude toward Europe demonstrated by the British press and a small fraction of the political class. Blair knows that British voters, trade unions, and business firms do not share these groups' extreme positions on such matters as withdrawal from the European Union, although they may have doubts about the desirability of a single currency. But Blair moves very cautiously on European questions out of fear of repeating Major's experience, in which these issues split and paralyzed the governing party for five years. The irony is that the Blair government, with an overwhelming majority in the Commons and broad popular support from voters, has few of the characteristics that weakened its predecessor.

Notes

1. Speech to the Konrad Adenauer Stiftung, Bonn, March 11, 1991.
2. Quoted in Paul Anderson and Nyta Mann, *Safety First: The Making of New Labour* (London: Granta 1997), p. 133.
3. Philip Stephens, *Politics and the Pound* (London: Picador 1996); James I. Walsh, *European Monetary Integration and Domestic Politics* (Boulder: Lynne Rienner 2000), pp. 120–124.
4. The government continued to support observing the Maastricht treaty's convergence criteria for fiscal policy, arguing that they were consistent with its goals of reducing public spending and debt in Britain and Europe. Interview with senior Treasury official, London, March 1995.
5. Conseil des Communautes Europeenes, "1604ème session du Conseil Economie/Finances," 8854/92, Brussels, September 28, 1992.
6. Walsh, *European Monetary Integration and Domestic Politics,* p. 163.
7. Hugo Young, *This Blessed plot: Britain and Europe from Churchill to Blair* (London: Macmillan 1998), p. 465.
8. "Joining Euro is 'Patriotic,' Insists Blair," *Independent* October 15, 1999, and Robert Peston, "Labour Leaders Unite Over Euro Entry," *Financial Times,* September 27, 1999.
9. *Financial Times,* March 29, 1996, p. 8.
10. *Livre blanc sur la défense* (Paris: Union Générale d'Éditions 1994) and David Yost, "France and West European Defense Identity," *Survival* 33 (1991), pp. 327–351.
11. *A Partnership of Nations: The British Approach to the European Union Intergovernmental Conference 1996* (London: Foreign and Commonwealth Office 1996), and Louise Richardson, "British State Strategies after the Cold War," in: *After the Cold War: International Institutions and State Strategies in Europe, 1989–1991,* eds. Robert O. Keohane, Joseph S. Nye, and Stanley Hoffmann (Cambridge: Harvard University Press 1993), pp. 148–169.
12. Foreign and Commonwealth Office, *A Partnership of Nations,* p. 36.
13. Richard Norton-Taylor, "Anglo-French Defense Links," *Guardian,* December 3, 1998.
14. Foreign and Commonwealth Office, "Joint Declaration Issued at the British-French Summit, Saint-Malo, France," (London: Foreign and Commonwealth Office December 4, 1998).
15. Norton-Taylor, "Anglo-France Defense Links," and Jill Sherman, "Britain Tries to Strengthen Relationship with France," *The Times,* December 4, 1998.
16. European Council, "Presidency Conclusions, Cologne European Summit, Annex III: Presidency Report on Strengthening of the Common European Policy on Security and Defense," (Brussels: European Council June 4, 1999).
17. Colin Hay and Matthew Watson, "Rendering the Contingent Necessary: New Labour's Neo-Liberal Conversion and the Discourse of Globalisation," paper prepared for the Annual Meeting of the American Political Science Association, Boston, September 1998; see also Joel Kreiger, *British Politics in*

the *Global Age: Can Social Democracy Survive?* (New York: Oxford University Press), pp. 20–23.

18. Leon Mangasarian, "Is This the Real Schröder?" *Deutsche Press-Agentur,* October 8, 1998.

19. Hay and Watson, "Rendering the Contingent Necessary."

20. Suzanne Berger and Robert Dore, eds., *National Diversity and Global Capitalism* (Ithaca, NY: Cornell University Press 1996), Geoffrey Garrett, *Partisan Politics and the Global Economy* (New York: Cambridge University Press 1998), and J. Rogers Hollingsworth and Robert Boyer, eds., *Contemporary Capitalism: The Embeddedness of Institutions* (New York: Cambridge University Press 1997).

21. Robert Taylor and Ralph Atkins, "Schröder Attacked by Union Chief," *Financial Times,* July 1, 1999.

Chapter 9 ❧

Old Bones for New Bodies: The Geopolitics of Franco-German Europe

David Calleo

Introduction: Back to the Future?

Germany's unification, together with the disintegration of the Soviet Union, marked the end of Europe's postwar era. Those entrapped within the "evil empire" greeted its collapse with joy. But in the West, at least, joy over the end of the bipolar system was tempered by fear of returning to what had preceded it.

In the first half of the twentieth century, Europe's traditional state system had revealed itself to be murderously unstable. This instability, combined with modern armaments and the techniques of totalitarian control, had threatened to destroy Europe and much of the rest of the world besides. The solution after World War II was to import two outside "superpowers" to partition Europe between them. That external dominion was doubtless a galling experience for some Europeans, but it was a better fate than yet another European war. The collapse of the bipolar order raised the prospect that Europe's state system might once more be on its own. The question was whether it would prove as unstable as before.

The Old German Problem

Europe's historic instability arose from the crowded coexistence of several gifted and ambitious peoples, who were mobilized in nation-states. Much of

Europe's history has been a repeated cycle of wars provoked by the hegemonic ambitions of one indigenous great power or another. By the later nineteenth century, Germany had become the principal pretender to European hegemony. The instability of the European state system became identified with its "German Problem."

For the rest of Europe, Imperial Germany was too big, too dynamic economically, too ambitious, too authoritarian, too militaristic, and too unstable. Needless to say, the behavior of the Germans under the Nazis confirmed and augmented these fears. Many historical analysts have tied the aggressive and unstable aspects of German behavior to pathological features of German geography, history, and culture. "Realist" analysts, however, are inclined to find more general and prosaic explanations for the so-called German Problem. For them, it has less to do with the special faults of the Germans than with general European geopolitics. Bismarck's Germany, with its late-developing but dynamic economy, was too big, new, inconvenient, and threatening for the rest of Europe. Germany's neighbors were bound to ally against it. Bismarck's Germany was born encircled. His "nightmare of coalitions" was a realistic expectation of the way other nations in Europe's crowded state system would probably react to Germany's strength.[1]

In the Realist perspective, Germany's principal enemy, France, was similarly trapped by geopolitics: As the French saw things, if Germany were not contained by a hostile coalition, it would be bound to dominate Europe, France included. To survive, the French made it their vocation to create an anti-German alliance. They succeeded in World War I, but at a terrible cost to themselves and their allies, as well as to the Germans. Victory brought only temporary relief. The French had hoped to confirm Germany's defeat by bringing in the Americans as Europe's external balancer—a role that the Americans soon abandoned, together with the League of Nations. The French lost not only their new ally, the United States, but their primordial continental ally, Russia, which had descended into its long communist nightmare and was unavailable for the old anti-German strategy. Meanwhile Britain was flirting with appeasement, while Italy was in the hands of a dictatorial regime with diffuse resentments and designs, mostly to be achieved at France's expense. More than ever, France seemed doomed to be dominated by Germany.

It was in these circumstances that the French turned to a radical alternative—*Paneuropa*—a project to reconstruct the European state system into a confederacy led by France and Germany together. The project's geopolitical rationale was laid out and tirelessly promoted by an influential Hungarian diplomat, Count Richard Coudenhove Kalergi.[2] According to Coudenhove, Europe's traditional state system condemned it to recurring rounds of increasingly destructive warfare. As a result, Europe's states were almost certain to lose their place in the evolving global system, and indeed to lose their own political and economic self-determination. The solution was a confederacy led by France and Germany together.

For a few years in the 1920s, the French and German foreign ministers, Aristide Briand and Gustav Stresemann, worked to foster a new partnership.[3] But neither country could ignore its own competitive geopolitical imperatives sufficiently to make the partnership durable. Germany, for example, was willing to renounce territorial claims against France and the other Western neighbors, but not to give up its lost territories in the East. More fundamentally, the collapse of the Austro-Hungarian Empire, as well as the alienation of the Soviet Union from the West, meant that Germany's national ambitions in the East could not easily stop short of the old vision of Germanic Mittel-Europa. Achieving that vision meant not only a very large Germany but seemed to ensure the eclipse of France, for it implied German hegemony over all of Europe regardless of whatever agreements were meanwhile made in the West with France. With basic geopolitical relations even more radically unbalanced after World War I than before, the old antagonisms reasserted themselves and Europe began preparing for another round of fratricidal war. To counteract the German threat, the French tried to cultivate the new states of Eastern Europe and the British, as well as to build up their overseas empire. But the French now held a weak hand. The expedients available were inadequate to replace Russia, America, and Italy as allies. Britain itself was an uncertain friend.

Events in the 1930s followed their predictable geopolitical course, except that the prospect of German hegemony grew all the more sinister thanks to the vicious lunacy added to it by the Nazis. Not only was French independence at stake, but also the liberal and humane values that France had championed in Europe since the Enlightenment and the Revolution. World War II was a great catastrophe for France and for Europe, as the French knew it would be. They themselves were rescued only by a series of miracles—the belated heroism of the British after Dunkirk, Hitler's attack on Soviet Russia and the unexpectedly tenacious resistance that followed, and the eventual awakening of the Americans; and later, Charles de Gaulle's political sorcery that partially rescued French honor and morale.

The Postwar Solution:
Franco-German Hegemony Inside a Tripolar Europe

Postwar French policy set out to reverse the fundamentally unfavorable geopolitical conditions that had led to World War II, and to France's defeat in 1940. The French joined with the British in promoting NATO, and the American protectorate that was its essence—not only to keep the Russians at bay but also to suppress the Germans. In other words, the Cold War was used to resolve the traditional German Problem. The American protectorate in NATO precluded any serious military threat to France—from either the Soviets or the Germans. Nevertheless, France soon chafed at American hegemony, mistrusted its reliability and durability, and began working for a more "European" solution. Early in the postwar era, the "father" of European integration, Jean Monnet, and soon thereafter General de Gaulle, resurrected the old project of *Paneuropa*. French policy found a willing ally in Germany's great postwar leader, Konrad Adenauer. Like Stresemann, although with more conviction, Adenauer used the project of a European confederacy to regain defeated Germany's sovereignty.[4] Unlike Stresemann, however, Adenauer did not vigorously pursue Germany's old ambitions in the East. He was inhibited not only by his own pro-Western inclinations, but by the Soviet occupation of East Germany and most of Mittel-Europa, as well as by the Federal Republic's own Western allies. In effect, the conditions set by the Cold War gave *Paneuropa*'s confederal strategy much improved chances for success. German aggressiveness was doubly contained. So long as the Cold War framework continued, the old German Problem existed only in the future. Meanwhile, France and Adenauer's Germany found it easy to collaborate in building and leading a continental community, because—among other things—NATO made it unnecessary for that community to assume military responsibilities.

There was, to be sure, still a German Problem—"reunification." Resolving that new German Problem threatened, of course, to restore the old, big Germany. But nothing would happen so long as Europe was bipolar, and the bipolar structure seemed to have a long future ahead of it. The Soviet regime seemed firmly rooted in Russia and its leaders sufficiently powerful and ruthless to preserve the Soviet East European empire. And in spite of various transatlantic strategic and burden-sharing quarrels, the Western Alliance seemed even more firmly implanted. In short, German reunification and, with it, resurrection of the old German Problem, seemed a remote worry.

A much more immediate concern lay in the penetration of Europe's markets and industries by the giant American economy, together with the growing European and international monetary disorder that Europeans tended to blame on the Americans. These pressures pushed West Europeans to build an economic bloc to give themselves the scale and weight needed to compete with the Americans. The European Union, led by France and Germany, grew into an economic superpower, while remaining an American military protectorate. This was the grand transatlantic compromise of the Cold War. It allowed Europe to be both America's protectorate and its own confederacy. The compromise worked surprisingly well, despite a growing agenda of transatlantic quarrels and grievances. Its success was owed, above all, to the

Soviets—who provided the common threat needed to secure American protection, limit American and European disagreements, foster Franco-German partnership and, with it, West European unity. In effect, postwar Europe rested on a tripolar balance.

The Soviet Shock and the European Reaction: Maastricht

The unexpected sudden collapse of the Soviet Union naturally ended this tripolar balance and thereby severely challenged the two poles that remained. How, for example, was American military hegemony to be justified without a Soviet threat? Or how was Franco-German partnership to continue, now that Germany was reunited, Russia weak, and Eastern Europe wide open? How were NATO and the EU to fit together within the new Pan-European space? Recognition of these challenges prompted the French and German leaders of the time, François Mitterrand and Helmut Kohl, to press for major new steps toward European integration, sketched in the Maastricht Treaty of 1992.[5] The first fruit of their joint strategy was European Economic and Monetary Union (EMU)—a project that advanced Europe's economic integration without directly challenging the American military protectorate. But Maastricht's other major project— Common Foreign and Security Policy (CFSP)—implied major changes in NATO that pointed toward ending American management of European security problems. It implied returning to a European system that was once more autonomous.[6]

By the end of the 1990's, EMU seemed well on its way, but the success of CFSP was far from certain. Many European leaders were reluctant to part with the comforts of the American protectorate. NATO was bolstered by a large military and civilian bureaucracy related to it, in both Europe and the United States, as well as by large academic, commercial, and industrial interests.

American Triumphalism

Not surprisingly, American elites grew bemused by the idea of a "unipolar" world order, with the United States as the "indispensable" superpower. But with the decisive defeat of George Bush in the presidential elections of 1992, the population as a whole seemed to turn its back on these "triumphalist" enthusiasms in favor of repairing the country's serious fiscal crisis and addressing neglected domestic issues. Accordingly, the Congress cut the military budget severely—by roughly a third in real terms in the 1990s.[7] Given this large peace dividend, America's fiscal problems rapidly disappeared and the economy began to blossom.

America's economic success stood in painful contrast to conditions in Western Europe. During the Cold War, most European governments had spent much less of their national income on defense than had the Americans and therefore were not in the same position to reap a fiscal benefit from the peace. Europe's fiscal problems stemmed from bloated welfare states, from which the end of the Cold War offered no particular relief. Meanwhile, the economic problems imposed upon Europe by the costs and financing of German reunification, together with meeting the criteria for EMU, meant that Europe in the 1990s suffered from relatively stagnant economic growth combined with very high unemployment.

As the decade proceeded, America's success juxtaposed with Europe's difficulties came to revive American triumphalism. Ironically, the shift occurred within the Clinton administration itself—whose election in 1992 had seemed to signal the public's lack of interest in the triumphalist agenda. The administration's domestic weakness, with the President impeached in 1998 (although he remained in office and retained his influence), had strengthened its enthusiasm for external assertion. It also made it easier for parochial domestic interests, as well as the oversized but threatened imperial bureaucracy, to hijack foreign policy.

American tendencies toward globalist interventionism gradually took on a European focus. By the end of the decade, the United States had not only grown deeply involved in the Balkans but was wrestling with a weakened Russia for influence throughout its "Near Abroad" (the countries on its border). NATO was enlarged and apparently had hopes for much wider expansion. The United States pushed to transform it into a transatlantic intervention force under American direction. By the end of the century, these trends were clearly suggesting revitalized American hegemony—not only in Europe but now extended into Eurasia. What had once been a bipolar Pan Europe was now to become firmly unipolar.

By the end of the century, however, it was increasingly evident that these American tendencies were coming into sharp conflict with Europe's aspirations for its own self-determining confederacy. American hegemony and European confederacy were at loggerheads. In any such contest, Europeans seem likely to prevail, provided that they can overcome their own bad habits.

A significant integration of European diplomatic, security, and defense policies is probable, along with a serious upgrading of collective European military capabilities. And barring unforeseen shocks, a considerable American disengagement seems more likely than not during the first decade of the new century, together with a redefinition of transatlantic relations.

It seems best to begin with the long-term reasons for a probable American disengagement.[8]

Pressures for Transatlantic Adjustment:
Europe's Changing Security Problems

Europe's security problems after the Cold War have not been particularly suitable for American management. America's Cold War leadership was in response to the highly visible external threat of an alien superpower in the center of Europe. The situation naturally called for a friendly superpower to compensate. The American role was self-evidently legitimate—not only to most West Europeans but also to most Americans. In today's new Pan Europe, by contrast, security threats are not so much external as internal—neighborhood ethnic wars, drugs, crime generally, gangsterism, and terrorism. In many respects, these are police and intelligence problems. It is uncomfortable to have a foreign power taking charge of them, no matter how friendly that power may be. Nor is there any reason to think the United States will prove adept at managing such problems. Unlike the threats of the Cold War, these threats to Europeans are not also urgent threats to Americans. The United States has no vital interest in keeping its mind focused on Europe's problems. It also lacks Europe's ample means for dealing with most of these problems, which are often more susceptible to political and economic pressures and blandishments than to military intervention

Diverging Transatlantic Interests

A second fundamental reason for American disengagement pushes in the same direction. European and American geopolitical interests have become much more divergent than they were during the Cold War. The outcome of World War II, making the Soviets a Central European power, soon made the Americans a West European power. The retreat and disintegration of Soviet Russia has restored a more traditional kind of geopolitics. Without the Soviets, America, to paraphrase de Gaulle, becomes, once more, another world. This more distant America has quite different perspectives toward Europe's near neighbors—in particular Russia and the Middle Eastern states. A United States dedicated to protecting Israel has long remained incapable of delivering some reasonable settlement for the Palestinians, or a stable settlement between Israel and its neighbors. Partly in consequence, U.S. policy remains preoccupied with "rogue states"—like Iran, Iraq, and Libya. Europeans, for whom these "rogue states" are important neighbors and promising commercial prospects, would much prefer a policy of "constructive engagement" rather than one of unremitting hostility. Over the long run, Europe cannot afford to be stuck in a posture of barren and unproductive enmity toward its principal Moslem neighbors. Letting European relations with those neighbors be dominated by the United States is bound to seem an ever more unproductive course. The European tendency to play regional "good cop" to the American "bad cop" will grow more and more pronounced. Given the huge commercial interests and rivalries involved, mutual irritation is only to be expected.

The same mutually alienating transatlantic pattern is also visible in American and European approaches to Russia. It is difficult to imagine any promising future for Europe that does not include intimate regional cooperation with a strong, prosperous, and politically civilized Russia. To leave an American-dominated NATO in charge of Europe's relations with Russia means to continue emphasizing an abrasive military preponderance—a posture bound to antagonize and embitter the new Russia. The long-range costs of such negligent shortsightedness seem likely to be high, for Europe above all. Unless Russia turns, once again, into a major menace, Europeans will tend to bypass the Americans and to seek their own modus vivendi within some cooperative Pan-European structure that gives Russia the respect and the voice that it craves and, almost certainly, must ultimately have.

America's East Asian Vocation

Other long-range geopolitical factors are also working to draw America's attention away from Europe. The end of the Cold War has left the United States as the hegemonic power in East Asia. To give up that role now would not only leave a large commercial position exposed, but would almost certainly mean a competitive proliferation of nuclear weapons among America's current allies in the region. But to continue in the hegemonic role would mean building a regional security structure to contain China. This seems likely to be America's principal geopolitical project in the new century. As NATO's evolution during the Cold War indicates, such a task is not only dangerous but grows progressively more expensive over time. As China gradually develops into a nuclear superpower in its own right, the United States, its homeland at high risk in any serious confrontation, will be compelled to adopt an Asian version of "flexible response" strategy. This requires not only American conventional forces but regional allies with serious conventional forces of their own. Arguably, it is better when such allies are also conservative nuclear powers—like Britain and France in Europe—since this takes some pressure off American "extended deterrence."

In Europe, of course, extended deterrence is what cemented America's relations with its principal ally—the Federal Republic of Germany. The Germans were NATO's principal source of conventional forces, together with the Americans themselves. By contrast, the British and especially the French, both with nuclear deterrents of their own, limited their conventional-force contributions to the Alliance. In Asia, Japan is the obvious parallel to Germany. But it seems questionable that Japan, an island, will embrace the German role with much enthusiasm.

Ironically, America's principal Asian ally should probably be Russia, whose huge Asian empire is highly vulnerable to the Chinese. At the moment, however, America's maladroit enlargement of NATO has driven the Russians and the Chinese into each other's arms. Arguably, America's security imperatives in Asia ought eventually to lead to a reconsideration of American policy in Europe. The growing need for Asian security should encourage American policy to favor a more autonomous and self-sufficient European confederacy, particularly one that has developed a balanced but cooperative relationship with Russia and can take primary responsibility for maintaining its own regional order.

The American Republic

The evolution of America's domestic politics further reduces American capacity for its old European role. Many people throughout the world like to imagine the United States as a sort of surrogate United Nations, endowed with a highly professional imperial bureaucracy dedicated to maintaining order everywhere, and backed by a stable political system committed to this role. While the rhetoric of American politicians may encourage such a vision, the country's domestic politics of recent decades do little to encourage such exalted imperial expectations. Americans have other political values. Playing a global imperial role requires an imperial presidency. Since the administrations of Lyndon Johnson and Richard Nixon, the American constitutional balance has been shifting away from such a presidency. The other constitutional branches—the Congress, the courts, and the states—have all collaborated to return the presidency to its pre-imperial dimensions—to the "normalcy" of Presidents Harding and Coolidge rather than the norms set by presidents Wilson, Franklin Delano Roosevelt, Truman, Kennedy, Johnson, and Nixon. This widely shared constitutional impulse to cut down the presidency has been manifest during the Clinton presidency, but it was also at work during the Bush and Reagan administrations. Both were tormented in their last years by a plague of judicial inquiries and threatened indictments—most concerning the "unconstitutional" overextension of presidential power in foreign affairs.

Dynamics of European Integration

Fortunately, domestic trends in Europe and America seem to be working in opposite directions. Paralleling the dispersion of constitutional authority in America is Europe's recent dynamic progress toward political-economic integration, deliberately accelerated by the French and Germans at Maastricht. One of the Maastricht Treaty's great projects—EMU—has, as of early 2000, come close to fruition. That achievement has its own dynamic consequences. The euro has the potential to make Europe a monetary superpower. Having a major alternative reserve currency will greatly complicate America's once hegemonic capacity to finance its habitual external deficits. These complications will not only condition America's ability to finance global military pretensions, but also limit its hegemonic role as the world's "consumer of last resort"—a role of critical importance for the American position in Asia. A Europe whose defining monetary project has such inconvenient consequences for the United States cannot expect to continue comfortably as an American military protectorate. As the planners of Maastricht seem to have understood, EMU (European Monetary Union) points to CFSP in the EU (European Union) and ESDI in NATO. Europe's further evolution as a confederacy seems in keeping with the world's unfolding geopolitical framework after the Cold War. But it demands a renegotiation of the transatlantic compromise.

Prospects for the New Europe: Can the Franco-German Partnership Survive?

Following EMU, the European confederacy is bound to be tested as to whether it can bear the pressure of its new geopolitical pretensions. The fundamental test will be whether the Franco-German partnership can be sustained as the EU tries to transform itself into an effective security alliance. That transformation cannot be obtained without full German participation. But such participation implies ending the special military disabilities imposed on Germany during the Cold War. Arguably, these disabilities made the postwar Franco-German partnership possible in the first place. Completion of the EU thus requires eliminating the conditions that made the EU possible. Now that the partnership has been so long established, can this feat of historical legerdemain be accomplished? Can a half-century of cooperation change the traditional geopolitics of the European state system?

At present, Germany's "normalization" back to great-power status is progressing slowly and reluctantly. Certainly the Germans cannot yet be accused of excessive zeal. It has taken the whole decade of the 1990s, with two shameful wars in Yugoslavia, for the Germans to shed the constitutional provisions forbidding their forces to participate in foreign interventions. Psychologically, however, the Germans seem to have taken an important step: From "no more wars" to "no more Holocausts."[9] This suggests that Germans no longer expect to fulfill their obligations to Europe merely by staying home to defend their own territory. Instead, as the EU's biggest and richest member, they will take a leading military role, through the EU and NATO, to enforce a civilized peace throughout Europe and its surroundings. Before the Germans can actually play such a role, however, they will need to reorganize their armed forces. This means supplementing the current conscript army—organized for territorial defense under NATO command—with a professional army able to project force elsewhere.

If plans for common defense and ESDI go forward, major European powers are supposed to be able to act independently of American direction.[10] Possibly, the European partners will develop a separate European version of NATO—with its own hierarchical command structure to match that headed by the American Supreme Allied Commander in Europe (SACEUR). Such a structure would presumably be organized through the EU or WEU. More likely, Europeans will prefer a more ad hoc coalition structure, with EU institutions promoting common general planning beforehand but tailoring any actual command structure to the particular situation.[11] Arguably, such a coalition structure has actually been characteristic even of NATO's actions in Yugoslavia. Such coalition-building, however, implies the prior existence of independent national commands and staffs. To participate, the Germans will have to reconstitute a national general staff that is able to plan and direct operations independently—something that has not existed since World War II. It is difficult to see how they can otherwise play the role of a major partner.

Whereas Britain and France, by the end of the century, were well on the way to developing professional intervention forces and amply endowed with command and staff capabilities, the Germans were not yet fully committed to professionalization, let alone to reconstituting their general staff. Germany's shortcomings naturally inhibit the development of separate European defense capabilities. Security is thus the weak link in the Franco-German partnership. Were it up to the Germans, progress would be very slow toward CFSP and effective common defense. The Kohl coalition was divided on this and reluctant to confront it, and Schröder's Red-Green coalition has referred the question to a commission, due to report in the year 2000.[12] Perhaps it will favor a more rapid evolution toward the professionalization needed for CFSP. Meanwhile, however, it has been Britain's unexpected conversion to the European security project that has given CFSP its current strong impetus. But the project is unlikely to come to fruition without the full participation of the Germans.

The EU's present situation thus seems full of historical irony. The postwar restrictions on German military structures were not random accidents of history, but reflected the deliberate and deeply rooted views of Germany's neighbors. Lasting peace in Europe, they believed, was a goal well served by having Germany divided and especially by having it disarmed.

No More German Problem?

Why should no one fear re-endowing a united Germany with the military capabilities of an independent great power? Why is this not a formula for resurrecting Europe's old German Problem? Today's resurrected big Germany is, now as in the interwar years, looking outward to a Mittel-Europa that has once more become a political and economic vacuum. Thanks to the weakness of Russia and its retreat from Central Europe, this unhappy analogy with the 1920s seems compounded by erratic American behavior. Triumphalist inclinations lead the United States to quarrel with Russia, as well as to take offense at efforts to tighten and expand the scope of Europe's confederacy. At the same time, there is a curious and recurring American enthusiasm for "bigemony"—for expecting the reunited Germans to become the surrogates of American power. There is, of course, nothing new about America's courting the Germans. It has been part of the long struggle with the French to define postwar Europe. Successive American administrations have seen Germany as comparatively liberal and "outward-looking" toward the world economy, and hoped for a partnership to offset the baleful influence of the French on the EU's economic policy. These expectations have been regularly disappointed, and EMU should presumably lay them to rest. Today's hopes for bigemony lie with the bilateral "special relationship" that grew up between the two military establishments during Germany's long postwar dependency.

The United States may be unrealistic about keeping Germany as a dependent military partner, but are the still broader expectations harbored by the French any more realistic? Why, in fact, do the descendants of Talleyrand seem so eager to see the Americans off from Europe? In pursuing their mostly theatrical rivalry with the Americans, have the French foolishly opened the way to a revival of the old German Problem? Do they really believe that *Paneuropa* alone gives them adequate protection? The question has eaten, worm-like, into Western policymaking since the Two plus Four Talks put the old Germany back together again.[13] But despite some distinguished academic soul-searching, continental policymakers—the French above all—seem to prefer building a stronger European bloc as opposed to reinforcing ties with their transatlantic protector.

A Different Germany?

Many arguments are invoked to justify Europe's apparent disregard for a reviving German threat. Probably the most popular is that Germany has now become a genuine democracy, and that democracies do not go to war with each other. "Realist" analysts of international relations find this old Kantian bromide intrinsically less convincing than do many historians, political scientists, and so-ciologists. In the Realist perspective, all states tend to be aggressive—particularly when they feel threatened by their neighbors or, conversely, when the disarray of their neighbors invites expansion. Realists are therefore not so inclined to find the sources of Germany's historic aggressiveness in its suppos-edly wicked culture or dysfunctional institutions. By the same reasoning, how-ever, they are not so easily convinced that something like the old problem cannot recur now, simply because German political culture is more liberal. Sim-ilarly, Realists are often relatively skeptical about the belief that different do-mestic institutions make a great deal of difference in countries' external behavior. They are therefore less impressed that the German state is now much more of a pluralist democracy than in 1914 or 1920. In the Realist optic, if Eu-rope's former geopolitical conditions return, the old German Problem may well also return. Some see Germany's reunification, Russia's retreat and weakness, and America's growing isolationist diffidence all suggesting a return to earlier geopolitical conditions. Such changes do not, therefore, seem to result in a geopolitical framework favorable to continuing postwar Franco-German part-nership in *Paneuropa*. For the Realist, denying this logic requires explaining how other changes have made a repetition of past patterns improbable. Ar-guably, such changes have, in fact, occurred.

Europe's New Politics:
the EU, National Identity and Interest

In recent years, many theorists contend that under the pressure of European and global integration, Europe's old national identities have become so at-omized and Europeanized, and European national interests so fragmented and globalized, that nation-states are less and less the ultimate sovereign ac-tors. Within Europe, where cooperative bargaining goes on at many levels, the notion of a distinct "national" identity or interest is said no longer to have much practical relevance.

Undoubtedly, five decades of close and increasingly structured intergov-ernmental cooperation in the EU have left their mark. Nevertheless, it seems unlikely that the EU's institutional development has gone so far as to con-stitute an irreversible loss of national sovereignty for states like Germany or France. Indeed the EU is more accurately described as a "pooling" rather than a surrender of national sovereignties. Claims that national interest and national identity are insignificant seem belied by the EU's inner workings, where states are still very much in charge of amalgamating and advancing the interests of their citizens.

National identity, moreover, seems robust in both France and Germany, even if one of its more fashionable expressions lies in the special claims of both countries to embody a new European consciousness. French nationalism, for example, often expresses itself in a particularly vigorous form of European geopolitical self-assertion. For many Germans, who often deny any distinct national identity of their own, German identity comes clothed as a distinctively assertive form of European cosmopolitanism. Underneath these fashionable costumes of the moment, the Realist still sees France and Germany, alive and watchful, despite fifty years of intimate cohabitation.

Europe in the Global System

Even Realists doubtful that the EU has deprived France or Germany of its sovereignty, or that European sentiments have seriously undermined French or German national identity, must nevertheless admit that radical changes in the geopolitical environment alter significantly how the two nations perceive their interests. Throughout much of the twentieth century, Europe had ceased being the dominant center of the global system. Europe found itself demoted from a "history maker" into a "history taker." Coudenhove Kalergi's *Paneuropa* project for the 1920s assumed that the French and the Germans, realizing the futility and mutual destructiveness of their rivalry, and the danger of external domination, would ally to unify Europe together. The project had only a brief and anemic half-life in the 1920s. It could not overcome the asymmetry between French and German power and prospects. World War II eventually led to a more promising environment, but the end of the Cold War has threatened to recreate the old asymmetry. Even assuming that the lingering machinery and habits of the EU will prevent any dramatic explosion of antagonism, the old partnership may well be severely weakened.

One outcome might be German hegemony at last. More likely, given German inhibitions and Europe's openness to outside influence, the decline of the Franco-German partnership would leave the EU quarrelsome and paralyzed and therefore incapable of managing European security. For reasons discussed at length earlier, American hegemony is unlikely to prove a satisfactory long-term solution. Given these unhappy alternatives, Europe's best hope would be to keep its Franco-German partnership going.

But is the shared danger of external domination enough to keep that partnership going? The answer would seem to depend on three issues. The first is the actual asymmetry between France and Germany, whether or not it is too great to permit a balanced and stable partnership. The second is whether the "New World Order" evolving after the Cold War still gives Europeans, and France and Germany in particular, a strong national incentive to cooperate. The third is whether the rest of the world, in particular the United States and Russia, will accommodate a strong European Union.

Franco-German Asymmetry?

The degree of French/German inequality depends on the elements being compared. Before 1989, French and German populations and economies were roughly equal. After reunification, Germany became roughly a third larger in both respects. The change, however, is not as much of a shock to the EU's inner balance of power as might be expected. In some significant respects, Germany is weaker as a result of its reunification. Although the accession of the German Democratic Republic (GDR) to the Federal Republic has significantly increased Germany's overall Gross Domestic Product (GDP), it has also notably decreased the quality of the economy. The federal government has made enormous investments in the Eastern *Länder*. After a decade, the results are still disappointing. Hopes that a *Blitzkrieg* of huge investments would quickly bring the East to Western levels have been cruelly disappointed; in many instances, Western generosity has not so much energized the East as left it dependent and demoralized. Over the long term, the harmful effects will presumably diminish as the huge investments begin to bring their benefits. But the whole process has already taken much longer than most experts believed it would. Very probably, one or two generations will pass before the new Germany realizes its economic potential. Meanwhile Germany's fiscal balance has deteriorated sharply, with no significant improvement yet in sight.[14] Germany's competitive position has also deteriorated. Labor costs, for example, are dramatically higher than in France, whereas overall productivity is not.[15]

Accession of the East has also weakened Germany politically. After a short honeymoon, voters in the East have grown disaffected with the major Western parties and have voted increasingly for their own resurrected communist party, the PDS (*Partei des Demokratischen Sozialismus*). Meanwhile, the Greens have become a significant force and the liberal FDP has nearly disappeared.[16] These trends may well make it much more difficult to form stable coalitions in the future. This unaccustomed political instability occurs at a period when resolute tax and labor reforms are badly needed.

France also went through a difficult period in the 1990s. It had great difficulty meeting the EMU criteria. Doing so meant tight fiscal and monetary conditions and high unemployment. In part, the cause lay with the high interest rates that resulted from heavy German borrowing to finance reunification. The result, however, is that French public finances and industrial competitiveness have been significantly strengthened. In effect, the 1990s put France through a period of austere discipline that seems to have strengthened it. Germany, by contrast, has been through a period of fiscal self-indulgence that leaves it weaker.[17]

The French, too, had volatile coalition politics in the 1990s. But on balance, this does not seem to have weakened their capacity to govern themselves effectively. In 1995, after fourteen years of Mitterrand in the presidency—much of the time with Gaullist prime ministers—the country elected a Gaullist president, Jacques Chirac, together with a Gaullist-Centrist parliamentary majority. Within two years, however, new parliamentary elections returned a socialist government. In short, cohabitation now seems the rule rather than the exception in French politics. The prospect of such cohabitation used to be seen as the Achilles Heel of the Fifth Republic. Two decades of frequent cohabitation now suggest a different view. Under the Fifth Republic, France has proved able to sustain consistent and coherent national policies through several alternations of majorities and periods of divided government. France's joining the EMU, for example, required consistent long-term European policies and rigorous, unpopular domestic economic discipline. These policies were nevertheless sustained under both Mitterrand and Chirac and through several governments.

On balance, France's domestic record in the 1990s probably compares favorably with Germany's. Both countries have needed major reforms of labor, tax, and pension laws. In Germany, neither Kohl's old coalition nor the new SPD-Green coalition headed by Schröder has been able to push through such reforms. By contrast, the French, disciplined by unemployment and the *rigueur* imposed to meet the EMU requirements, do seem to have made changes that leave France with more competitive costs than Germany.[18]

Analyzing the relative strength and prospects of highly developed states is inevitably an elusive exercise. Much depends on the creativity and enterprise of the system over the long run. It is very difficult to make any serious reckoning, except to note that the French economy, although smaller, is not notably inferior to the German in these aspects. In short, reunification has not yet resulted in any radical new economic imbalance between the partners. If anything, France seems to have strengthened itself relative to Germany. And France has, of course, retained its military advantages. It has a well-developed nuclear deterrence and its conventional forces are much further along in their "professionalization."

Over the longer term, unified Germany's natural weight seems likely to be felt more strongly. But in any purely bilateral reckoning, at least, Germany's present disabilities seem unlikely to disappear quickly, and any imbalance seems unlikely to be radical and disruptive. The greatest danger, as suggested earlier, lies in the weakness and disorder of Eastern Europe—a condition that threatens to restore Germany's fatal attraction for Mittel-Europa, and to alienate France and overwhelm the EU's confederal structure at precisely the moment when it will need strong leadership. The significance of this threat probably depends on the relative weight of other considerations—the challenge to Europe from globalization, and the place of Russia and the United States in the evolving Pan-European system.

Globalism and European Integration

This brings us to a second broad issue likely to determine the fate of Europe's confederacy: Will the unfolding "New World Order" following the Cold War continue to encourage Franco-German partnership and European integration generally? This is a question that needs to be answered from both global and regional perspectives. The end of the Cold War does not seem to have reduced the old global incentives for Europeans to band together to assert their own interests. Quite the contrary. The dramatic demise of the bipolar system has made the underlying pluralist trends of the past four decades all the more evident. The most obvious sign of the coming of a plural world is the spectacular rise of Asia. Following the explosive growth of Japan and the various Asian "Little Tigers," China is gradually emerging as an economic and military superpower. India, too, is a vast economy, some sectors of which are highly advanced and competitive. Both China and India bring enormous pools of cheap and skilled labor to the world economy, a development that particularly challenges Europe, whose labor is expensive and cosseted. The proper liberal prescriptions for rich Western economies is to specialize in industries and services that require highly skilled labor and pay their workers enough to sustain Western standards of living.

In pursuing this course, however, Europeans confront the Americans and Japanese, who are both hoping to dominate such industries for the same reason—to preserve their high standard of living. Competitiveness among the advanced countries is already intense—as may be seen from the embarrassing prevalence of industrial espionage among Western countries.

Heightened competition presses Europeans toward alliances to achieve the scale and global reach of giant American firms. Hence the rush of European mergers and acquisitions in recent years. Obviously, not all this activity is directed to forging partnerships within Europe, let alone between France and Germany. It is too early to tell how much this globalist corporate behavior will strengthen European integration itself. But common sense suggests that, on balance, it will do so. National governments and the elites gathered around them resist losing national control over major firms that occupy leading positions in their economies. When transnational amalgamation cannot be avoided, governments now seem more inclined to press for European rather than transatlantic outcomes—perhaps because they hope to retain some degree of control over corporate behavior through the apparatus of the EU. American firms seem more alien and difficult to control. The imperial tendency of American courts, as well as Congressional attempts to control technology transfers, all work against permitting American firms to gain control of critical European firms. On occasion, the same tendency is notable on the American side as well, particularly in the defense industry. This does not, however, prevent American firms from investing heavily in Europe, or European firms from investing heavily in the United States. In short, the issue is complex. Nevertheless, several decades of huge mutual direct investment does not seem to have seriously eroded the instinct to resist American domination by pooling Europe's economies.

Other aspects of globalization certainly seem to encourage European integration. EMU seems a classic illustration. By the 1980's it was increasingly clear that the global integration of financial and currency markets left Europe's own closely integrated economies highly vulnerable to erratic changes in exchange rates—above all to changes amongst themselves. The monetary shocks to Europe, often originating in the vagaries of American macroeconomic policy in the Nixon, Carter and Reagan years, greatly reinforced the tendency to amalgamate. Ultimately it led Europeans to EMU—to a common currency and a European Central bank (ECB). France and Germany were the leaders in creating EMU. Its dynamism is geopolitical as well as economic. EMU points toward CFSP, common defense, and ESDI. The partners are now approaching the critical stage of military cooperation. Perhaps this is the phase where they can finally incorporate Britain.

How well the old partners succeed will depend upon more than their own skill, luck, and determination. It will also depend on the reaction of the rest of Europe and its neighbors. And it will certainly also depend upon finding a comfortable place for the remaining elements of the Cold War system in Europe—Russia and the United States.

Russia, America, and Franco-German Europe

It is difficult to imagine a happy future for Europe that does not include a prosperous, liberal, and friendly Russia, cooperating to sustain a broad Pan-European peace. What makes Russia so critical to Europe is not only its own great size and potential resources, or its role in Asia, but its role in preventing the revival of Europe's German Problem. Despite its accompanying horrors, a strong Soviet Russia did solve the German Problem for half a century. Today, with the Soviet empire gone, Western Europe is inevitably drawn eastward, as the ambitious proposals for enlargement of the European Union indicate. The problem with such an enlargement is that it threatens, once more, to make Germany disproportionately powerful and France more contentious, and thereby threatens to destabilize the balanced hegemonic core around which the European Union has been formed. In short, it is not so much German reunification that threatens to destabilize the EU, but Europe's general opening to the East in a period when Russia is extremely weak.

If this analysis is valid, Europe's fate probably depends ultimately on Russia's revival—preferably as a successful and friendly nation-state drawn into close cooperation with the EU. But resurrection of a strong Russia, friendly or not, also calls for the continuing presence of the Americans, as Europe's insurance policy. In effect, something is needed in today's *Paneuropa* to replace the old bipolar structure that limited Germany's yearning for Mittel-Europa, while also keeping each of the superpowers in check. The Cold War system was hardly an optimal solution. It kept the peoples of Central and Eastern Europe—and the Russians themselves—in miserable bondage to an outrageous tyranny. In addition, huge resources were wasted on arms. But all these deplorable costs were better than another European war.

The Soviet collapse has given Europe a chance to find something even better. But the new opportunity also carries the old risk. The German Problem still lurks—as it has all through the twentieth century. In the EU, today's version of *Paneuropa,* France and Germany have been preparing their own solution. With the dawn of the new century, their moment has come. But the success of this new *Paneuropa,* like that of the Cold War system it succeeds, requires not only the Franco-German couple, but a balanced Russian-American presence as well. The new *Paneuropa,* after all, has the same basic players as the Cold War system. With luck, the great advantage of the new dispensation will be a Russia not only strong enough to play its essential role, but transformed enough to play it as a liberal and responsible member of the European family. The great danger is a Russia that will be permanently weak, as well as quarrelsome and dangerous. Here, the Americans still have their old Cold War balancing role to play. But this requires an America that has not lost its head to visions of its own Eurasian hegemony.

From a Realist perspective, the problem with these unsettled moments in geopolitical systems is the tendency of major actors to misjudge their ultimate roles. Those who feel strong, like the United States, are inclined to "overshoot" their roles; those who are exceptionally weak, like Russia, invite them to do so. As always, the problem is timing. Before America grows tragically committed to its own Eurasian ambitions, *Paneuropa* needs to assert mastery in its own space. For better or for worse, France and Germany once more find themselves at the center of world history. We can only hope it is not for the last time.

Notes

1. For an elaboration of these arguments and accompanying bibliography, see David P. Calleo, *The German Problem Reconsidered* (Cambridge: Cambridge

University Press 1978). I also suggest that Imperial Germany's penchant for unstable and authoritarian governments can be explained less by the peculiar culture of Germans than by the newness of the Empire, its diverse population, so recently and forcefully amalgamated and not yet reconciled to living together.

2. Richard Coudenhove Kalergi, *Paneuropa 1922–1966* (Vienna and Munich: Herold 1966).

3. Arnold Wolfers, *Britain and France between Two Wars* (New York: W. W. Norton & Company 1966), pp. 60–66.

4. Hans-Peter Schwarz, *Konrad Adenauer* (Oxford: Berghahn Books 1986), pp. 610–621.

5. For illustrations of how Maastricht was conceived as the European solution to German Reunification and Soviet collapse, see François Mitterrand, in *Europa Archiv* 6/46, 1991, pp. 143–149: Jacques Delors, *Our Europe* (London: Verso 1992); Helmut Kohl, "Regierungserklärung" after the European Council's meeting in Maastricht, 13/12, 1991, in *Aussenpolitik der Bundesrepublik Deutschland* (Koeln: Verlag Wissenschaft und Politik 1995).

6. Besides the two major achievements of Maastricht, EMU and CFSP, the treaty provided for closer intergovernmental cooperation in justice and home affairs, introduced more majority voting in the European Council, and enhanced the influence of the European Parliament. For an overview of the treaty's main provisions, see Andrew Duff, John Pinder, and Roy Price (eds.), *Maastricht and Beyond* (London: Routledge 1994), pp. 19–36.

7. Total national defense spending decreased from 371.7 billion dollars in 1990 to 263.4 billion dollars in 1999. These figures are from *The Military Balance* 1997/1998, The International Institute for Strategic Studies (Oxford: Oxford University Press).

8. David P. Calleo, "The Strategic Implications of the Euro," in *Survival*, Vol. 41, No. 1, Spring 1999, pp. 5–19.

9. This redefinition of lessons from the German past can be traced through German reactions to the major international crises of the post–Cold War world. The decisive turning point came with the Kosovo crisis, in large measure due to the active advocacy of Green Party foreign minister Joschka Fischer, who supported German participation. See Joschka Fischer, *Die Zeit*, 16/1999 and 25/1999.

10. According to an Anglo-French plan endorsed at the Helsinki Summit in December 1999, the EU should be able to deploy up to 66,000 troops within 60 days for peacekeeping and peacemaking tasks by 2003, independently of NATO.

11. According to the Anglo-French plan endorsed at Helsinki, a number of Brussels-based committees will provide military expertise in the EU Council, and promote and monitor progress on creating and maintaining the EU force. For an overview of the plan, see *Financial Times*, July 12, 1999.

12. The "Zukunftskommision," composed of 20 independent experts, was supposed to come up with recommendations for Bundeswehr reforms. But

whatever its recommendations, severe budgetary constraints are likely to hamper the process of reequipping the Bundeswehr for new out-of-area tasks. The German government is in the midst of an attempt to impose austerity measures on the German economy.

13. The old German Question figured prominently in the considerations of all major actors in the 2+4 negotiations. See Harold James and Marla Stone (eds.), *When the Wall Came Down* (New York: Routledge 1992); Stephen F. Szabo, *The Diplomacy of German Reunification* (New York: St. Martin's Press 1992).

14. Germany's fiscal balance deteriorated in the wake of unification. The Schröder government has embarked on a policy of consolidation aiming at a balanced budget by 2006. The success of this plan, however, depends on the government's ability to push through social security and tax reforms. *Economic Survey of Germany,* 1999. OECD Policy Brief.

15. Relative German labor unit costs have exceeded French since unification. Whereas costs have decreased in France from 101 in 1991 to 93 in 1997, they have increased from 103 to 112 in Germany in the same period. *OECD Economic Outlook,* June 1998, p. 268.

16. For a discussion of how this has made Germany less governable, see Russell J. Dalton and Wilhelm Buerklin, "The Two German Electorates," in *German Politics and Society,* Vol. 13, No. 1, 1995.

17. France has experienced a sharp improvement in macroeconomic performance since the elections of 1997. The growth rate has been around 3 percent per year, competitiveness has improved, the trade balance is in surplus, inflation is low, and unemployment has decreased. *Economic Survey of France,* January 1999, OECD Economic Surveys.

18. See note 16 above.

Conclusion ✤

Patrick McCarthy

I n late January 2000, when all of this book except the Conclusion was already written, the news broke in the Italian press—never reluctant to publish reports of political corruption in other countries—of a large sum of money given by Mitterrand to Kohl to finance his successful reelection campaign in 1994. The channel was the state-owned French oil company Elf, which bought a company in the ex-DDR and added the bribe to the price it paid. Does this mean the cement of Franco-German cooperation was bribery? No, it is almost the other way around. Since the French and German political systems were riddled with corruption, the Franco-German relationship could hardly remain immune. Kohl accepted illegal financing from many sources; why should the French government constitute an exception? As for Mitterrand, in the posthumous revelations of his sins, this is a fairly minor one. Nor is it a surprise that he was helping a center-right candidate running against the SPD. Ideology plays little part in the Franco-German relationship: Schmidt supported Giscard d'Estaing against Mitterrand in 1981 and Kohl supported Mitterrand against Chirac in 1988. In each case, personal sympathy counted for something but the banal fact of "the devil one knows . . ." was just as important. This is not meant to imply that corruption in the Franco-German relationship does not matter. But it is not specific to that relationship and should be examined in the context of French and German politics as a whole.

In early February came another shock: the entry into the Austrian government of Jörg Haider's *Freiheitlichen* (Freedom Party). Although in my opinion this is an Austrian problem, linked with an ambiguous attitude toward Austria's role during the Hitler years, it also was a warning to France, Germany, and the other European countries. One could imagine the Front national, especially if led by Bruno Mégret, forcing its way into a French coalition government; and if the German Christian Democrats were to be gravely weakened by the financial scandal, this could leave space open to the Republikaner or some other group on the far right. Such developments would render the Franco-German relationship much more difficult.

Of more real significance are the impressions gained from reading Erik Jones's chapter on economic cooperation, and Anand Menon's on defense. Jones points out that France and Germany are no longer drawing economically closer to each other and that, while this is perhaps an effect of the economic problems that plague both countries, it is surprising because economic collaboration was the area where cooperation, from the now distant ECSC onward, worked best. Moreover, if one shares the view that, with the euro in place, progress toward greater European union will come via economic rather than political actors, then Jones's findings take on greater importance.

Menon is dubious about security cooperation, seeing more rhetoric than military might as well as the continuing survival of old habits and differences. He notes that France did not consult Germany before it abandoned the draft: a nation's right to make whatever security decisions it can is not easy to give up.

On the positive side, Erik Jones notes that the Franco-German relationship gives the couple a power within the EU that neither would possess without it. Moreover, in the past there were cases—like the Elysée Treaty or the FAR—in which France and Germany cooperated on their own, outside of the EC-EU structures. But such cases are now rare and the EU is the setting where Franco-German cooperation unfolds. The Lamers letter of 1994 suggested that a select group of countries move ahead on their own, but this letter aroused much discussion and was then not acted upon, which was probably what its author intended.

Jones's theme leads naturally into Roger Morgan's chapter, which describes how the French and the Germans led the EU in the 1990s. Here the effort of political imagination mentioned at the end of chapter 1 was not made, and France and Germany stumbled through a very difficult decade. Morgan notes that the agreement on monetary union gave way to a struggle about whether power would go solely to a European central bank, animated by anti-inflationary zeal, or whether the bank should act in a context set by political leaders who also worried about unemployment and growth. This difference between the German view and the French one had been present since the debate about monetary union began again in the 1980s.

It grew sharper after the high anti-Maastricht vote in the French referendum of 1992 and the crushing defeat of the French Socialists in 1993. In Germany, where Kohl did not want to hold a referendum, opposition to monetary union came from an odd mixture of elites like the editor of the influential weekly *Der Spiegel,* and ordinary Germans who did not want to give up the Deutsch-mark. The solution, on which Kohl could agree with the Bundesbank, was to go ahead with monetary union but to insist on a strict interpretation of the German version. Hence the Stability Pact, which Roger Morgan explains. Were the French and Germans, after forty years of heeding Kessler and François-Poncet, going to switch to an admittedly non-violent interpretation of Bainville?

The answer was, not quite. Both Kohl and Chirac stopped in time: Kohl held fairly firm on the financial prerequisites but agreed to a milder version of the Stability Pact; Chirac watered down the populist rhetoric of the first months of his 1995 presidential campaign and spoke more about the joys of deflation and strong money. Occasional disputes, like the Duisenberg-Trichet affair, revealed that the underlying difference was still there. Agreements in the Franco-German relationship, and even more so in the EC-EU, are made in a certain political context; as this changes, the words of a written text may alter their meaning.

Two unforeseen circumstances have made it possible to bridge the gulf between France and Germany. The first is that reunification has weakened Germany, which is no longer dominant enough either to stray off down some *Sonderweg* or to get its own way in Europe. Kohl had to resort to creative accounting to meet his own requirements. The second is that the financial markets do not yet believe in the euro, which is, as of early 2000, hovering around parity with the dollar. At a time when crude oil costs $25 a barrel this creates inflation, but it also works wonders for European exports.

Roger Morgan notes that talks on modernizing EU structures to make them more democratic and more capable of housing new members have not gone far. Here again both Germany's federalism and France's *l'Europe des patries* block development. Institutional change was bequeathed by the Irish presidency to the Dutch, where it found expression in the very vague Amsterdam Treaty and was bequeathed to the French in the year 2000, when it will be a theme of the French presidency. This has been a period of concessions on both sides, but it did not produce much except an outline of what a European security plan would look like, along with some progress on immigration and police issues out of which the Schengen Treaty emerged.

Ulrike Guerot is critical of France and Germany but believes the two have learned at least to limit their disagreements. This was apparent in the question of the EU's Eastern expansion. According to conventional wisdom, the accession of Poland, Hungary, and the Czech Republic should benefit Germany. So at the Essen Summit of 1994, France won an agreement that pledged money too for the EU's southern border. The disagreement between the two slowed up Eastern expansion but did not prevent it from happening.[1] The two countries seem to have divided up the work of establishing a zone of stability on the EU borders—except where armed conflict breaks out and every hand is needed. Germany takes the East, which involves establishing good relations with Russia. France, with help from Spain, looks southward especially toward Algeria, where there is less question of joining the EU, and European effort is put into avoiding wars with Islamic fundamentalists and restraining the flood of emigrants leaving for the other coast of the Mediterranean. Economic help is restricted by maintenance of the Common Agricultural Policy (CAP), on which France insists.[2]

Franco-German leadership is stronger in some areas than others. In general the more publicity an issue gets, the greater is the Franco-German effort to find a common position and the greater the likelihood that other countries will accept it. Agriculture, an important part of the original bargain struck in the Rome Treaty, is still considered vital to France—and Germany, whose self-interest seems quite different, recognizes this and helps out. Similarly, Germany toils to reconcile French and American views on NATO or the GATT.

Within this context the behavior of Britain, Italy, and Spain becomes important. In Britain the fundamental question is whether the Blair government really is different from previous governments in substance as well as style. Blair's frequent trips to Washington, and his help in the useless bombing of Baghdad, are not encouraging. To borrow David Calleo's (chapter 9) phrase, Blair is flattering American triumphalism. One can hardly blame the French for wondering how much the Saint-Malo meeting is worth.

James Walsh, in chapter 8, however, takes a more optimistic view of security cooperation than of any other issue. He demonstrates that, on the euro as on the measures to combat unemployment, the Blair government is closer to Thatcher than to Jospin or Schröder. The most exasperating feature that Walsh points out is that the British public is not, as it is often depicted, the chauvinistic bulldog that recoils from a Europe where people eat their fish and chips with mayonnaise. A prime minister with Blair's majority could be bolder.

Italy has the opposite problem. To the Italians, Europe is a myth of modernity and efficiency; it is the anti-Italy. Italian governments are determined to cling to the Alps rather than drift into the Mediterranean, as Anja Dalgaard-Nielsen puts it in chapter 7. There is a danger here, which we have discussed elsewhere, that the longer Italy stays in the EU the harder it grows for the Italians to see Europe as the anti-Italy, and the more likely it is that the myth will collapse.[3] Anja Dalgaard-Nielsen makes the original point that Southern Italy needs quite a different Europe from Northern Italy: interventionist rather than liberal, giving priority to unemployment rather than to the strong euro.

When Romano Prodi was prime minister, he often gave the impression that getting into Europe was all that mattered; France and Germany would then impose reforms on Italy. The reverse, however, is true: to retain its place in Europe, Italy must reform its state. On this point Massimo D'Alema, who used the Kosovo emergency to demonstrate that Italy was a reliable partner, is on the right track. There is no reason why Italy, provided it completes the reform of its political system, should not play a strong supporting role to the Franco-German couple. As Anja Dalgaard-Nielsen points out, Italy exports much to Central Europe and is also a Mediterranean actor. Her goal should be to unite Europe—or rather, since Italy does not seek to lead, to help unite it.

One might take off from Guerot's (chapter 3) and Stürmer's (chapter 2) chapters to ask oneself what the future holds for Franco-German cooperation. Stürmer's chapter is ironically pessimistic: In the postwar period, Germans hoped they might become Europeans who just happened to speak German; neither the European Community nor Franco-German cooperation has any clear goal, although both have been viewed as historical destinies; reunification did not turn out as expected; and the jury is still out on monetary union. Implicit in Stürmer's analysis is the theme that Germany should conduct a debate about what it is and where it wants to be. As I argued in chapter 1, such a debate was avoided for the first twenty years after the war by intense anticommunism. From the late 1960s a minority of Germans opted for a green-pink blend of neutralism, improving relations with the DDR, and minimizing Soviet aggression in Afghanistan. The majority clung to NATO, the EU, and the D-mark. Kohl, in the boldest foreign policy move since Brandt's *Ostpolitik*, negotiated reunification directly with Gorbachev, obtaining along the way the approval of the United States but not of the Europeans. Was Kohl about to abandon the Stresemann approach?

Not so. He reverted, offering to give up the D-mark now that he had Deutschland. Sturmer's point is not that this was wrong but rather that it did not form part of any design. The German part of the Franco-German engine seemed exhausted. Ulrike Guerot argues that France was exhausted too.

Yet this is a moment when France and Germany will have to act together to shape their own and Europe's future, because the collapse of the Soviet Union means there is no reason why the United States should do this for them, and no pretext for them to allow the United States to do it. David Calleo is suspicious of the American tendency toward triumphalism: certainly George Bush did not think that the end of Communism meant the end of America, the superpower. In Saddam Hussein he found the perfect enemy—even more belligerent and foolish than General Galtieri, who had served Margaret Thatcher so well. The United States electorate, however, was not very impressed by the Iraq victory and felt that Bush had neglected the domestic economy. They elected Bill Clinton who has run the economy well, even if Calleo attributes much of his success to the peace dividend. But in Clinton's second term, the old demons of the imperial presidency returned. Clinton ventured into the minefield of Northern Ireland, where he has been successful, although the Irish continue to demonstrate their flair for snatching defeat from the jaws of victory. Clinton was tough on Russia and willing to undertake the bombing campaign over Kosovo.

Meanwhile France and Germany were moving at a snail's pace toward the CFSP and a European force that will be able to act without U.S. leadership. It is true that much is demanded of Germany, especially of an SPD government with a Green foreign minister, Joschka Fischer. It is also true that the Gaullist worldview is being put to the test for the first time, whereas it has hitherto been operating behind an American shield.

How will the Franco-German Europe fit into the post–Cold War world? Calleo attaches much importance to Eastern Europe and to a Russia that is strong enough to be a stabilizing influence. But Russia is at present weak, aggrieved, and unpredictable, and Europe has no clear policy toward its former enemy. Just as important, in my opinion, is the European dialogue—such as it is—with Islam. The European record is bad: religious, cultural, economic, and geopolitical reasons and prejudices combine to create incomprehension that can at any moment turn into hostility. Learning to live with the followers of Islam, inside their boundaries as well as just outside, is the great task that young Europeans will have to take up. It will be easier if the Franco-German couple can provide clear and enlightened leadership.

We have deliberately left for the end—to underline its importance—a brief discussion of the link between domestic politics and Franco-German cooperation. As already stated, governments of different ideological or political hues have had no more difficulty than governments that belong to the same political family. Trouble comes when cooperation does not work properly: a vicious cycle occurs, in which the electorate punishes its government for not bargaining more successfully, which often further weakens the government, making it more intransigent or less able to sell the next results of its bargaining to the electorate.

Since Maastricht, the French political system has been weakened. A simple journey through election results shows this. The anti-Maastricht vote in 1992 included virtually half of the electorate and demonstrated the leadership capacity of Philippe Séguin. In the parliamentary election of 1993, the Socialists were reduced to approximately 20 percent of the vote and suffered heavy losses in almost every sociological and geographical sector and almost every age group. In 1995 Chirac campaigned for the presidency promising to use the power of the state to integrate *les exclus*. Once in power he reversed gears and made cooperation and the strong franc his priorities. Despite populist gestures, such as inviting French youth to the Elysée Palace on Bastille Day, Chirac and his prime minister, Alain Juppé, were confronted with a massive strike in the autumn of 1995. In 1997 Chirac gambled on early elections and was rewarded with a clear if not overwhelming victory for the left.

The electorate was manifesting its dissatisfaction with whomever was in power and also with the austerity measures that the Maastricht agreement imposed. Paradoxically, Chirac, although he lost control of his own party in the 1999 European elections, has fared relatively well in the polls. For this there are two reasons: firstly, Chirac is a good politician for this period—constantly changing his mind, devoid of both a sense of tradition and a vision of the future, and with energy undiminished by repeated setbacks. Secondly, the public has learned that in periods of cohabitation it is the prime minister who governs. The Socialists have benefited from a mild upturn in the economy since 1997, and Lionel Jospin is also good at selling austerity. His Protestant background serves him well.

The French electorate remains disoriented. This is revealed in the mild increase of votes for the Far Left; in the sustained ability of the Front national to get 13 to 15 percent of the vote and, as Ulrike Guerot points out, to play king-maker in 1997; and in the uneven but substantial share of the vote in the European elections that went to the Hunters and Fishermen's Party—as much as 20 percent around Bordeaux and 27 percent in the Somme department. This was a vote for traditional French life and against unwelcome Brussels modernization. The swing from state to market has not been welcomed in any European country—few Europeans *like* the market as Americans do—but in France the adjustment has been more difficult than elsewhere. To the *dirigiste* tradition that goes back to Colbert, unfettered market forces seem like a "Darwinian nightmare."[4]

Meanwhile German politics was marked in the early 1990s by a growing distrust of Kohl's policies but the lack of a credible alternative. Eventually the alternative emerged in the person of Gerhard Schröder and the Red-Green coalition. The SPD victory in 1998 was in the order of things: the Christian Democrats had been in power for sixteen years. A series of defeats in regional elections showed that Germans felt no great enthusiasm for the SPD. Schröder's embracing of Blair and of New Labour's "third way" marked an absence of new thinking, rather than anything else. The much-criticized Oscar Lafontaine at least understood that the emphasis on the strong euro and the independent European Central Bank was unsuited to the new Germany, and in conjunction with his French counterpoint, Dominique Strauss-Kahn, he tried to increase political input and confront the issue of unemployment. Lafontaine's departure from the government marked a victory for Schröder's more conventional approach; and Strauss-Kahn's more recent departure marked the end of what might have been, but was not, an interesting piece of Franco-German cooperation.

There is much talk about a decline in cooperation because of Schröder's pragmatism and his lack of ties with the Second World War. Certainly there is little of Stresemann or Adenauer in him. But the need for a partner in the new Europe holds Germany and France together. Certainly the relationship is not going through an innovative period, but a Germany where a Green Foreign Minister has carefully brought the electorate around to the realization that it must do much more in the security sphere can hardly do without a close tie to a France where the notion of national defense is well-implanted.

The autobiography of Joseph Rovan, one of the leading intellectuals of the Franco-German relationship, was published in 1999. Of German-Jewish background, Rovan's family fled to France when he was in high school. He switched languages and continued his education. During the war he was in the Resistance, was imprisoned at Dachau, and joined the *Esprit* group. After the war he devoted himself to the organization of Franco-German projects like *Documents/Dokumente*. In 1940 Rovan had turned down a chance to leave for the United States where he would have been safer. He consciously chose France and Germany, helping to free them from Vichy and Hitler.

Rovan's book makes admirable reading, as its title promises.[5] But it belongs to the heroic period of Franco-German cooperation. We shall not have the good fortune to see another generation of Rovans or of Alfred Grossers, for Franco-German cooperation has become a matter of business rather than of principles and morality. But it continues.

Notes

1. Patrick McCarthy, "France, Germany and Eastern Enlargement" in Douglas Webber, ed., *The Franco-German Relationship in the European Union* (London: Routledge 1999) pp. 41–57.
2. Enzo Grilli, "Con il Mediterraneo quale futuro? in *Politica internazionale* 6/1998 (November-December) pp. 87–111.
3. Patrick McCarthy, "Cambia l'Italia, cambiano i miti," paper presented at conference organized by Department of Sociology at University of Bologna, Fall 1998.
4. Alain Minc, *La grande illusion* (Paris: Grasset 1989), p.149.
5. Joseph Rovan, *Mémoires d'un Français qui se souvient d'avoir été Allemand* (Paris: Editions du Seuil 1999).

Index